BLESSED ALI

'When I prayed to God, it always came into my mind that a new house for girls must be set up, wherein all possible good should be done' – the words of a young woman east of France who, with her parish priest, Pierre Fourier, founded an order to set up schools for girls. Within twenty-five years the schools run by the Congregation of Our Lady, Canonesses of St Augustine, were established from the Duchy of Lorraine to Paris.

Newly translated into English by Janet Shirley, Marie-Claire Tihon's book brings close to us Alix as a woman of great vision and spiritual life, and as woman of action, an exceptionally gifted organiser. We also get close to her darkness as we read her own writings: 'I cry out from the depths of my emptiness and nothingness to the God of incomprehensible majesty and greatness'.

'Make him grow': Alix's practical religion, perceptions, love and teaching show us today how we can value each person, the unsheltered, and love God and ourselves.

Tihon portrays Alix weaving through the obstacles of established religion whilst integrating her work and prayer in shared religious life.

Blessed Alix Le Clerc

MARIE-CLAIRE TIHON

Translated by
JANET SHIRLEY

COOL-CSA Publications
Congregation of Our Lady
Canonesses of St Augustine
2014

First published as *La Bienhereuse Alix Le Clerc*
Les Editions du Cerf, Paris 2004
This edition, by permission of Les Editions du Cerf
24 rue du Tanneries, 75013 Paris, France,
first published by
COOL-CSA Publications,
Congregation of Our Lady, Canonesses of St Augustine,
35 Maude Terrace, London E17 7DG

English edition edited by
Christina Brown and Anne Tennant

A catalogue record for this book is
available from the British Library

ISBN 978 0 9930957 0 2

Typeset in Garamond by Antony Gray
Printed and bound in Great Britain by
TJ International, Padstow, Cornwall

The cover shows the portrait of Alix Le Clerc by
Claude Deruet, 1622, together with Alix's autograph
injunction 'Que Dieu soit votre amour entier'
(*May God be your only love*)

Cover photograph by Maria LE thi Thanh-Nga
[The painting is at present held at Fontenay-sous-Bois]

The editors would like to express their thanks to the author Marie-Claire Tihon who has shown eager interest and vigour in our Englishing of her work on Alix Le Clerc and has moreover graciously written a new epilogue for this edition.

The translator Janet Shirley has patiently borne with our sounding out and correspondence concerning seventeenth century and contemporary religious notions and practice thrown up by Alix's life and writings.

We are indebted to Teresa de Bertodano, the Canonesses of the Holy Sepulchre and Pauline McAloone; Chris Dolan; Mme Laurence Rondinet and Frére Eric de Clermont-Tonnerre of Les Editions du Cerf; Sisters Emma Athill, St Paul Evans, Geraldine Hall, and Odile Guyot-Sionnest, sisters of the Congregation of Our Lady and especially, Martina Boylan whose enthusiasm for an English version of this work sparked the whole.

Our thanks above all go to that pair of educational and spiritual seers and doers, Alix Le Clerc and Pierre Fourier.

Contents

Main References and Abbreviations

Vie, 1666 Anon., [probably Angélique Milly] *La Vie de la Vénérable Mère Alix Le Clerc, fondatrice, première Mère et Religieuse de l'Ordre de la Congrégation de Notre-Dame, contenant la Relation d'icelle, escrite et signee de la mesme Mère, par commandement de ses supérieurs; les esclaircissement sur ceste Relation: avec les remarques des commencements de la Congrégation, tirées sur les Escrits propres du R. P. Fondateur et quelques Mémoires des actions principales de la dite Mère. Dédiées à Son Altesse par les Supérieures et religieuses de la Congrégation à Nancy.* Nancy, 1666.

[The Life of the Venerable Mother Alix Le Clerc, foundress, first Mother and nun of the Order of the Congregation of Our Lady, containing her own Relation, written and signed by the same Mother, at the command of her Superiors; clarification of this Relation: with remarks on the beginnings of the Congregation taken from the Writings of the Reverend Father the Founder and some Recollections of the principal acts of the said Mother. Dedicated to his Highness by the Superior and nuns of the Congregation at Nancy, 1666.]

Ecrits spirituels Alix Le Clerc, *Ecrits spirituels d'Alix Le Clerc*, extracts presented by Madeleine Cord'homme, Congrégation de Notre-Dame, 1968 (spelling and punctuation modified).

Relation/Rel	Alix Le Clerc, *Relation d'Alix Le Clerc (1576–1622), fondatrice de la Congrégation Notre-Dame*, complete text, edited with commentary by Paule Sagot, Congrégation Notre-Dame, 1990, abbreviated *Rel.* and paragraph number.
Rel./Cahiers, 2004	Alix Le Clerc, *Relation autobiographique* and *Notes de ses cahiers,* edited with introduction by Paule Sagot and Marie-Claire Tihon, Paris, Ed. Du Cerf, 'Sagesses chrétiennes', 2004.
Derréal, 1947	Hélène Derréal, *La Bienheureuse Alix Le Clerc et ses Ecrits,* Société d'impressions typographiques, Nancy, 1947.
Correspondance/C.	Edited by Hélène Derréal assisted by Madeleine Cord'homme, *St Pierre Fourier: sa correspondance 1598–1640,* 5 vols, Nancy, Presses Universitaires de Nancy, 1986–91. Vol.1: 28 November 1598– 25 December 1624; Vol. 2, early January 1625–6 May 1628; Vol. 3, 11 May 1628 – 29 December 1633; Vol. 4, 3 January 1634 –1 March 1640; Vol. 5, 1 March 1640– 12 December 1642, with Tables and Index.

Spelling has been modernised. If a letter is undated, abbreviations such as (*C.* 1, 122) read as (*Correspondance*, vol. 1, p. 122).

TRANSLATOR'S NOTE

Bible quotations are taken from the 1966 Jerusalem Bible published by Eyre & Spottiswoode.

Introduction

Why should Blessed Alix Le Clerc (1576–1622) be so little known? One reason must lie in the mishaps which affected her reputation after her death. Four years before she died she wrote at her confessor's request a short and invaluable autobiography, a *Relation*, composed in order to describe everything God had done for her which was 'rather unusual, for the good of her soul'. Her sisters collected together their memories of the woman they knew as Mother Teresa of Jesus, and in 1666 they published in Nancy the first biography of the Blessed Alix, including in it her *Spiritual Writings* and the *Relation*. In this way they bequeathed to later generations a revised portrait of Alix, as they improved her autobiography. They paid little attention to the shining graces of her mystical journey but took pains to emphasise, as they said, to 'clarify', what were then considered the main criteria of sanctity, miraculous events and the machinations of her enemy the devil. Later biographers, three in the eighteenth century and four in the nineteenth, wrote in the same hagiographic tradition. Among these her most fervent admirer was Count Gandelet, who in 1882 issued a new edition of the 1666 Life, in which he took remarkable liberties with the text of the Relation. Eventually in 1935 Canon Edmond Renard wrote about Alix as an historian, but alienated many of his readers by attributing only minor importance to the influence the founder of the Order had upon its foundress and instead stressing that of the primate of Lorraine, Antoine de Lenoncourt. The various approaches taken by biographers have done much to disguise Alix's true face. One such, Bedel, in 1645 made no reference to her whatsoever in his biography of

Pierre Fourier, instead emphasising the role of Gante André, one of the early sisters, as if the founder thought her more important than Alix. Ever since then there have been some who refuse to acknowledge Alix as foundress.

In 1937 came a providential discovery. In the city library at Evreux Sister Hélène Derréal found a manuscript copy of the *Relation* which is nearly contemporary with the original, and shows what changes the early editors had made. Now Alix's greatness blazed out in the light of truth. On 4 May 1947 Pius XII announced her beatification. Then on 2 May 1950 her coffin was found, which had been lost after the upheavals of the French Revolution, during which the convent of Nancy had been seized by the state. Her coffin, for safekeeping, had been moved a few feet from its original position. In 1960 the remains of the blessed Alix Le Clerc were officially identified and made available for veneration. In 1976 the painting by Claude Deruet of Alix on her deathbed was also found and given to the Congregation. Scholarly and fervent publications accompanied these various discoveries. Sister Marie-Lucienne de Lorgeril, writing as A. de Remiremont, in 1946 and 1947 published two charming *Lives of Alix*, one of them 'told to little girls in France and everywhere'. In 1965 Sister Hélène Derréal published the first volume of her masterly biography of Pierre Fourier, *Un missionaire de la Contre-Réforme et l'institution de la Congrégation de Notre-Dame* (*A Missionary of the Counter Reformation and the Founding of the Congregation of Our Lady*). A second volume was to include the founder's *Letters*, but Sister Hélène died in 1989 before the later volumes appeared. In 1990 Sister Paule Sagot published the complete text of the *Relation*, based on the Evreux manuscript, together with a commentary which sets the work in the context of its own time and of the author's life. This work is indispensable for all who want to understand Alix Le Clerc.

What more could any one want? Nothing, so people said, but a biography of Alix. I was glad to undertake this task because it would enable me to write for the foundress the same sort of work I had already written on Pierre Fourier, published by Editions du Cerf in 1997. I soon saw that it would not be easy. Some fifteen Lives of Alix had already appeared, all giving different pictures of her according to the periods and opinions of the different authors. Most of them were such as would appeal to readers with a taste for tales of the marvellous and demonic attack. Then a fresh idea came to me. After all, I thought, the Holy Spirit, then and now, spoke and still speaks to us through the saints. Through them he can reach us. If his hearers are to understand his message, I must use their language. If I am to paint a picture of Alix, I must make clear the characteristics proper to her historical setting, so that from it her own shining self may emerge, transcending all times. Because the Relation is a piece of typically seventeenth century spiritual writing, it is essential that we distinguish between the heart of our faith and the dress it wore in the fashion of those days. In it Alix describes supernatural interventions in ways which now we may find disconcerting but then were acceptable. She may talk of dreams and imaginary visions, but this does not matter. These images furnished her mental world and God used them to touch her heart. Her resistance to sin takes the form of a battle in which she challenges the devil, a devil perverse enough to disguise itself as human. Her devotion allows her to feel comfortable with the Virgin, the Lord Jesus and the saints. She encounters them, talks with them, and such conversations will sometimes lead her to 'most high things in the knowledge of God'.

If, as Karl Rahner said in connection with Teresa of Avila, 'personal experience of God is more urgently needed than ever', the present is the right time for hearing the message given by Alix Le Clerc. She reminds us of the near presence of the Lord who dwells in our soul and inspires all we do. Her mysticism is the more attractive to us from the very fact that she was a woman of action and an exceptionally gifted organiser. She and her women friends formed a well knit team who fought for the recognition, almost unthinkable at that time, of their vocation as teaching nuns. Energetic but humble, Alix founded the Congregation of Our Lady, bought houses, opened schools, taught children, came to the help of the poorest, stirred up her communities. Everywhere she spread the love of God which burned in her. She expressed the rules of her life in pithy phrases which we can make our own if we want to tread in her footsteps – 'Do all possible good', 'Do all that most pleases God, even if it means death'.

BLESSED ALIX LE CLERC

The Duchy of Lorraine in Alix's time

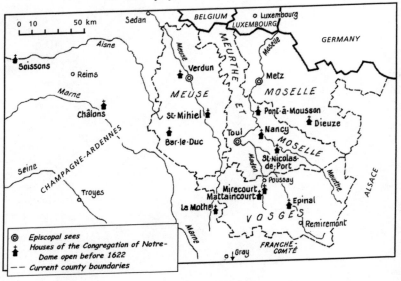

The Duchy of Lorraine, founded in 959, was a independent duchy roughly corresponding with the present-day region of Lorraine in north-eastern France. Slight changes to the boundaries occurred over time but, following the War of the Polish Succession, Lorraine was annexed by France in 1766. Lorraine is now a region of France, which in turn is divided into four counties shown on the map above. Alsace once part of the Duchy is now a separate region of France.

CHAPTER ONE

'A good and devout girl, in everyone's opinion'

1576

Alix Le Clerc was born at Remiremont on 2 February 1576. A biographer looking for information about her childhood cannot find much, but this very fact of her being rooted in Lorraine is significant. At this period the duchy of Lorraine, both independent and staunchly Catholic though it was, had been severely shaken by repercussions of the Wars of Religion which ravaged her two powerful neighbours. Eastwards, the formidable empire of Charles V had collapsed at his death in 1558, but his successes against the Protestants had fixed the pattern of Germany's religious divisions, leaving the Lutheran princes free to impose their own religion upon their subjects. Westward, relations between Lorraine and France were unstable, affected by the ambitions of both parties. Matters began well when the King of France, Henri II (1519–1559), brought to his court the young Duke of Lorraine, Charles III (1545–1608), and in 1559 married Charles to his daughter Claude. The Duke of Lorraine was now son-in-law to the king of France. While the French crown passed in turn to two of the sons of Catherine de Medici, Francis II (1559–1560) and Charles IX (1560–1574), the Duke of Lorraine kept out of the Wars of Religion which caused such bloodshed in France, but when another of her sons, Henri III (1574–1589), came to the throne, the Duke abandoned his neutrality and flung himself into battle. In France the cadet branch of the house of Lorraine, Dukes of Guise, took the lead. Henri, third Duke of Guise (1550–1588), like his father known as *Le Balafré*, Scarface, instigated the St Bartholomew's day massacre (24 August 1572), then later defeated German Protestants at Dormans, but in the following year he could not prevent the king signing the peace of Beaulieu, which gave considerable advantages to the Protestants. Treason! cried the Lorrainers, and in their disgust drew closer to Henri of Guise, who on 8 June 1576 established the first League. This was both a political party, seeking to restrict royal power in France, and a religious one, eager to fight Protestants wherever they might be. It is no coincidence that Alix Le Clerc was born in the year that the League was formed and drew her first breath in Lorraine, homeland of supporters of the League. It was also the time when Charles III became increasingly harsh, indeed intolerant, towards Protestants.

Remiremont

Echoes of distant events came quietly to Remiremont, nature has set the town in such a pleasant place, encircled as it is by the beautiful and thickly forested slopes of the Fossard massif. It is well watered too, as the Moselotte here joins the Moselle, which flows broadly on, dividing Remiremont from its neighbour Saint-Etienne. The roads carry more traffic than do the rivers, enabling travellers to journey north or south. Merchants from Trèves or Cologne can reach Basle by way of Metz, Pont-à-Mousson, Nancy, Epinal and Remiremont.

To these gifts of nature Remiremont adds a greater one: it is an important spiritual centre, one destined to welcome saints. It was Romaric who first chose this mountain in the Vosges, an area well suited to contemplation, which became known as the 'mount of Romaric', and soon as Remiremont. In 620 together with St Amé he founded two monasteries, one for men half way up the hill and the other for women right at the top of the holy mountain. In the ninth century the nuns moved down into the valley and settled on the left bank of the Moselle opposite the original mountain. The town grew around their convent. At about the same time they abandoned the harsh rule of St Columbanus and adopted the kinder one of St Benedict. Some two centuries later they ceased to live in common, gained exemption from episcopal control, becoming subject in spiritual matters only to the Holy See, and transformed their community into a Noble Chapter of canonesses. Now an enclave in the heart of Lorraine, the chapter depended directly on the Empire, to the great annoyance of the dukes of Lorraine. In 1566 Charles III, tired of being nothing but the abbey's protector – the Advocate, as he was called – and infuriated by the fact that the Noble Ladies had set up the Empire's armorial bearings over the abbey doors, announced the confiscation of their very considerable property. The canonesses made a show of resistance but then decided to submit – la Guerre de Panonceaux (the War of the Escutcheons) was over.[1] The duke made his solemn entrance to Remiremont on 2 August 1579.

The Le Clerc family

Alix must have become more and more aware of events as she grew up. Certainly they affected her relatives, who are described as 'well known and among the best families of those districts.[2] The archives are full of references to the brothers and nephews of Jean Le Clerc, Alix's father, but as for he himself, his wife and his children, not one document remains. The very identity of Alix's mother is uncertain – some call her Lagoutte, others Anne Sagay or Sagard.[3]

Alix certainly had a sister, Philippe, who married first Claude Perrin and later a second husband, Nicolas Bonlarron. We know that her brother Jacques (1575–1637) had six children.

Pierre de Gonneville uses hundreds of notarial records to show that the family originated in Hymont. He begins their family tree with Demenge Le Clerc, 'the older', and declares that he had six children, of whom Jean was the eldest. Alix's uncles and her aunt are of interest because they became 'friends and well-wishers of the Good Father' and benefactors of the Congregation of Our Lady. They were: Didier Le Clerc of Domèvre-sous-Montfort and Hymont; François Le Clerc from Adompt; Demenge Le Clerc the younger from Hymont; Catherine Le Clerc, wife of Nicolas Guillerel of Derbamont; and Nicolas Le Clerc from Epinal.

What we know of the younger members of the family casts light on the older. Well known in the village, they were agricultural workers or traders or both. Such of their many children as settled in the town were merchants, butchers or clothiers rather than craftsmen. Some entered the liberal professions, becoming advocates or notaries. Soon some aspired to enter the ranks of the nobility. They were mayors of their villages, and each generation gave sons and daughters to religious orders and the priesthood. They took care to have their children educated, sent their sons to university in Pont-à-Mousson, and contributed to the increasing strength of the middle class of which they formed part.

In Jean Le Clerc we find the same sort of profession, the same work ethic, the exact and practical mind. It seems that he sold meat or traded in cattle, a considerable business at that period, one which involved travel to local fairs and markets and the handling of money like a banker or money-broker. According to family tradition he was closely involved in local government, as is shown by his ascent through the ranks of municipal administration in Remiremont. In 1582, when Alix was six, he was *doyen de justice,* in charge of the administration of justice, it was his duty to implement decisions made by the tribunals, such as the issue of summonses, arrest warrants, orders of compulsory attendance, and the arrest or release of prisoners. In 1587 he was chief magistrate, *grand échevin*, presiding over the tribunal of civil and criminal justice, and also acting as the corporation's receiver. It is in this role that we see him in action during the 'disturbance caused by war', a tragic episode due to Lorraine's situation, open as it was to the passage of armies as the Wars of Religion moved to and fro. A second League had been formed in 1584, one which constantly harassed the Huguenots and openly supported the duke. Armed conflict seemed inevitable, to the point where the opponents thought good to appeal for help to foreign forces, in this case calling in an army of 30,000 or 40,000 German reiters. These crossed through and ravaged the country on their way to join the troops of Henri of Navarre, thus revenging themselves for Charles III's promise of support to the Leaguers.[4]

Nothing is more dreadful than the transit of men of war, and the Lorrainers already knew this only too well.[5] As was common practice at the time these men lived off the country and committed the vilest atrocities – houses burned, women raped, crops laid waste, cattle slaughtered. Lively alarm was felt in Remiremont, because the mercenaries, avoiding Nancy and Toul, were making their way south. In the crisis committee gathered in the town hall the chief magistrate, Jean Le Clerc, dealt with the costs of defence.[6] He paid the sentinels posted on the ramparts and the look-outs on the tower of St Peter's church. He sent men to find out where the reiters were moving – they had reached Blâmont, Bayon, would soon be at Vézelise. His brother Didier kept watch for him in Mirecourt. At last on 12 September 1587 the invaders, having laid waste the district of Vaucouleurs and Neufchâteau, left Lorraine.

Their passage had affected only part of the country and cannot be compared to the later horrors of the Thirty Years War, but it terrified people and must have struck hard at an impressionable child such as Alix, then aged eleven.

One year later in January 1588 there came a new alarm – plague, following in the soldiers' footsteps, broke out in Remiremont, where it made swift progress, in spite of the winter cold and the purity of the air.[7] Great bonfires of juniper wood blazed at crossroads and in the almost empty streets, from which the inhabitants had fled to the countryside, where they would stay until the plague was halted.

In the shade of the abbey

The Le Clerc family played its full part in the town's joys and sorrows, but Alix is always discreet and says nothing of this. None the less her father's career must have involved her in town events, particularly in official ceremonies such as those accompanying the handover of posts. In 1591 Jean Le Clerc became mayor, or more exactly, the abbey's mayor. People remembered in Remiremont that the Noble Ladies in fact controlled the administration of the town. It was therefore the abbess, Madame Barbe de Salm, who chose Jean Le Clerc from the three candidates presented to her by the inhabitants and solemnly invested him with this office in the abbey hall before a gathering of the authorities and a good number of local people. Having received his staff of office, the new mayor made his oath, vowing to exercise his powers rightly under the authority of the abbess. The day concluded with a feast to which were invited ladies, canons, the mayor, town and lawcourt officials *(jurés et gens de justice)*, various citizens of whom Madame de Salm approved, and surely the new mayor's family.[8] At fifteen, Alix would take an interest in her father's new responsibilities and thus extend the boundaries of her world. In a small town of two thousand inhabitants and at a time when temporal and spiritual were mingled, necessary business still had a certain humanity, free from undue bureaucracy. It was the mayor's duty to maintain roads and defences, to ensure that gates, roads, inns and markets were policed. He oversaw the town's food supply, checked the prices and quality of foodstuffs on sale, bread, wine and meat. He had to provide a family council for orphans and supervise the administration of their property. Of course there were difficult cases, and he would talk about them with his children, and so young Alix came to learn the realities of life.

Her parents, says the chronicle, 'were virtuous and feared God. Alix was brought up in the piety and civil behaviour of the best houses of the place'. These formulaic phrases allow our imagination free rein. Her father and mother were certainly well enough educated to be able to teach her to read, write and reckon, as there was no school to which they could have sent the child, but it is quite likely that one of the canonesses of the abbey may have helped her to further study.

Undoubtedly the presence of the Noble Ladies brought fame to the town, even though their easy way of life was much criticised. We wonder what young Alix thought of these canonesses who can hardly be called nuns, living as they did, each of them in her own house among her numerous servants.[9] But they are properly called 'canonesses', since the rich prebends[10] they held enabled them to form a chapter dedicated to St Peter and ensured, or should have ensured, the celebration of services in the their monumental and magnificent church. The most appropriate name for them was that of the Ladies, *les Dames*, from the Latin *Domina*, because of their illustrious birth. Each one had to prove her right to at least eight quarters of nobility.[11] They wore sumptuous and worldly garments, and to the amusement of Montaigne, who passed that way, their veil was a mere piece of light crepe worn on the head. They took no vows, went out as much as they liked and could leave Remiremont to get married. Looking more closely at their history, we can see that after adopting the Rule of St Benedict, they allowed their abbey to become a house of education for girls from noble families, or even, as has been said, 'a seminary for marriageable girls'. The fact that the canonesses were free to welcome guests means we can suppose that Alix went visiting there, and perhaps received the education she would later demonstrate. When she herself came to create a completely new form of religious life, she knew, having seen them at Remiremont, what faults to avoid, and she understood the need for and approved the reforms attempted by her contemporary Catherine of Lorraine (1573–1648), daughter of Duke Charles III.

Meanwhile in her adolescence Alix preferred to meditate in her baptismal church of Our Lady rather in that of the Noble Ladies, where the altars were as neglected as the souls and all the canons were ignorant men, incapable of celebrating the sacraments properly, including especially that of penitence.[12] Alix liked to go to quieter sanctuaries and visit the many saints of her home town. One such was the chapel of St Mary Magdalene attached to the leper house, where not so long before, only in 1579, two leper women had been enclosed to lead a life of penitence. In the former priory on top of the Holy Mountain, looking out at the sublime landscape spread below her, she would turn her mind to thoughts of heaven, and in the chapel of St Sabine she would glory in the memory of the girl who was martyred by the Huns.

In the light of 2 February

Every year as the Feast of the Purification of Our Lady drew near, Alix prepared to observe it as well as she could, because, she said, 'I have an especial devotion to that day because I have been told that it was the day of my birth and my baptism' (*Rel.* 23). A marvellous conjuncture, the baby is no sooner born than filled with God! On the same day that the most pure Virgin submitted to the purification imposed by law, the light of baptismal grace shone upon Alix. All her life she tried to keep fresh the glory of this day, longing as she did for purity and seeking to offer God a single-hearted love.

In Alix's time 2 February was a public holiday, not so well known as the Presentation of Christ in the Temple but called Candlemas and very popular. The office included a candle-lit procession and in the church of Our Lady where Alix had been baptised this feast was the crown of the year. In that church, indeed, every day was a small Candlemas, for an oil lamp was kept burning in front of a very ancient statue of the Virgin and in the vault hung a large chandelier, on which the *chatoliers* (the churchwardens whose duty it was to administer the church's possessions) every day lit the many candles offered by the faithful. In the year Alix was born they had granted to certain privileged farmers, 'the guests of Our Lady', the monopoly of making *brizien*, the mixture of wax and honey from which were made the candles that would light the church all the year round.[13] In the clarity of 'Our Lady's light' Alix was glad to renew the grace given her at baptism and to tell Mary how much she longed for purity. She was still very young, and in that church she could study as if in a great picture book, receiving lasting impressions, creating her mental world. Statues, windows and tapestries gave her close acquaintance with those

who dwelt in heaven, Anne, Nicholas, Peter, Paul, the angel of
the Annunciation and others too. What struck the child most
were the great 'christolles', the hangings showing the Christ
which hung behind the altar during Lent. On Ascension Day
she had been moved to see the figure of Jesus disappear
before her eyes. This naive faith, rather backward in relation
the Council of Trent (1545–1563), left the teenager hungry.
Referring later to 'the town of Remiremont, her birthplace',
Alix pointed out its failings. 'There was nothing there,' she
wrote, 'but the darkness of ignorance, no church people who
could teach the way to virtue' (*Rel.* 3). It was this lack of
teachers, felt so painfully, that later would lead her to 'teach the
way to virtue' to little girls.

'Sin and fear'

At that point she had no one to guide her, no one and nothing
but the grace of God, who is always ready to use mere chance.
'It was luck,' said Alix, describing the event. She was ill in bed
with a persistent fever when a young friend came to see her. He
scornfully tossed on to the bed a book full of terrifying accounts
of the fate of penitents who had made incomplete confessions,
too ashamed of some of their sins to mention them.[14] Then
came the tragic result of a sacrilegious confession: eternal
damnation. This guidance based on fear moved Alix, so deeply
that as soon as she had recovered she went and made confession.
This was, she said, the 'only good confession' of that period,
'good', she felt, as being complete, since a minute examination
of her conscience had led her to list every sin of her childhood
(*Rel.* 2). Exactly how old was she, perhaps fifteen or sixteen?
Alix wanted to share the benefit of this full confession, one
which could halt the sinner sliding as Delumeau says, on a
'tobbogan of sacrilege', with her closest friends, and began by

filling them with her fears of hell. This reaction shows how much she was already a teacher: a book shows her a light, she instantly makes use of it, and eager to spread this flame, she uses it to enlighten others.

The darkness of the past is swept away but the present is still not right. 'This confession,' she said, 'was not enough to deliver me from the sins and vanities which I was committing, because I was so ignorant' (*Rel.* 3). It is a clear diagnosis: not knowing how to give meaning to existence, her life seemed empty to her, as if wrapped in a vain outward show. That is the sense of the word 'vanities', a word very often used by authors of the period.[15]

The attraction of vanities

But how intoxicating Alix found these vanities! A beauty in the terms of that age, she was very attractive, tall, slender, with fair hair and delicate features, her white skin enhanced by the brilliance of her blue eyes. Aware of her good looks, she enjoyed the admiration they brought her, but maintained a reserve which inspired respect and made her still more attractive because of the depth her friends could see in her. She had a charm, they said, which you felt before you even spoke to her. Her character was at one with this 'pleasant manner'. She was, said those who knew her, 'of a sweet and obliging nature, sparing of her words, with a calm and always equable humour',[16] but always lively and cheerful. Naturally she was much liked, especially by young people, the boys and girls she met and danced with. Alix was an excellent dancer, notable for her grace and distinction. Intoxicated by the music, eager to discipline her body to the rhythm of the chaconne or the pavane, she was more eager still to intensify her feelings as the dancers crossed hands and exchanged looks. But she had an absolute safeguard against excess: 'All that was best in me,' she wrote, 'was that I loved honour'. Out of pride, she added, 'I concealed my vain and youthful behaviour'. This sense of honour would not allow her to give way to what she called her 'light behaviour in company', so that her devotion to Our Lady and to St Anne meant that people considered her 'a good and devout girl according to the world' (*Rel.* 3). Two girls were at war in Alix, one frivolous, one devout. Which of them would win?

'Come!'

Fresh graces came to Alix after she had made the confession aroused by that terrifying book. The first came in a dream which she describes in her *Relation* as straightforwardly as she does the other messages God was to send her. Why should we be surprised at this form of communication? The Bible is full of prophetic dreams in which God speaks to those who are searching for light. As she slept, Alix saw herself present at the mass in the church of Our Lady in Remiremont. Just as she was moving towards the choir to make her offering in the ancient way, she saw the Virgin herself dressed in a religious habit which later, in memory of this vision, became that of the Sisters of Our Lady. Feeling her unworthiness, Alix did not dare approach her, but Mary encouraged her, saying, 'Come, daughter, and I will make you welcome, for when you were sinning you did what pleased my Son by making your confession' (*Rel.* 4). Later when Pierre Fourier was writing the preface to the Constitution for his nuns in 1640, he remembered the scene the future foundress had described to him and placed Mary on the threshold ready to welcome, 'accept and keep in her noble family' the woman who asked to come in. But at the time Alix was not inclined to attach importance to a dream. None the less it brought her a double benefit: 'I resolved,' she decided at once, 'to be more devoted to Our Lady and to make my confession more often' (*Rel.* 4).

Now it was not fear of hell bringing Alix closer to God, it was Mary who took the initiative. She will welcome Alix and take her to her Son. The chosen girl's spiritual adventure was beginning. The Lord Jesus had looked at her and his look made her frivolous life ridiculous. 'My soul was very sad among the vanities', she acknowledged, 'and I had some inclination to leave Remiremont where I was so much in company with vanity and youth' (*Rel.* 5). Providence brought a response to her wish – in 1595 the Le Clerc family moved house. Alix's father was ill, ill with a long-drawn-out disease, and he was advised for his health's sake to try the air of his natal home and to settle himself and his household at Hymont. Remembering what this would bring, Alix thanked Providence for this move, for her parents, she tells us, 'died in the grace of God', as she had hoped they would, 'through the happy end they made' (*Rel.* 5). Reading between the lines we can conclude that the Le Clercs, having become parishioners of Pierre Fourier, at the end of their lives enjoyed the pastoral care of the priest of Mattaincourt.[17]

At nineteen, Alix imagined that to live in Hymont was to 'withdraw from the world' and was delighted to do so, because the world troubled her, though she did not know why (*Rel.* 6). But she soon discovered her mistake. Who would have thought that in this small village, tucked away behind the encircling Madon, there could be 'more vanities, more worldly pleasures, than elsewhere'? The Le Clerc family's way of life was not quieter, quite the contrary, for they had recently received a considerable share of the inheritance left by their Demenge grandfather and Alix noted that at Hymont her father had 'the power to live and stay there as long as he should like'. As soon as she reached Hymont she was welcomed like a queen and 'companions surrounded her there just as much as elsewhere' (*Rel.* 6). Nothing could be more tempting than to join in and share in all decency and honour in the festivities to which Hymont's young people flocked. Among them were her cousins, dozens of them, six at Uncle Didier's, mayor of Hymont, ten at Uncle Francis', at least five at the younger Didier's and three at Aunt Catherine's house. It is not surprising that Alix, young and lovely, was sought in marriage. But no, a fresh and 'especial grace of God', she said, meant that she was 'not drawn to the vocation of marriage'. She even acknowledged, being of an independent nature, that she felt 'an aversion to subjection to a husband' (*Rel.* 6). Two years passed in this way, with Alix in love with 'vanities' but deriving from them only sorrow and injury to her soul.

filles)', who wore these, she said, when they wanted to make their communion.[22] Already her love for poverty and humility was clear.

Also clear now was her devotion to God alone, for 'without taking any advice' she made a vow of chastity. The *Relation* says no more about this, but some biographers have claimed that it was during a wedding that she consecrated her virginity to the Lord. We can surely suppose that in some such joyous celebration of a newly married pair Alix would know what it was she was giving up. A sudden whim, people may say. No, a heartfelt impulse, a prelude to her mystical betrothal.

Encounter with Fourier

Like many saints, Alix could use the well known expression, 'God does exist, I have met him'. As God called to her, she heard his commands and obeyed them, obeyed them exactly but in her own way. She was obedient but self taught, and needed now to use the words of St Paul, 'Lord, what do you want me to do?' God answered by sending her his chosen guide, Pierre Fourier.

This man whom she visited during the summer of 1597 she would afterwards refer to as 'our good Father', because when she wrote her *Relation* almost twenty years later, he had founded the Congregation of Our Lady and the word 'good' was firmly attached to his name. In the event no title would better suit the role of priest, confessor and spiritual director he was to play in her life. Later on their friendship would become richer in many ways but we may feel sure that all of them were present in potential from the very start. He as teacher and she as pupil agreed to listen together to the Spirit. Sometimes they may have changed these roles and the astonished priest would perceive God at work in Alix's soul.

Stimulated by the walk from Hymont to Mattaincourt, and encouraged by her priest's welcome, Alix began to explain her plans to him and said that she would do everything he would tell her to do that would 'be pleasing to God'. Admirable docility, and he responded by advising the normal remedy of the time, a general confession. Easy, thought Alix, 'not being very sinful, she would be soon done for that time'. But the priest did not stop there. He put into her hands a book on the examination of conscience which plunged Alix into the depths of despair. She wrote, 'I found myself described there, so full of sins that I became bitterly unhappy and wept day and night'. Well, we may think, there's a young inexperienced pastor who prescribes the same remedy day in day out – to examine one's conscience according to the rules of his Jesuit masters. Inappropriate as we may feel this direction to be, seeing what a drastic effect it had on Alix, we still have to admit that it would give rise to essential graces. Very soon Alix would catch up on her years of ignorance and establish her spiritual life on firm foundations. Hard work, then, and 'costly', yes indeed! She was in constant anxiety because hidden sins lurking in some dark corner of her conscience would come back to her, 'always more sins recurring to her mind'. The more she meant to renounce them, the more she saw how serious they were. And to her own faults was added the whole fallen sinfulness of humankind. Because our first father Adam had sinned, she concluded that he had made 'the whole human race subject to sin'. The injustice of this disgusted her and drove her to 'great temptations of blasphemy and against the mercy of God' (*Rel.* 10). This almighty God who is said to hate sin, does he allow evil to triumph over good?

Fourier was sorry for Alix's distress and did not avoid the visits she made him, which she describes like this: 'Every day I spent some time in confession before him during a period of six months' (*Rel.* 9), a practice which was not improbable in those days. Just what that spiritual therapy was can be clearly seen in the benefits Alix drew from it then and later as they flowered. The first was an understanding of herself, of her profound grief and her past faults. This sharp sense of sin, which never left her, made her greatly regret that she had not kept the purity of soul she had had as a child.[23] To recover this she was ready to follow the example of Christ who shed his blood for the remission of sins and to offer herself as an expiatory victim. She declared, 'I offered him my body to be crushed into a thousand pieces, if only he would re-establish my soul in its first purity' (*Rel.* 10). By meditating on sin she acquired an 'extreme apprehension of offending God or of displeasing him, however slightly'.[24] From this came the violence of her struggles with temptation, from this her devotion to the Immaculate Virgin, model of purity, being free from the original fault and from all sin. Educationist that she was, she would pass on to others the fruit of her experience, wanting these teaching women to make it their principal care to 'keep little girls in a state of innocence, impressing on them at an early age the fear of God and the horror of sin'.[25]

Fourier, for whom humility was second nature, supported Alix in the painful life of her spiritual sorrow, but he gave her a calming remedy, that of divine mercy. He showed her the Christ who was the friend of sinners, the physician who came to heal the sick. The young theologian, later a passionate apostle of salvation in Jesus Christ,[26] revealed to Alix the unfathomable mystery of God's love. When she rebelled against the thought that sin entered the world because of one man, Adam, he would oppose her with the words of St Paul, 'If it is certain that through one man's fall so many died, it is even more certain that

divine grace, coming through the one man, Jesus Christ, came
to so many as an abundant free gift' (Rom. 5:15). He exerted his
remarkable teaching gifts to instruct Alix and she, greedy for
knowledge, reflected and prayed. She does not mention Fourier's
help here, but it was decisive. A very right intuition made her
feel that God in his goodness had not created sin, and she
acknowledged that she had been wrong to consider this idea,
'not knowing', she said, 'that this was a temptation'. But who
had told her that it was a temptation, if not Fourier? To see that
the Holy Spirit used the priest to enlighten his penitent, we
need only read the preface to the *Relation*, and measure the
distance travelled. She confessed her faults to God, 'acknow-
ledging', she wrote, 'that I was most unworthy to receive even
one of his graces but rather worthy of much hell for the many
sins I had committed, the time I remained in the world, and
since sixteen or seventeen years of age when I had felt the light
of his grace, so many offences and so many failures to co-operate
with that grace'.[27] At the time she was writing her *Relation*,
however, the joy of salvation had done away with all fear of hell.
Even if fear of the judgment did touch her for a moment,
confidence would instantly triumph. At the opening of the
Relation addressed to her confessor, Fr. Jean Guéret, she wrote:

> I tremble and blush often when I think of this before [the just
> Lord]; but looking the other way to see his infinite mercy and
> kind goodness, granted to me through the merits of my Lord
> Jesus Christ and the help of his blest Mother, not only do I
> hope and raise my trust in him but I receive great solace,
> rejoicing that on the great day of judgment his mercy will rest
> more fully on me than on all the rest of the world, as also I
> shall see it shine on all the other sinners who have turned
> from their sin.

Remembering the sinner who was a guest of Simon the Pharisee, Alix knew that much was forgiven her because she had loved much (Luke 7:47).

The parable of the 'three states'

Schooled by Fourier, Alix moved on from fear of hell to trust in God. During the months after her conversion the Holy Spirit flooded her with experiences of light, of which these are some of the most striking –

One evening as it was getting dark and Alix was deep in meditation, she felt 'suddenly seized by a great fear', caused by a strange and quite new experience (*Rel.* 11). At first she felt that she was 'monstrously big' and heavy, so much so that she could not 'even move a finger' or make a sound. The meaning of this parable in action was revealed to her at once: 'This is the state of a sinner who cannot move without the grace of God'. The lesson is clear – just as paralysis prevents all movement, so sin renders the soul incapable of action, but God's grace restores life to the sinner. Alix would remember the healing of the paralytic at Capernaum who got up and walked as soon as Jesus had forgiven his sins (Matt. 9:1–8) and that of the dumb demoniac of whom the evangelist says, 'And when the devil was cast out, the dumb man spoke' (Matt. 9:32–33).

Then in the second scene of this vision there comes a devil who advances upon Alix and an angel dressed in white who brandishes a sword at him and with a tremendous noise puts him to flight. This angel-devil battle appears often in the iconography of the period and Alix would certainly have known the image of St George defeating the dragon or St Michael trampling on the devil. A more likely image for us, less familiar with those representations, is that of the angel with the sword of flame guarding the gate of Paradise (Gen. 3:23), or the battle of the Apocalypse in which Michael and his angels fight the ancient serpent (Rev. 12:7–12). Whatever the origin of the images, Alix suddenly felt so light that she rose into the air, with nothing she could see supporting her, while an inner voice explained, 'This [is] the state of grace'. The feeling of weightlessness led her to interpret the scene: in the fight against the forces of evil divine grace guarantees victory to the Christian soul and lifts it up into the heights where the wind of the Spirit blows.[28]

The third scene used the symbol of fire. Alix's body came gently down, rested motionless, then was consumed by fire 'from the feet to the head' and rose up 'like smoke'. This devouring flame manifests the presence of God and purifies. It consumed the offering Alix had made of her life, lifting it towards God like smoke from incense. 'This', said her inner voice, 'is the state of perfection which consists of rendering the flesh subject to the spirit and the spirit to God, seeking and loving him above all things and cleaving to him alone'. Thus with a brief wing stroke young Alix in God's clear light touches the genius of Pascal and his famous hierarchy of the 'three Orders': 'All the bodies there are, all the souls, and all they can produce are not worth the smallest movement of charity. This is of an order infinitely higher'. It is remarkable that from the moment of her conversion Alix so beautifully ranks the worth of body and of spirit, and above them places God alone, dearer than all.

This vision of the three states, that of the sinner, of the soul indwelt by grace and of the Christian walking towards perfection, illumined Alix so profoundly that it banished her temptation towards blasphemy and led her to fresh progress. She now reached the stage of 'great desires', in which her generous nature, never half hearted, took command. 'This left me', she says, 'with a great longing to obliterate myself and to endure for the love of God, because it seemed to me that suffering was a more divine way to God' (*Rel.* 12). She adds, 'Oh how easy this seemed to me then! But practice has made me think very differently'. Fair-minded Alix acknowledged that this excessive longing for pain was a sign of self will. She expressed this by a striking word, being still, she said, 'crouched' (*croupie*) within herself and co-operating badly with the 'great desires' Our Lord was sending her. Nor was she more indulgent towards the 'great desire for penitence', which she hoped would last all her life. She worked hard, she tells us, with the nuns of Our Lady, for five or six years after they came to Nancy in 1603, until eventually their Jesuit confessors brought them to greater moderation. We are grateful to Alix for describing her journey complete with its faults. As a new convert she at first thought of goodness as a series of heroic deeds. Soon she would realise that the essential is to let God act and abandon the self to him.

CHAPTER THREE

'This vocation is from God'

An imperative vocation

Working through these various 'great desires', Alix reached what seems to be the normal conclusion. She wrote, 'I told our good Father everything that was happening within me and the great longing I had to be a nun' (*Rel.* 14). This personal calling was so important to her that she used it in her *Relation* to date events in her life. 'This was at the beginning of my calling', she says (*Rel.* 62). To implement this longing, a 'vocation of attraction' as Count Gandelet called it,[29] there was not a great deal of choice. Convents were almost all in need of reform and the only house Fourier could suggest to Alix, suitable because reformed, was that of the Poor Clares at Pont-à-Mousson. At first young Alix liked the idea, but then she changed her mind. Moreover her parents were against it – the Order was too strict, the Rule too harsh, the enclosure too rigorous. Let their child enter a 'non-cloistered *Religion*'[30] and they would accept that. But their daughter heard this suggestion 'with horror'.

As often happens, the solution came from above, and Alix received the light of revelation. 'When I prayed to God,' she said, 'it always came into my mind that a new house for Girls[31] must be set up, wherein all possible good should be done' (*Rel.* 15). A fundamental declaration, where every word engages the future. God had spoken, Alix listened and understood. 'Set up a new house for Girls' – this was to invent a new form of religious life, something quite unlike that unsatisfactory one led the Ladies of Remiremont. It should be a new Order in which virgins consecrated to the Lord would gather with a purpose already defined, 'there to do all possible good'. Thus without worrying about the hindrances that canon law was creating by the dozen in her time, Alix anticipated the institutions of the Church and founded an apostolic congregation. Her boundless objective was to build the Kingdom of God, which would be at the service of all humanity, while taking account of the available material. As she prayed, the project took shape and Alix felt herself urged 'with so much vehemence' that she set off to tell Fourier about it, 'begging him,' she said, 'to let her make this decision'. It was for her to do so, she was sure. Fourier refused – not surprisingly. He recited a litany of objections – 'the difficulty of finding girls who had what would be needed to undertake this new vocation and many other reasons'. Alix listened but was stubborn, displaying much greater trust in God than Fourier had done. 'Nothing is impossible to God, if such is his will', she retorted. Arguments done, he sent her away, saying, 'Find some companions, and then we'll see'. She wouldn't find any, he thought, and that would be that. How little he knew Alix, how little he knew God, master of the impossible! Alix tells us what happened next: 'Six weeks or two months later three girls[32] came one after another to see me and told me of the desire they had felt all of a sudden, they wanted to be nuns and to come with me'. Such vocations say much about the attraction Alix had for her friends. The attractiveness she had exercised upon her admirers she now turned into an apostolic bait. Without waiting to see how her three imitators would say goodbye to their parents and strengthened in her plans by the swift decisions, she led them off to Fourier, who, of course, required them to make general confessions. This done and absolution granted, they declared to him with one voice that they were glad to accept their friend's plan, to make a new house of religion and to do all possible good there. They wanted this apostolic calling to be communal, for we wish, they added, 'to live together and be in common'. Another refusal, 'They would not let us do this', as they must surely have expected.

Two foundation dates

Fourier, however, was driven by the same enthusiasm, and wanted to help these generous souls achieve their potential. But although the four girls knew nothing of what was needed to set up a women's congregation, Fourier understood it very well. If they wanted to lead a truly religious life apart, they would have to live in cloistered convents, expensive to build, necessarily located within towns, enjoying large and steady incomes and cut off from any hope of external mission work. Canon law regulations had been inescapable since Pius V in 1566 required all consecrated women to take solemn vows and accept enclosure, thus turning them all into nuns. It was therefore impossible to allow these new 'apostresses' as Fourier later called them, to devote themselves to 'doing all possible good', unenclosed, in small village placements. Like a careful Lorrainer, he weighed up the pros and cons, and very often found that 'pro' was winning. In his abbey at Chamousey he had indeed seen how the Canons of St Augustine opposed all attempts at reform. Very well then, if the old Orders refused to rekindle their original fervour, it would better, he thought, to start afresh. The words of Alix, 'to make a new house so as to do all possible good there', echoed strongly in his apostle's heart and encouraged him to rely upon the inexhaustible invention of the Creator Spirit.

With practical good sense, he adapted the plan to present needs. Having no house in which they could live together, the girls, now five in number,[33] lived in their own families and divided their time between prayer and works of charity. Fourier was training them to be excellent parish workers, and together they and he organised the care of the poor and the maintenance of the church building. It was already a novelty to entrust these tasks to women, and others soon followed. At midnight mass on 25 December 1597 he allowed the young women to bear public witness to their consecration to God. Watching these five girls, all dressed in black but blazing with joy and deep in prayer, people began to see that something new was coming to birth. Rightly and joyfully this feast of Christmas of 1597 is celebrated as the birthday of the Congregation of Our Lady. Bedel first pointed out the deep significance of this timing: 'It is a sight worthy of the eyes of Paradise', he wrote, 'and a happy concurrence to see an Order in its cradle at the same time that the Son of God is in his swaddling clothes, and the girls giving themselves wholeheartedly to the Majesty we adore just at the time that Majesty gives itself to the world'.[34]

Those who found new things disturbing did not hesitate to say that these 'new devotions' were nonsense (*Rel.* 16). Murmurs and calumnies harassed the little group to such an extent that Alix's parents reacted in exasperation and using their parental authority they transferred their daughter to the Sisters of Mercy at Ormes. In vain Alix protested that her vocation did not lie there 'and I have no intention of staying there', she had to obey. She said goodbye to her companions, assuring them that she would soon be back, and even hoped to make use of her stay; feeling some curiosity, she would see how people lived in a convent.

Six leagues from Mattaincourt, Ormes was a large village which had had its glory days: two suburbs, an imposing castle, a church and a monastery. But the war had passed that way, and the grey-habited Sisters of St Elisabeth, the Grey Sisters, had a fine convent house rebuilt in the style of day, with gardens, waterfalls and expensive works of art. So far from relieving Alix's distress, her observations plunged her into bitter depression, for nothing is more demoralising than mediocrity to a soul in love with perfection. 'There,' she wrote, 'I found none of the order or good example that I would have hoped for; seculars came in freely with many types of distraction,[35] with the result that all the time I was there I suffered many anxieties of mind and often wept, most of the nights I spent in prayer. I wrote frequently to our good Father to ask him to arrange my prompt return, for I was in greater danger there than in the world; which he did at once' (*Rel.* 16).

Fourier now needed to take action. As he always did, he looked for God's will and found signs of it in events and in prayer. As had happened for Alix, it was in talk with God that he was told to found a new house. His parish was a torment to him. It was not that there were more delinquents, ruffians, drunks or dissolute men in Mattaincourt than elsewhere, but that he feared for his parish. He feared that children and youngsters would be drawn into vice before they knew anything of virtue. He had just learnt with horror that the schoolmaster had raped one of his girl pupils. As mixed schools were the running sore of the district, he began to dream about schools which should enrol none but girls and the teachers would all be women. And now God was sending him these very women, Alix and her comrades, who wanted 'to do all possible good'. They would, he knew, be excellent schoolmistresses. He would train them to be teachers. He would invent for them a new form of religious life and would make education their principal apostolic mission. No little girl would be unable to attend their schools, because the teaching would be free.

Fourier spent the night in prayer and by dawn on 20 January 1598 the project had taken on in his eyes a universal dimension and a space as yet vacant in the Church. Humble as he was, he always claimed that his nuns were the first to exercise this mission. 'They were the first in our time', he wrote on 6 August 1627, 'at least in this area,[36] who thought of accepting as their dowry and the main purpose of their religious life the duty of instructing young girls faithfully and for no payment in the fear of God, having begun this new devotion in 1597 when as far as I know no one else had thought of it' (*C.* 2, 268).

With the utmost confidence in God, Fourier resolved on that night of St Sebastian to work for this project 'with all his strength and with complete dedication', so that he does indeed deserve the title of the founder of the Congregation of Our Lady. Does this mean, as some would say, that Alix was not the foundress? It does not, for no one can deny that the first suggestion came from her, and any such denial shows a narrow view of the possibilities inherent in a collaboration between a holy woman and a holy man. They worked together to establish a new Order, each with their own personality. The difference between their characters did not divide but complemented and enriched them.

A cradle, oats and a hammer

Alix and her comrades, determined to 'do all possible good', embraced Fourier's idea with enthusiasm. They did not see the teaching of young girls as a diminution of their apostolic hopes but as a very necessary way of responding to the needs of their time. In her *Relation* Alix makes this agreement clear by speaking from now on of their common vocation. She says, for example, 'the first or second year of *our* vocation' (*Rel.* 63). The chronology of events, however, is not easy to establish, as the writer did not intend to set out a linear account of her life but only to make a careful record of the graces which God had poured out on her. Careless of narrative order, she now and then harks back and introduces a vision with such words as, 'I forgot to say that as soon as I had made my first general confession, I seemed to see . . . ' (*Rel.* 45). This event should certainly be placed here.

Alix was now trying to decide in which religious congregation she should dedicate her life to God. In a setting inspired by the churches of her time, with heavy columns hung with 'fine cloth' she watched 'a procession dressed in white which she thought was of the Order of St Francis' which led her to St Clare and St Elisabeth, who were sitting between two columns. She asked each of these saints, 'Will you have me for your daughter?' and heard the same reply, 'No'. This encouraged her in her refusal to join the Poor Clares at Pont-à-Mousson or the Sisters of St Elisabeth at Ormes, where people wanted to send her. But then where was she to go? Another way would be shown her. 'The two saints', Alix went on, 'showed me something in the middle of the four columns, saying that my vocation was there. It was a cradle, and in the middle, as if planted, was a stalk of oats bearing stems and grains. Beside this cradle was a big iron hammer which struck of its own accord against the stalk every time the cradle rocked this way or that'. The symbolic meaning of the cradle seemed so clear to Alix that she described it only as 'a cradle'. She must have had in mind the devotional objects so common then arising from the cult of the Child Jesus and known as 'Jesus at Rest'. This involved a statuette of the Child whom devotees would rock in its bed as they sang holy songs.[37] But the cradle Alix saw was empty, or rather it contained one oat stalk with delicate stems bearing grains, evoking all the children yet to be born. The threatening hammer kept trying to hit the stalk which stood up again after each blow. Alix understood the scene clearly: 'It came into my mind', she wrote, 'that the vocation which I should follow would suffer much persecution without being destroyed, as was shown me by the oat stalk, so fragile in itself but not damaged or broken by the hammer, and that Our Lord would make it firm and secure'. It was a meaningful vision and prophetic: among many other Church missions it was that of education which fell to the new congregation. Persecutions were foretold, but Alix could count on the strength of the Lord who would ensure that her foundation would be secure and would grow.

At Poussay, election retreat

Fourier was quick to put an end to Alix's misery, held against her will at Ormes, by explaining the situation to two ladies of the abbey at Poussay, Judith d'Apremont and Catherine de Fresnel, who were full of admiration for the pastor at Mattaincourt, now their spiritual director. Knowing Alix and her plans (*Rel.* 16), they immediately suggested that she and her companions should come to the abbey. Glad to see her removed from 'the people's persecution', her parents agreed to this, and on 20 May 1598 these founder members of the Congregation settled at Poussay, where they would together confirm their chosen vocation.

About a league away from Mirecourt and slightly further from Mattaincourt, the abbey that welcomed them was not so rich or influential as that of Remiremont, but had a very similar history.[38] In about the year 1000 Berthold, bishop of Toul, founded here in the Madon valley a convent for women, which one of his successors, Brunon de Dabo, later Pope St Leo IX placed under the patronage of St Menne (Manne in the local pronunciation) by installing there in 1036 the relics of this

virgin saint, martyred in about the year 400. The nuns at first
followed the Rule of St Benedict but after changes in the
thirteenth and fourteenth centuries their successors formed a
noble chapter of lay canonesses. Noble quarterings were now
essential for admission to the abbey, but otherwise life was not
hard. No religious habit was worn except for the large mantle
worn in the choir, no vows were taken, there was no enclosure,
the Ladies owned individual prebends and private houses,
where Montaigne, visiting Poussay in 1580, remarked bluntly,
'Company is received there in all liberty and one sees gentlemen
coming to pay court to future brides'. There was nothing wrong
in this for in this 'seminary of marriageable girls' some were
staying there without a vocation, no vows taken, and could
leave whenever they wished. More regrettable was the resistance
of the ladies to all attempts at reform made at the end of the
sixteenth century. As soon as she was elected in 1576 the abbess
Claude d'Anglure tried to effect a return to the primitive Rule,
but the canonesses, much attached to their privileges, appealed
against her to the duke Charles III and won their case. The
noble lady then turned to Cardinal de Vaudémont who let
Rome decide on the secularisation of the chapter. Claude
d'Anglure kept up the fight but died four years later without
victory. Her successor Edmonde d'Amoncourt renewed the
battle but the discontented canonesses elected Françoise du
Châtelet in her place. This lady died a few months later, leaving
the post open to her rival. Exhausted by all this in-fighting,
Edmonde at last gave up hope of bringing the abbey to any
strict observance. Twenty years after this failed reform, after
effects may still have lingered in the community.

The chapter at that time consisted of seventeen canonesses,
whom Bedel, a severe judge, described as virtuous. Two of
them, Fourier's penitents, are notable for their piety and for

their kindness to Alix and her companions. Judith d'Apremont made all the arrangements and installed them in a house she owned in Poussay. It was and still is a small and precious house, one that keeps alive the memory of the first convent and the first school of the sisters of Our Lady. Immediately opposite stands the abbey church, not in fact beautiful with its solid square tower but attractive because of some of its treasures – a picture of the Nativity, a statue of the Virgin carrying the Infant Jesus, and the shrine of St Menne. It was there that Fourier gathered his protégées, for whom, following the example of St Ignatius and his Exercises, he had carefully worked out a programme, a method of choosing one's way of life. The young women spent the whole octave of Corpus Christi in retreat, praying and fasting in order to receive God's light on their vocation. Each day they were required to note down answers to questions asking them which of two options would be, as Alix had wanted since her conversion, 'most pleasing to God' – to marry or to stay with their parents, to live separately or all together in community, in an old Order or a new one, taking or not taking vows, without apostolic work to do or committing themselves to give free teaching to little girls. With each question came the phrase later so frequent with Fourier, 'See what you think', so concerned was he to make no decision without the sisters. The retreat ended, the notes were sent to him: in perfect unanimity all the retreatants agreed that they wanted to live out in the most demanding way the plan now laid out in its main lines. Now it must be developed and submitted to the Church.

The first official approval

Clearly the Jesuit fathers took a hand here. On the one hand Pierre Fourier consulted them, on the other he put Alix in touch with them, which led to their interventions which she noted in her *Relation*, as they were important.

Taught by Jesuits at school and at the university of Pont-à-Mousson, Pierre remained attached to his teachers. Called on to deal with this unexpected founding of a new Order, he turned to his cousin Jean Fourier, rector of the university, whom he had chosen earlier as director of conscience, as François de Sales was to do.[39] Alix tells us that she kept him informed of all the events at Poussay (*Rel.* 17) and he also consulted Father Nicaud[40] and other Jesuits. They all approved his plan and encouraged him in the methods he had chosen, especially that known as 'the notes retreat'. It is interesting to see this Jesuit influence, still stronger later on, already active when the Congregation of Our Lady was being formed. The young Company of Jesus had already proved itself; among the tasks in which the Jesuits fought 'for the greater glory of God' was that of educating young people and it was in 1599 exactly that appeared, after much thought and experiment, the work *Ratio studiorum,* setting out the method which was to ensure the success of their teaching.

Alix was to be deeply influenced by Ignatian spirituality, but for the time being she does no more than tell us how she first met the Jesuit fathers (*Rel.* 19). Whether it was the result of a vision or from what she had heard tell of them or because she met certain members of the Company, she came to the same conclusion: their direction was necessary and beneficial. This is how she describes it: 'Being one day in the Ladies' church, in a chapel called the Sepulchre, praying that our vocation should be strengthened, my senses vanished and I thought I saw before me two of your Fathers;[41] and I was told in my mind that these were the ones I should follow'. She accepted this instruction and adds, 'From then on I wanted very much to see them and be able to talk with them, because Monsieur our good Father and Madame d'Apremont constantly spoke about them and very much praised your Company'. Alix's need for communication is clear, and it was the deeper because she had always lacked it until she met Fourier. Now she spoke appreciatively of the two Jesuits she had met for the first time at Poussay, 'although at first', she admits, 'we found it hard to follow their advice as to moderating the penances and excessive austerities we were using'. She acknowledged that their warnings were right: the inordinate penances she and her companions were employing at Poussay were not right for the life they had chosen.

For his part, Fourier was anxious to work in harmony with the Church and to win the hierarchy's approval of the project. The first rung of the ladder to which he turned was the bishop of Toul, Monseigneur Christophe de La Vallée, to whom he sent a petition in which the ideal of the earliest sisters was already made clear. They were 'ready to do their poor best to embrace everything that they shall find to be the best and most expedient for the honour and glory of God, for their own salvation and perfection and for the relief, both bodily and spiritual, of their neighbour.[42] Here are clearly set forth the three basic aims of the future Congregation – the search for the glory of God, inspired by St Ignatius; the struggle for personal perfection so as to be pleasing to God; and the desire to help one's neighbour in both body and soul. Cautiously, the schools were not mentioned but Fourier was not the man to abandon his idea. In September 1598 he took Monseigneur de La Vallée a second document entitled *Provisional Rule*,[43] which in effect was the sisters' earliest Constitution. They spoke here in their own name, and this is no stylistic formula, for Fourier had made them work at composing this text. Now the essential

word was spoken – 'The first and chief part of our purpose',
they declared, 'through which we hope God may be honoured
and well served by many [...] is to establish public schools and
there for no payment to teach girls to read, to write and to use
a needle, and Christian teaching, seeking according to their
and our capacities to make them understand the catechism
and encourage them to piety and devotion, [...] to fly from all
kinds of vice and sins and to embrace virtue according to the
condition, age and capacity of each one of them'.

As far as the petition to set up free schools was concerned, the
learned persons[44] whom the bishop assembled at Liverdun to
discuss the project could only approve. The Council of Trent,
considering teaching to be an important factor in the renewal of
the Church, had ordered the setting up of free schools in all the
dioceses. But the rest of the *Provisional Rule* was another matter.
Who were these schoolmistresses Fourier wanted? They would
be, said the document, 'girls in a Congregation, trying to live
well, unpaid, giving an example of piety and of various other
things that could in themselves bring some small profit to
those who learned them'. The bishop and his learned advisors
instantly saw in this a third Order such as those Pius V had
ordered to vanish or else embrace the monastic life, and their
objections killed the project dead. What would they have said if
Fourier had revealed the heart of his plan, that he meant to
create schoolmistresses who would also be full time nuns . . .
but now, thought the prudent Lorrainer, it would be better to
have sisters who did the teaching work but without enclosure,
without solemn vows. He sprang to their defence, praising
them in the words of St John Chrysostom as women 'more
ardent than lions', sharing with the apostles the labour of
spreading the gospel. His plea touched one of the assessors,
Monsieur de St-Germain, precentor of Metz cathedral, who

exclaimed, 'God's hand is here!' The cause was won, but with a good number of reservations. These members of a Congregation must be 'perpetually enclosed in a new house (if this can be done) to live there under rule'. Monseigneur de La Vallée gave Fourier nothing more than a verbal authorisation, nothing written, no letters patent. Alix knew that a new stage of their common life was beginning, a successor to that in which she and her friends had shown that they were 'in agreement to pursue [their] hoped for plans'. The conclusion she came to was that, 'What I have said so far is to show that this vocation came from God' (*Rel.* 17).

CHAPTER FOUR

'Apparently small beginnings'

It was seen in the past, is seen now every day and will be seen
in future that very great and excellent things can take root,
foundation and strength from apparently small beginnings.

Pierre Fourier, 13 June 1630

Troubles at the end of the century

We might think that political events would scarcely touch Alix,
engrossed in the work of her new life in a village as tranquil as
Poussay, the very name of which means 'haven of peace' (*portus
suavitatis*). This is a false impression, if we judge by the episode
she describes in her *Relation,* one which occurred in the final
months of 1598.

Henri IV had just renounced Protestantism and been consecrated at Chartres. Since 1594 he had been thinking of
marrying his sister Catherine de Bourbon to the heir of Lorraine,
who would succeed his father Duke Charles III as Henri II
(1608–1624). This marriage, part of the French king's general
strategy, was considered iniquitous in Lorraine. Even worse
than the difference in age between the two or the degree of
consanguinity was the difference in religion, for the daughter of
Jeanne d'Albret refused to abjure Calvinism. Were reasons of
state to prevail, would they see an ardent Calvinist[45] on the
throne of Lorraine?

Alix was anxious about this. As devoted to her Catholic faith
as to the very Catholic ducal family which ruled her country,

she prayed, she said, with all the fervour she could 'that good Duke Henri would not marry Madame Catherine de Bourbon because she was a Huguenot'. Nothing had been settled, and Alix prayed the more earnestly because the discussions were almost concluded. Then her prayer turned into a vision, which she describes: 'I was drawn in the spirit out of myself and I seemed to see a great cloud of serpents with wings which they spread out as they flew over the countryside, where there were several persons, and these serpents were trying to get down on to each person's head to bite them. At the same time I understood that this signified the cloud of heretics who were to enter Lorraine' (*Rel.* 42). Following biblical tradition, Alix sees the serpent as the symbol of the power of evil, enemy of God and his people. But to represent heresy and show how fast it could spread and how dangerous was the contamination, her imagination offered her a cloud of winged serpents whose poisonous bite wounded assembled Catholics in the head. Undoubtedly the strongly Protestant town of Metz was extending its influence into Lorraine. Calvinism spread along trade routes, pastors travelled among merchants and books were hidden in their packages. Catherine de Bourbon herself was surrounded in her château of La Malgrange by preachers who threatened to promote the new faith in Lorraine. Alix prayed passionately 'that this evil should not happen', but her prayer would not be answered, not at least at that time. In spite of Pope Clement VIII's refusal to grant the necessary dispensation, the marriage was celebrated at St-Germain-en-Laye on 31 January 1599. Had Alix heard this news, and that of the events that followed? The end of her vision makes it seem likely. She wrote, 'I seemed to see a great precipice down which this lady wanted to throw the others but she herself, not noticing, fell down it'. The pope was angry, declared the marriage null, excommunicated Henri and remained deaf to all approaches from the king and duke. Prince Henri went himself to Rome in 1600 and at last in 1604 obtained a conditional dispensation. But it came too late; the messenger who brought the news only reached Nancy after the death of the princess on 13 February 1604.

Heresy remained a threat. Its echo occurs in the *Règlement provisionnel*[46] where the sisters undertake to pray 'for everything that most closely touches God's honour and glory, especially for the extirpation of heresies'. In 1598 this was a clear response to the political situation, but the same phrase is found in the *Rule* of 1617 and in the *Constitutions* of 1640. Right from the start both Alix and Fourier expected their nuns to be concerned about outside events, requiring them to pray for the great people of both 'the Church and the world, on whose prudence and good behaviour depends the tranquillity of the whole Church and the peace of the people'.[47] The sisters' prayers never lost this dimension of intercession 'for the glory of God and the salvation of the world', as had been asked of them from the beginning.

The first foundresses

Although the religious vocation of the earliest founding sisters owed much to the exceptional influence Alix had on her friends, it was also due to the immense love of God which inspired each one and united them all. We know nothing about their early religious training but can suppose that they were brought up in a solid traditional faith, one that would provide the good ground in which the divine seed would produce a yield of an hundred-fold. They were the 'brave and valiant girls' Fourier wanted and they knew what difficulties lay in wait, all the more so because three of them whose parents were of 'a very middling condition' were poor, and the other two could expect nothing from their

family but 'discontent and opposition'.[48] Best known of the
founding team is Gante André (1578–1645). She was the
daughter of a well off family of craftsmen in Mattaincourt, not
yet twenty years old when she made friends with Alix and
declared that she was ready to take part in her project. The two
girls were well suited to each other, for Gante had a generous
nature and was eager to do good, not counting the cost. We are
told that as a child she was so sorry for poor people that she
took things from her paternal home to relieve their poverty. It is
said too that when still very young she used a red hot iron to
mark a cross on her arm, to show that she belonged to Jesus
Christ and loved none but him. Bedel gives an excellent idea of
her: she had great strength of mind, good physical health,
courage to overcome difficulties without fretting over details
and such excellent common sense that the wisest men would
turn to her over confusion in matters of business.[49] Such
qualities marked her out for an important role in the new
Congregation.

Isabeau or Isabelle de Louvroir, often called Elisabeth (1581–
1628), was sixteen when the irresistible call to 'do all possible
good in a new house' stirred her to the point of leaving everything to form with Alix and Gante the trio of founding 'shock
troops'. She came from a humble Mattaincourt family and had
an elder sister, Jeanne (1579–1635), who felt the same call but
did not join the little group until after the departure from
Poussay.

Tradition claims Claude Chauvenel (1578–1633) as the
fourth founding sister. The daughter of a Mirecourt furrier,
she joined the others at Poussay when she was about twenty
years old.

There was a sixth companion known as Mademoiselle
Barthélemy, of whom one of Alix's biographers[50] says that

she began with fervour but soon tired of Poussay's isolation and made the village ring with her complaints. Madame d'Apremont, disturbed by the calumnies she was spreading about the sisters, took her to live with her for some months. Then Mademoiselle Barthélemy left for good.

Apprenticeship to the religious life

Now only five in number, the sisters set work with all the zeal of born leaders to put into practice the ideal of life set out in the *Règlement provisionnel*. Well aware that they were founding something new, they were apparently determined to set the standard very high, perhaps afraid it might decline later on. It is impossible to follow them in their acts of penance which the Jesuits in vain tried to moderate and which our weakness can scarcely understand, as a biographer remarks.[51] This is what he says: 'They fasted nearly all the time on bread and water, slept on boards, prayed throughout the night, only sleeping for one or two hours and arranging matters so that while one of them took a short rest the others continued in prayer and they did not stop praising God together all night long'. As for their penitential tools, sackcloth, hair shirts, scourges, chains and iron spikes, they horrified Fourier himself, who at the sight of a belt bristling with points expressed some doubt as to the use Gante would make of it, only to be told, 'Father, I have already tried it'.[52]

Alix was second to none in generosity of mind and received messages from heaven in response to her current anxieties. In one such, 'very much aware of offences against God' (*Rel.* 18), she was in the village church praying for one of her relatives whom she knew to be in a state of sin. The griefs of living overcame her to such an extent that she begged fervently to be allowed to leave this world, where, she said, 'so much is done that is displeasing to his divine Majesty'. Later it was impatience to be with her Lord that made her want to die. Today it was the ugliness of evil that disgusted her with the world. Drawn out of herself, she thought she saw Our Lord seated with his two apostles 'in a high place where the crucifix is normally set in the middle of churches'. With her usual enthusiasm she rushed towards Jesus who looked at her kindly but then she immediately fell downwards, while a voice told her, 'This is not the way you must rise to heaven'. What came next is more explicit: 'Then I was shown a little path like a plank, very narrow, covered with green; it began in a chapel in the same church dedicated to Our Lady on the altar very near her image and the other end touched the sky. [As] I wanted to start climbing by this way, I was told that it was not yet time'. For Alix, trying to understand ways towards God at the start of a great venture, this symbol of the path was eloquent. The one her imagination showed her was as green and humble as those of the Lorraine countryside and as narrow as that in the Gospel, taken by only a few. There was nothing sublime where the path began – it was at Poussay, in the chapel where she prayed, in front of an altar bearing an image of Our Lady. But its further end touched heaven. This was enough to tell her that her task here below was to complete the projected foundation. Meditating on the meaning of this vision, she came to see that the nuns of her congregation would lead a 'mixed life' in which action and contemplation would both have their place. Did not Our Lord say to Mary of Magdala when she wanted to stay near him, 'Do not hold me . . . Go and find my brothers and tell them . . . '? Alix also learnt through this vision that the Virgin Mary, whom she chose that day to guide her, would stay with her to the end of the road. Always ready to make good use of a grace received, she immediately made a resolution: 'Since then', she wrote,

'I have always devoutly longed to see our plans established under Mary's protection. And I have always relied greatly on her help, asking everything from God through her Son and through her'. The chronicle shows much evidence to support this statement. When Pope Paul V, for instance, in 1615 confirmed the Congregation under the name of the Daughters of Our Lady, Alix, we are told, felt great joy. The origin of the pope's decision may seem remote – it was the little chapel in the church at Poussay where Alix prayed to the Virgin Mary. Fourier certainly knew the details of the insights Alix received, and he later referred to this connection. In a letter to the sisters at Troyes dated 14 April 1631 he encouraged them to pray to Our Lady by reminding them of the original choice – 'You know, beloved Lady, how since the birth of our pious plans [...] we chose You [...] in heaven, most glorious Virgin, and took You for our dear Mother, for Our Lady, our protectress, our patron, our defender, our guide, for our mistress and for our advocate before God . . .' This 'we, our' is not a royal formula, it means Alix, her comrades and Pierre Fourier together working out the rule for their Congregation.

Services in the abbey church were conducted with an almost theatrical solemnity. As it was the first duty of the Poussay canonesses to recite the canonical hours, they did this with meticulous care, and Alix and her friends attended the ceremonies. The Roman rite and Gregorian chant did not call for them to join in, nor indeed did the ceremonial appropriate to the ladies. The abbess officiated under a dais and a crimson cloth, on her left her assistant (*la doyenne*), on the right the bursar (*la secrète*). When she entered the choir the ladies remained standing till she reached her stall.[53] The Apremont and Fresnel ladies gave their protégées lessons in liturgy to help them disentangle the rubrics. But although these girls, being so few in number, did no more than repeat together the Office of the Blessed Virgin, they did not find it easy to keep the rules in their heads. The story is told and repeated by several writers, of a marvel which occurred in this connection; Father Rogie tells us that,

> One day when they were together in the garden and were trying to recite the office but kept getting lost, there suddenly appeared among them a child of ravishing beauty with a radiant face who began to explain what they did not understand. As the child spoke, light dawned in their minds, the difficulties disappeared, and from then on all that had been full of difficulties and obstacles became as it were a smooth and well lit way along which they went forward without trouble.[54]

Some of the biographers attach great importance to this and other marvels, but taken in their own setting they only show that in their daily life saints pray in faith to God and receive the help they need. The story of the lost cow tells the same tale. Here it is, told by Edmond Renard.[55]

Chance, always malicious, sometimes enjoyed disturbing the teachers' tranquility. They had a cow which they used to put in the meadow. One evening as night was falling when they wanted to milk her, she was not to be found. Had some thief stolen her? Had soldiers passed this way? They looked for her. All five, with one lantern, scattered here and there, searching. But suddenly a mysterious voice, heard by Alix, whispered through the dusk, and: 'Go down into the valley, quite near', she said. There in the pasture beside the Madon lay the creature, heavy with her unused milk, waiting for the dawn.

The first school

If there is one reality which needs no fable to enhance it, it is the school at Poussay. This has its place not only in the history of Lorraine but, we dare to say, in that of all humanity. The year 1598 marks the beginning of free primary education for girls, and it was Alix Le Clerc and Pierre Fourier who achieved it. Certainly other such ventures arose at this turn of the sixteenth and seventeenth centuries. In 1592 in Provence Canon César de Bus founded the Daughters of St Ursula in L'Isle-sur-Sorgue, inspired both by the aims set out half a century earlier in Italy by Angela Merici and by the rules prescribed by Carlo Borromeo. In 1604 in Bordeaux Jeanne de Lestonnac, a young widow, niece of Montaigne, established the Daughters of Our Lady. The dating of these events is no coincidence because both these institutions, like Fourier's, all three intended for the education of girls, were part of the great wind of renewal that the Council of Trent (1545–1563) sent blowing through the Church. Fourier and Alix Le Clerc entered fully into the spirit of the council, being vividly aware of the importance of teaching, affirming that all knowledge, even profane, is a basis of faith and an essential means of evangelism. This was a principle for them both, but they also had the merit of bringing a true revolution to its practice. We have no way to check the soundness of their methods in those earliest days but we are told that their ideal of education shone in the Congregation's first school, brilliant as a flame which in a long relay is handed on from school to school down the centuries and across continents.

In order to educate the little girls at Poussay the first teachers began by learning. Madame d'Apremont, a well connected lady, taught them how to behave with simple good manners. Sometimes she would take them into the abbey's library to show them the precious manuscripts. Under their admiring gaze she would turn the pages of the most lovely item in the collection, an eleventh century gospel, and tell them how the movement of books in that period had brought it to Poussay. Fourier made regular visits, furthered their apprenticeship in the religious life, took an interest in their work, encouraged, taught, corrected, enthusiastically developed his ideas on education, and suddenly put an end to his visits. Dismayed by his absence, the children soon understood why he had stopped coming: like the master advised by Montaigne to make his pupil 'trot ahead of him to judge his gait', Fourier wanted to make sure that his disciples were making good progress themselves without his visible support.

Threat of schism in Poussay abbey

In fact the little group was making such progress that its fervent zeal was disturbing the older canonesses of Sainte-Menne, anxious because some of the younger ones were calling for a return to a more demanding religious life. The group of older ladies had no intention of giving up any of the privileges they had worked so hard to win twenty years earlier, while some of the younger ones were wanting to leave the Chapter and join a stricter Order.[56] Faced with the threat of schism, the abbess Edmonde d'Amoncourt, remembering the difficulties at the time of her election, asked Madame d'Apremont to find a solution. Reluctantly she and Fourier decided that Alix and her comrades should leave the abbey, which they did on 22 July 1599 after a fourteen month stay at Poussay. They went to Mattaincourt, 'so as to be close to our good Father,' said Alix, 'as we had so much wished' (*Rel.* 20).

CHAPTER FIVE

For or against 'a new house'?

Mattaincourt 1599

The arrival in Mattaincourt was full of promise and hope. Judith d'Apremont, supporting the new life coming to birth, without hesitation pawned her silver to buy the sisters a house which she also 'furnished and made comfortable' (*Rel.* 20). Thirty years later Fourier recalled with emotion how this 'tiny house' was blessed, room by room, by the provost of the canons of La Mothe, already drawn to the light shining from this 'poor little cradle' (*C.* 3, 496). The town still keeps its memory, for though the house has vanished, an inscription marks the place where it stood.[57]

This cult of the past is right, for the small house really was the prototype of the initial project, as Pierre Fourier and Alix Le Clerc wanted it to be before canon law stepped in and blocked the way. The presence of the two founders was a guarantee of this success, essential for a good start.

Undoubtedly the little house did not look like a convent shut in behind high walls, but in it the sisters worked hard at their vocation as nuns and as teachers. Several young women joined them – Isabelle's sister, Jeanne de Louvroir (1579–1635), and Jeanne Brégeot, daughter of a master draper in Mattaincourt.[58] Others came too. With her companions Alix organised their communal life, and it was natural that the charge of the household and of the sisters' conduct should also fall to her. She acknowledged that she did not want this, as for one thing she did not feel that she was capable of being a Superior and for another, she thought that obedience had advantages, which she described like this: 'I would rather have obeyed, so as to have more help and a better way of making myself pleasing to God' (*Rel.* 21). Independent character that she was, all that mattered to her were the 'more' and 'better' which would please God! But it was precisely God's will that she should accept this task. An inner voice told her so: 'It seemed to me', she wrote, 'that the foot of a cross was placed in my heart and the rest of it projected at my side; I imagined this for many days, thinking it was really so' (*Rel.* 21). Was there in fact a physical wound? She herself did not know, but as always this 'imagination' made God's will clear to her. Alix, accustomed to meditation, would remember among the Gospel scenes the one which the Church celebrates on 2 February when Mary brought her Child for presentation in the Temple and Simeon in prophecy said to her, 'And a sword will pierce your own soul too' (Luke 2:35). Sharing her Son's mission, his Mother bore the suffering as well. She accepted the pains of motherhood, not knowing what they would be, with the generosity she had shown at the Annunciation. Taking Mary for her example, not knowing what it would cost her, Alix accepted her task. She would be the 'Superior' but with 'the beautiful name of Mother', the only title the Rule would allow.[59] We know that in this role she would not fail. Statements made by her companions bear this out, as do the remarks in her own hand found in a notebook which reveal the method she used. In these pages, forgetting herself, she never mentions the difficulties of the task but emphasises the 'tender' and 'more than motherly' affection a Superior must have for her nuns.[60] Pride does not come into it. The obedience the sisters owed her was not in her eyes a means of exercising any kind of power over them but a channel for the grace of God. On this point the way she healed one sister in the name of obedience is significant. This is what she wrote:

> In the first or second year of our vocation, while we were at Mattaincourt, one of our sisters was very ill with indigestion in her stomach caused by the austerities we were using. As soon as she took any nourishment, she brought it up again with such violent pains as were pitiful. I felt moved to command her upon her obedience not to do this any more, not that I meant to force her to hold it back but hoping that through this virtue God would heal her. And this did happen; at that very time she was freed from this infirmity. (*Rel.* 63)

Thus under Alix's direction the first community tried out in advance what the Rule of 1640 later expressed in these words: 'As love is gained by loving, as soon as her sisters are convinced that the Superior loves them like a mother, they in return will love her like daughters'. [61] If we remember the natural charm of this young ruler, we can see how easy it must have been for her to draw her sisters towards the demands of holiness. Bedel, who was so good at 'sketching', as he said, 'a brief picture of the first nuns and their goodness', describes them as 'poor almost to the point of need'. 'They subsist on nothing but the little they can earn' working outside the classroom, for Fourier had forbidden them 'to accept anything from their relatives, to prevent slanderers saying that they had drawn in their daughters so as to get hold of their property'.[62] The sisters not only ate poorly but added extreme mortifications and a total disregard of comfort – so much so that one of them was overcome by discouragement and announced her departure. Fourier, skilled teacher, made her understand her decision and let her draw her own conclusion. He gave her a letter which she was to read at the foot of the statue of Our Lady, a letter which read:

My Lady, I am here to thank you for the honour you have done me in accepting me as one of your daughters. I am tired of this favour and think that the world is more worthy of love than you and your Son. This is why I am leaving you both. Let those serve You who want to. I have had enough.[63]

The chronicle tells us that the fugitive rejoined her companions and only quitted them in death.

The sisters shared in the transformation of Mattaincourt begun by its young parish priest. Parish auxiliaries, they took care of the dignity of church ceremonies, attending to the maintenance of the objects used in the services which Fourier believed must be magnificent in order to give an idea of God's greatness. As they were not hampered by enclosure, they could take on the many social tasks he had created, catching his burning charity and desire for their success. Alix was allotted the care of the poor, and as Fourier advised, made a list and considered the needs before working out how to deal with them. There was not one poor, sick or infirm person, no neglected old man or woman, no unloved child, whom she did not visit, bringing with her the light of her smile, words of comfort, and remedies, teas and potions, preserves, of her own making.

The teaching vocation challenged

The sisters' essential duty was to teach children in a new kind of school. There was already a school in Mattaincourt but it was mixed and fee-paying. The sisters' school was free and took only girls. Fourier even exercised the authority given him by the municipal offices he held in his parish, as was usual at the time, to make attendance compulsory. In doing this he anticipated Jules Ferry by more than two and half centuries. But in this

large village of some thousand inhabitants, the opening of a
school for girls was not welcome to all. One woman even tried
to throw her bunch of keys at the priest's head because he had
dared to change village ways. Like it or not, however, pupils
flocked into the classes and soon, won over by their teachers'
affection, little girls blossomed like flowers. With a thirst until
now unheeded, they drank in the rudiments of the Christian
faith, of reading and arithmetic.

Adults did not give up. Evil tongues chattered to such as
would listen – 'If these women were real nuns, they would be
enclosed in a convent. What they are trying to do is dangerous'.
Alix's father, who may have thought much the same, could not
endure the ridicule and decided to take action. Remembering
Ormes, he again began to look for a convent where the Rule
was properly kept. Some men of the Church and other persons
in authority told him about the recently reformed Poor Clares
at Verdun, and he informed his daughter that he would come
next day and take her there. Alix at once appealed to Fourier
who unhesitatingly told her to obey, bringing many arguments
to support this advice. At Verdun, he said, the safety of her soul
was assured, whereas the plans she had embarked on did not
seem at all likely to succeed. What was more, they 'were perhaps
a temptation' (*Rel.* 22). No, Alix did not agree. She believed in
the future, stood firm and rebelled. But when Fourier told her,
'In conscience you must obey', she gave in and had recourse to
her last hope, prayer. 'Seeing myself pressed on all sides', she
wrote, 'I turned to God and his holy Mother, most urgently
referring this whole affair to our sisters' prayers'. This mention
of the community's prayer shows how strongly the little group
were united around this project. But Alix did not pray for their
plans to succeed. She said that she only asked for one thing,
'That it should please God to touch his heart to fulfil his holy

will, if it was such as was said'. The divine answer was given her in a vision of which this is her sober account: 'Suddenly I was seized with fear and trembling; being drawn out of my senses it seemed to me that one of our sisters or rather the Virgin Mary in her likeness put little Jesus into my arms and I was told that I should persevere in my first vocation and that he would be my hope. My spirit took great comfort, holding this Child'. A marvellous spectacle, wherein Alix, having lost touch with the outside world, becomes totally open to the divine message which strengthens her in her 'first vocation', that of teaching. What could be more significant than the sight of Mary, her model, in her most maternal aspect, that of a mother holding a child? The Virgin hands Alix this precious treasure, the infant Jesus, because she wants to confirm Alix in her role of mother and teacher for all those whom this Child represents. Sure now that the presence of Jesus would never leave her, Alix found peace again, peace and heartfelt hope. But a doubt attacked her – was she basing her plans on the kind of revelation that is only an illusion? Time and again Fourier had said to her, 'Unusual methods are subject to illusion. It is better to seek true and solid goodness'.[64] With endearing simplicity, she put her Lord to the test. If he granted her prayer, it would prove that it all came from him. He had told her that he would be her hope along the chosen way – then let him change her father's purpose. He has, she told him, absolute power to do this. In this way she would be sure of doing his will. The result was just what she wanted. While Monsieur Le Clerc was climbing the hillside at Hymont he wondered whether he was right to compel his daughter to join the Poor Clares, when she was so certain that her calling came from God. To oppose it would offend him. He therefore decided not to intervene in Alix's spiritual life any more but to leave her entirely 'free in her determination, without wanting to take any further part in it'. A tremendous change of heart, if we remember the power of paternal authority in those days.

Having won this first victory over her father, Alix then had to battle with Fourier himself, all the more redoubtable an adversary in that he had on his side the Jesuits of Pont-à-Mousson and a certain Father Fleurant Boulangier, a Recollect from Verdun,[65] fiercely supportive of the decrees of the Council of Trent and now engaged in reforming the Poor Clares in his town. His party brought out the same arguments – the reliability of an established Order as opposed to the precarious situation of a 'new house' – and reached the same conclusion: they should abandon this rash project and send the pseudo-nuns of Mattaincourt to the Poor Clares. Fourier, full of deference for his former Jesuit teachers and humbly ready to renounce his venture without showing how much it cost him, urged his young followers 'with all his strength' to take the advice of those who knew better than he did (*Rel.* 46). Alix admitted that this was 'one of the greatest contradictions' her soul ever felt. How could anyone, especially Fourier, deny the will of God, so plain to her eyes, and call their plans a temptation? Her comrades shared her feelings and 'I' becomes 'we' in her account. There they were in a tug of war between submission to God who wanted them, so they were told, to go to the Clares, and their certainty that this was not their vocation. They could none of them, Alix said, endure the idea and they 'called upon Our Lord without ceasing for half a year'. As for Fourier, they attacked him with the same resolve: 'We told Monsieur our good Father that we would not be able to enter into a vocation towards which we could not feel drawn' (*Rel.* 46).

Answers from heaven

Among these conflicting signals Alix like a good pilot held a steady course and made note of the messages from heaven. One day she seemed to be in a Jesuit convent where monks were walking in procession along a cloister (*Rel.* 47). While her sisters sat in a corner near the door, she was using 'a rake with which one gathers hay in the meadows', collecting 'so as to profit from them' all the little straws lying on the ground. Seeing this work which they thought nonsensical, the men in the procession expressed some scorn, except for one of them, a man of venerable appearance, no doubt their Superior, who looked 'kindly' at Alix and signalled to her to persevere in what she was doing. Once she was herself again, she heard a voice explaining to her that this was St Ignatius encouraging her to teach young girls, 'who are not much valued, like little straws'. And the voice added very clearly, 'I want these little souls, who are like bastard children abandoned by their mothers, to have a mother in you'. Thus heaven spoke out in favour of Alix's calling as a teacher and specifically commissioned her to teach little girls. Without examining the question of abandoned children or the status of bastards at that period, the voice simply used the vivid metaphor of the 'little straws' treated as rubbish. The humble use of a rake, despised by the masculine cohort, is promoted to serve as a symbol for the work of education: gathering up those whom society excludes or marginalises and enabling them to become their true selves. The only way of putting into action this continuous creation we call education is the way of love, here shown in its highest and most feminine form, a mother's love.

In this period of conflict over her project, Alix prayed and meditated on spiritual motherhood, inseparable from the vocation to which she knew she was called. She took pleasure in contemplating Mary and Joseph as they watched over the growing Child. Using the method described by St Ignatius in his *Exercises*, known to her through her Jesuit contacts and Fourier, she applied herself to setting the scene, that is of visualising 'through the eyes of the imagination' [66] the Holy Family, or as she called them, the 'little household at Nazareth' (*Rel.* 24). Her gaze lingered on the modest furniture and on each of the persons, 'much comforted', she said, 'to see them'.[67] Angélique Milly, thinking Alix's remark too short and rather obscure, expanded it in her *Clarification*, writing that 'Alix had great tenderness for all the events of Our Lord's childhood. She reflected on them and talked about them very gently and sweetly', so much so that the nuns remembered her very words. To one of them she said, 'What an astounding marvel, to see the Son of God leading such a poor life, thought of as a carpenter. What mysteries to wonder at!' To another who asked her about her recollection in the workroom, she said, 'Don't you think it's more than enough to think about Jesus working there near the Holy Virgin and great St Joseph? I watch them, I listen to them. I wonder at them and in the little family I see all the greatnesses of the earth'.[68] In this way Alix, accustomed to mystical methods, moved from the visible to the invisible and gave her companions a simple and satisfying means of prayer: look, listen, wonder.

Alix's devotion to Mary may owe something to the Jesuits, but she was also influenced by Franciscan spirituality, which at this period emphasised the maternal aspects of this cult and gave rise to the creation of so many winsome soft smiling Madonnas, the Child playing with a bird or a flower or fondly caressing his mother's cheek. The visions of Alix's imagination must owe something to these images. She kept their tenderness but discarded the sentimentality, using them to provide both

food for her inner life and a motive for action. It even happened
at times that these images led her to an infused and silent
awareness of the greatness of God.

One such vision shines if possible more brightly than the
others. On Candlemas eve, the day before the anniversary of
her own birth and baptism on 2 February, Alix was preparing
to solemnise the feast as well as she could, when suddenly her
prayer came alive. 'Our Lady', she wrote, 'showed herself to me
holding her little Son and gave him to me, telling me to nurture
him till he grew up, meaning that I should procure his glory'
(*Rel.* 23). Here again education is seen in the role of the mother
and her primary function, to feed the child so that it can grow.
Alix understood that in the words 'Make him grow' Mary had
set down for ever the whole purpose of her congregation, not
just to provide children, rich and poor, with the food they
needed for physical growth but to offer lavishly to all, old and
young, what was needed for them to grow in intelligence and in
love, to help them 'to live, and live well', as Pierre Fourier later
said. Faced with the needs of such a mission, Alix felt that she
would have to find ways of doing it excellently, but for the time
being her vision of Mary handing her her Son drew her to other
depths. A scene from the Gospel stayed in her mind, the one
where the Lord says to the good workmen in his Kingdom, 'In
so far as you did this to one of the least of these brothers of
mine, you did it to me' (Matt. 25:40). A stupefying equivalence,
this, which brought her to another dizzying truth – to help
teach someone so that they become a true Christian is to help
them resemble Christ. The glory of the Resurrected Saviour
will be reflected, will shine out, and he or she in their turn will
reveal the glory of God.

In Alix's spiritual journey this vision, at first as simple as a
meeting between two women when one hands her baby to the

other, marks a stage which brings her to the level of the greatest mystics. For as soon as the scene vanished the narrator adds, 'And my spirit was much humbled and lifted up to matters very high in the knowledge of God. I cannot say anything about this, except that God is a pure spirit and that I encountered only a tiny part of his greatness and perfection, understanding still something of the Holy Trinity whom I adored Three in One and above all the love and union there' (*Rel.* 23). With ordinary every day words Alix gives her account of an exceptional favour. After revealing her teaching mission to her, Mary, link between human and divine, led her into contemplation of the Holy Trinity, which she perceived then through her intellect, not through any image. Having begun by establishing the lowliness of her own mind, Alix recognised that she could only grasp 'something', 'a tiny part' of God's greatness. She could say nothing about this except that these were 'matters very high in the knowledge of God'. She adored God, the 'pure spirit, Three in One', tirelessly discovering the love which unites the Father, the Son and the Holy Spirit. From then on the light of this three-fold Presence did not leave her. She herself tells us of her confidence which is, we must repeat, that of a true mystic. 'This greatness', she wrote, 'stayed with me always as if imprinted on my mind, and this purity, which drove me to desire it for my own soul and to have compassion on the souls which rebelled against the will [of God]; I wanted to endure and to give my life several times so that they should return to their first origin' (*Rel.* 23). This reaction is Alix through and through. She longs for her own soul to be clad in the glorious purity of God, but in her zeal for souls she wants the same for sinners. Her burning generosity compels her to suffer and to offer her life not once but many times to win their salvation and in so doing to win also the glory of God.

Resistance rewarded

With Alix to stimulate their resistance, the little group stubbornly refused to give up their plan and go and join the Poor Clares. Now began a battle of attrition, as Fourier, keeping to his normal practice of not giving in too soon to other people's haste in matters of God,[69] required six weeks of prayer and penance to obtain light. Delay followed upon delay and six months passed without result. After that he changed his tactics – let the sisters set down their feelings in writing and the Jesuits and Father Fleurant would decide according to their replies. Without exception every one of them wanted 'a new house' – their firmness saved the Congregation. Their frustrated adversaries hinted that this stubbornness arose from an excessive attachment to Fourier. If he did not go to see them, they would change their minds. Respectful of his masters' opinions, the priest bowed to this manoeuvre and for one year he gave his penitents only the minimum of care. Now without the founder's help but trusting in that of the Lord, the sisters made faithful progress in their calling. This test was convincing and Fourier laboured to 'make them competent in all aspects of infant teaching'. He was careful, says the chronicle, to teach them to read well and correctly and to ensure that they understood the principles of spelling and the rules of arithmetic by means of one short lesson every day.[70] Soon the school at Mattaincourt was too small, as the pupils came in crowds and new postulants arrived. Madame d'Apremont, concerned for her protégées' needs, had a solution: they had a presbytery which was too big for the priest and a school which was too small for the children – why not exchange them? But the town officials, in spite of the payment she offered them in compensation, refused. Annoyed that they seemed so unaware of the benefits of a school which in fact only existed because of her, the lady closed down the classes and decided to install the teachers in a private house she owned at Saint-Mihiel. While the house was being prepared, she took the sisters back to Poussay. There they relived with emotion the beginnings of their consecration to God, but did not reopen the school for fear of upsetting the abbess, who had wanted them to go. They made use of this period of recollection by making a pilgrimage to St-Nicolas-de-Port, going the twelve leagues on foot. In this town, which had fourteen thousand inhabitants and drew traders, money-changers, merchants and thieves from all over Europe, the sisters were only interested in the great church, with its front and towers then just fifty years old. Under the flamboyant windows, within the dazzling white limestone walls, they joined the pilgrims who came to venerate the relics of the patron saint of Lorraine and of children, 'Monsieur Saint Nicolas'. To him they entrusted their future, still very uncertain.

Fourier did not want them to leave his parish, but to keep them in Mattaincourt. Madame d'Apremont wished to hasten their departure and meanwhile she kept Alix at Poussay until agreement should be reached. Two novices and Elisabéth de Louvroir were to stay in Mattaincourt. Alix, Gante, Jeanne and Claude would go away to Saint-Mihiel.

CHAPTER SIX

The first flight

Saint-Mihiel, 1602

Madame d'Apremont managed matters briskly and sent Fourier the draft of the deed by which she gifted her house at Saint-Mihiel to the congregation, adding, 'I wish you had seen it' (*C.* 1, 2). Fourier felt the same, and stopped at Saint-Mihiel on his way back from Verdun, where the bishop, Monseigneur Erric de Lorraine, had granted him permission to settle the sisters in his diocese. Among the handsome houses in the town centre he noticed one and said to himself, 'Good heavens! That one would be just right for our plans!' And it was that very one which was to become 'the Congregation's first certain home'.

The town itself offered many advantages. The duchy's highest tribunal met there for the assizes known as 'les grands jours', great days, and to them came some of the most exalted members of the nobility and clergy, and sometimes the duke himself. The Benedictine abbey of St Michael, Saint-Mihiel, around which the town had grown, was an intellectual centre famous for the riches of its library. But at that time it was half in revolt against the reforms demanded by the bishop of Verdun. It was still some years before it would join with the Congregation of St Vanne and St Hydulphe [71] which at the instigation of Dom Didier de La Cour re-established observance of the Benedictine Rule.

The situation of their new home put the sisters right in the heart of the town. There were expensive buildings all around them, including a fourteenth century Gothic house known as the King's House ever since René of Anjou, duke of Bar, 'le roi

René', bought it in 1428. Opposite stood the d'Apremont
mansion, an old and spacious dwelling, grand and elegant.
Nothing remains today of this elegance but a slender turret
containing a spiral staircase under a conical roof, and a few steps
leading down to a deep cellar. Their residence in this ancestral
home brought the sisters close to the d'Apremont family. In
1602 Madame de Ligneville, sister-in-law of Louise d'Apremont,
one of Judith's three sisters, asked Fourier to allow Isabeau de
Louvroir to visit her. From the lady's letter, in which she
describes herself as overwhelmed by 'various bodily pains and
many other afflictions of the soul' (*C.* 1, 3), it seems likely that
a visit from the young sister would be a comfort and help to
her. Monseigneur Jean de Maillane and Monseigneur Chrétien
de Gournay, nephews of the canoness of Poussay and successive
bishops of Toul, showed the young Congregation the same
kindness as did their aunt. Fourier, always grateful to benefactors, recalled with emotion in a letter of 19 February 1633
how Madame de Gournay had used her credit to help this
'poor little tiny Congregation, trembling in its small cradle in
those former days, thirty-two and thirty-three years ago'.

On 7 March 1602 the d'Apremont carriage took Alix, Jeanne
and Claude to Saint-Mihiel, where Fourier gave them Gante as
their Superior. Alix was glad that she now only needed to obey,
but in fact all decisions were taken jointly. They would not use
the letters of recommendation or the credits opened for them in
shops nor any of the facilities offered by their benefactress.
They hastened to store in the attic all the valuable pieces of
furniture, chairs and games tables, curios, silver and porcelain,
to give a more monastic appearance to this magnificent interior.
Alix chose 'to put her bed in the smallest and most inconvenient
part of the house', under a wretched staircase, and still thought
she was 'better off than she deserved'.[72] In their longing to

be both active and contemplative, but without any of the compromises experience would teach them, Alix and her companions yearned for penances. They slept on boards, ate only coarse bread, fruit and milk products and drank water. They punished their bodies with liberal use of scourges, hair shirts and spiked belts. Having given God the first hours of the day in Divine Office and the mass, they devoted the greater part of their time to teaching. Their pupils belonged to the educated upper-middle class (*la bourgeoisie de robe*) which was well represented in Saint-Mihiel, and they soon came in such numbers that the sisters were able to try out Fourier's teaching methods. Each mistress had her own class of little girls whose progress in reading, writing and arithmetic she followed with patience and kindness. The catechism and prayers were first taken to heart and then learnt and recited. In response to requests from the families, the sisters took in some as boarders, and though the teaching was free for them as for the day-pupils, a contribution was asked for the cost of meals.

The town of Saint-Mihiel soon congratulated itself on the presence of the teaching nuns. One parish priest even said that he could easily identify girls taught in their school and declared that they would later become 'good mothers of a family'. Even so, this very priest was one who had at first shown some distrust of the sisters and especially of Fourier. Not pleased to see a religious directing and confessing penitents in his parish, his territory, he one day asked Fourier if his studies in theology gave him this right. Always humble, Fourier stammered an evasive reply and saw himself forbidden to hear confessions either from the sisters or from the children. At this news Gante exploded. Fourier tried in vain to calm her, extolling the pastor's merits. She took her complaint to the bishop, who granted the founder power of absolution, even in reserved cases.[73]

The foundation in Saint-Mihiel marks a happy stage of development for the sisters. Their vocation was acknowledged and they were living their ideal to its fullest height. It was now that the test came upon Alix, attacked by 'strong temptations against the faith'. 'It was at the beginning of my time in Saint-Mihiel', she says soberly (*Rel.* 41). The source of her doubts may perhaps be found in the intellectual currents running through the town, 'an entry point', said René Taveneaux, 'for the main ideologies of modern times, humanist, Calvinist, Cartesian and Jansenist'.[74] From a ragbag of ideas, Alix retained fragments, not fully grasped and contrary to true doctrine, on various topics which she lists as, 'grace, free will, immortality of the soul, the holy sacrament of the altar, ceremonies used by the Church and many other heretical points which I did not know to be such'. Harsher still than these dispersed attacks was a fundamental blade slashing at the basis of her faith, God himself. 'I was desperately tempted,' she said, 'to believe that the sun was God'. How could this taint of animism have reached her? Was she overcome by the life force of the sun? Was she taking a stand beside the defenders of Copernicus, whose heliocentric system was then a matter of debate and soon, on the basis of the Bible, to be judged heretical? For a soul so much in love with God as Alix, sun worship seems an impossible betrayal. But being ignorant she had no defence in the face of error. With justifiable pride she notes in her *Relation* how subsequently she did her own research and defeated similar temptations. 'Later,' she wrote, 'I learnt from sermons and spiritual books how I must resist these'. She did certainly find in Saint-Mihiel 'some good Fathers' among the Benedictines, Discalced Carmelites, Minims, Capuchins and Jesuits who thronged the place to whom she could confide her doubts, but the chronicle tells us that none of them was any help to her. As inescapable as a cloud of infected air, her temptations besieged her and stuck fast in her mind. She wore herself out, fighting them, and was afraid of offending God. She kept away from people, reserved and almost secretive, trying not to let her sisters see how unhappy she was. But they noticed and one of them gave this description:

> She withdrew to a place some distance from the house and spent the greater part of the nights in tears, praying and sighing after God. Being one day at the last point of her affliction, lying full length before God, she began to complain softly to him about the pitiable condition to which her sins reduced her, considering what a burning desire he had given her to seek and please him. While she could not tell which way to turn to find the right road, at that very moment she found herself free and entirely delivered from all her temptations, with such great calm in her mind that she felt as if she were another person. From then on she received so much grace and so much light as to the mysteries of faith that she was never again attacked by one single contrary thought, and there remained with her always a great depth of that infused faith which did her good service all her life in enduring the great afflictions of mind which came to her and the obstacles she encountered in the affairs of her Congregation.[75]

In this way God was shaping the foundress' soul, supplying her with strength for the future and heaping upon her spiritual treasures which she would give to others, especially to the children in her schools. One of the few texts in which her biographers show her intervening in the classrooms, deals with exactly this point, the teaching of the faith:

> She said she drew real comfort from the fact that the chief aim of our institute was to teach children about the holy

mysteries of the faith according to Christian doctrine. She
liked to go frequently into the classes to ask the children
questions and teach them herself, always choosing the poorest
girls and those who appeared the dullest because, she said,
they were usually less apt at learning and piety than children
from good families. She used to encourage the nuns employed
in the classrooms to take care first and foremost to teach them
well about the mysteries of the faith.[76]

Nancy, 1603

'In the year 1603', wrote Alix, 'the cardinal of Lorraine wished
us to go to Nancy' (*Rel.* 48). His wish was an order, coming
as it did from the highest religious authority in the country.
Charles of Lorraine (1567–1607), son of the reigning duke
Charles III, was simultaneously bishop of Metz and of Stras-
bourg, cardinal, papal legate for the whole of Lorraine and the
Three Sees (Metz, Toul and Verdun), and since 1602 he was
also primate of the primatial chapter of Nancy. This post was
meant to compensate him for the lack of a bishopric in Nancy,
capital of the duchy, where the pope, under pressure from
France, had refused to create an episcopal see. Pierre Fourier
and the Jesuit fathers supported the prelate's wish, and Alix and
Claude Chauvenel got ready to go in the name of obedience,
but experiencing 'great repugnance'. Until then they had felt
safe in their various settlements, although each place was larger
than the one before, moving from the hamlet of Poussay to
Mattaincourt village and then to the small town of Saint-Mihiel.
But what would it be like in Nancy? 'It seemed to us', explained
Alix, 'that this town was wrong for us because of the court and
so many people whom we could not help seeing, not being
enclosed'. The presence of the dukes did indeed bring constant
activity to Nancy. Around their magnificent dwelling, the ducal

palace, came and went a motley throng of officers, lawyers, religious, ladies in waiting, shopkeepers, in an incessant to and fro of riders and carriages. Jousts and tournaments took place on the Place de la Carrière, while processions and triumphal entries invaded the narrow streets of the town. This noisy society, greedy for the 'vanities' which she had renounced, was in no way to the taste of Alix, whose habit of contemplation fed upon silence. But a voice warned her as she slept that 'it is good to go there'. The reward offered was convincing: 'I was told as I slept that we would suffer many troubles there and much calumny, and that we would do and also receive there all possible good for the glory of God'. Sustained by this prospect, whatever the cost, Alix and her companion arrived in Nancy in the spring of 1603. Entering by the La Craffe gate, they crossed right through the Old Town and came out on to a building site. Charles III had decided that his capital was too small. He had the suburbs levelled and where they had been he began to build a New Town alongside old Nancy. Between the two stretched an esplanade lined with lime trees and surrounded by shopping booths and small poor houses. One of these, narrow and inexpensive, was reserved for the new arrivals. Close by stood the new hospital of St Julian and not far away was the large house of the Grey Sisters, nursing nuns like those at Ormes.[77] In less than fifteen minutes Alix and Claude could reach the Jesuit noviciate near the building work by the St Nicolas gate. Fourier had recommended them to the rector of the novices, Father Baccarat, who became Alix's confessor.

The school was soon opened and little girls flocked to it despite its small premises and out of the way location. But the foundress did not lose sight of the greatness of her vision. God would help her to make it good, she knew that. Moreover she was blessed with a knowledge of the future which was in fact the response God gave to the trust Alix had in him. One day, coming away from prayer, she called her companion to come and look through the window at the panorama spread out before them. Beyond the rue St Julien where they lived, the shady walk of the esplanade vanished into a formless area cluttered by the demolition of fortifications now being rebuilt further east to allow for the building for the primatial premises. 'Do you see that wide space?' she asked her. 'One day we shall have a fine convent there and in it you will see many nuns singing and praising God'. Claude laughed and said, 'Providence is great, but there is not much sign of all that!'.[78] The cardinal legate also believed in the work's future and Fourier, strengthened by his good will, on 8 December 1603 obtained from him the first official approval of the Congregation.[79] First giving the names of the five founding sisters, the prelate described their way of life with admiration and praised the results of their teaching of 'girls of the province' and 'young ladies of distinction'. As for those who had to earn their living in sordid trade, they, once educated at no cost, themselves became teachers in towns and villages, where they taught using the methods they had learnt. There was no mention in this text of solemn vows or cloistered convents, nor of nuns; but the cardinal allowed Pierre Fourier's sisters to build houses and schools anywhere in the whole area of his legation. They would work there, he said, 'according to the practice of the best regulated convents' with 'the sort of enclosure that they shall think most suitable'. This praise of the present and opening up of a future free from narrow restrictions was a great help, and as Fourier soon told the sisters, the cardinal had done more for them than he would ever have dared to hope (*C.* 1, 7).

Pont-à-Mousson, 1604

As the teaching of girl children made progress, the approval of
the Lorrainers for these new teachers, consecrated to God and
to the public, also increased. In 1604 Pont-à-Mousson wanted
such teachers too. The request was put forward by Servais de
Lairuelz, a former fellow student of Fourier's at university and
now his imitator in the difficult task of reforming an ancient
order, that of the Premonstratensians, by inspiring them with
new ardour. Appointed Superior of the abbey of Ste-Marie-au-
Bois in 1601, Servais embarked in 1608 on the construction of
a new monastery nearer to Pont-à-Mousson so that his religious
could there pursue their intellectual studies. This second abbey
was placed under the patronage of Sainte-Marie-Majeure, with
the result that Servais was never called anything but 'Monsieur
de Sainte-Marie'. The town of Pont-à-Mousson was as lively as
Nancy but differed from it in having a more cosmopolitan
population, spread along the two banks of the Moselle but
linked by the bridge over the river. The university attracted
students from every country in Europe and the religious
establishments had houses there for their scholars. At first
Fourier's humility made him doubtful about opening a school
in this university town, but eventually the presence of the Jesuits
there helped him decide. Judging by the letter he wrote to
the sisters at Pont-à-Mousson on 11 August 1622, he never
regretted his decision. 'Who could ever have thought that you
should lack solace in a town where [are] the Reverend fathers of
the holy Company of your good Jesus, and especially at Pont-à-
Mousson, fountain of every sort of learning and solace, which
spreads over the whole country and sends its waters much
higher, much further and into many more places than does the
Moselle'.[80] For this important settlement, he chose as Superior

Isabelle de Louvroir, who set off with some novices whom she
had trained at Mattaincourt, sending Alix and Gante with her
to help get the school started. It was all very well, says the
chronicle, to welcome them 'like angels', but their life there was
no paradise. For beds, a straw mattress and a cover, and in the
common purse, six francs *barrois*.[81] In order to keep access to
their school free, the sisters turned themselves into laundry-
women and before lessons began would take bundles of linen
down to the river and beat it with paddles to wash it there.
Their friends once gave them a turkey poult, meaning them to
enjoy a good fricassee, but the unshakeably abstinent sisters
saved its life and kept it to amuse the children. These enjoyed
competing to throw the bird bits of bread, which one evening
when food was short the sisters picked up for themselves.
Monsieur de Sainte-Marie had found for them a house so
inconvenient that they needed to be careful not to upset him
when they looked for somewhere better. Some girls, however,
attracted by the sisters' renown, were asking for admission. 'It
seems to me (lacking better advice)', said Fourier, 'that you
should not be in a hurry to open the door to Françoise and still
less to Bastienne and her sister at present, as foodstuffs are dear
enough and your house is small, cold and not well patched up
against the winter'. In the admission of applicants, he wanted
the sisters to use 'maturity, counsel and good advice, otherwise',
he joked, 'you will see huddled round your fire and shivering in
your badly floored rooms a boatload of similar girls not at all
appreciative of your vocation' (*C.* 1, 16). After Alix and Gante
left in 1606, Isabeau de Louvroir faced a difficult financial
situation as well as the impossibility of taking day pupils in such
an inconvenient school. It was for the community to decide. 'I
understand', wrote Fourier, 'that the opinion of your Reverend
Father, which is also yours, should be preferred to mine in this

instance'. The letters he sent to the sisters in these foundation years, a surprising number of which we happen to have, show how astonishingly attentive he was to material details, never short of practical advice – buy as much grain as possible when the price is low, get bread baked at the baker's 'while the household uses so little' (*C.* 1, 27). His visits to the sisters filled him with delight. 'I left Pont-à-Mousson thoroughly happy, comforted and strengthened', he wrote on 16 May 1605. Our only regret is that we do not have the letters the sisters wrote to him, letters he demanded of them and read, he said, 'with devotion'.

St-Nicolas-de-Port, 1605

From 1602 onwards the young Congregation of Our Lady opened a new house every year. In this accelerated rhythm, St Nicolas followed Pont-à-Mousson in 1605. This time the initiative came from Alix, recipient of a mysterious message. 'Our St Nicolas house', she wrote in her *Relation*, 'was shown to me in sleep. I was told that we must pick flowers in our garden in Nancy to transplant them to St Nicolas' (*Rel.* 51). The plan met with encouragement, receiving 'much advice and good counsels', and Claude Chauvenel left the capital of the duchy in August 1605 together with Jeanne Guarnard from Nancy, Jeanne Géry from Mattaincourt and Claude Mangenot who came from Pont-à-Mousson. Gante presided over the new beginning. This new shoot, plucked from the flourishing branch at Nancy, took root in a town doubly remarkable for religion and for trade. Pilgrims flocked there to pray to 'Monsieur Saint Nicolas' and long caravans of merchants converged upon its annual fairs where they bought wool, cloth, glass and other goods to take away to the Netherlands, Champagne, Switzerland and Germany.[82] Now for the first time the new congregation,

in spite of having no income, had to pay 7,000 francs to the
Jesuits. Although the sisters had received 'excellent help from
Saint-Mihiel' they still, thirteen years later, were 2,000 francs
in debt (*C.* 1, 122). The moment they arrived they were in a
hurry to open the school, but Fourier, worried that they might
disappoint the good people of St Nicolas, kept telling them,
'Don't be in too much of a hurry' and 'Better too late than too
soon' (*C.* 1, 6). In these letters, sent as term was beginning, he
sent all kinds of advice. 'Let our Sister Jeanne prepare good
pens, well cut, a good penknife, a ruler to rule straight copies,[83]
and good ink for her, as it adds a shine to the writing' (*C*, I, 6).
He tells them to buy tables and benches (*C.* 1, 8) but not to
keep asking the fathers of the little girls[84] for money, for they
had none to give them (*C.* 1, 28). To the sisters who asked him
about timetables, he replied, 'Send your boarders to bed at eight
o'clock' (*C.* 1, 14). He insisted on the priority of Christian
teaching: 'Teach mainly the catechism and piety to these little
ones. Make just as much of the poorest girl as of the most
admired' (*C.* 1, 8). He went so far as to sketch out the few
words the mistress would say to the pupils: 'Start your school
with these points, and on the first day give them a talk in which
you'll emphasise that you do not in the least want to keep or
display bad girls (and let them therefore do better and quit their
bad habits) and that your main purpose is to teach them to be
really good, to win heaven and become saints, etc.' (*C.* 1, 6).
Here already are the principles he would develop in his treatise
on education included in the *Constitutions de 1640*, as too his
idea of grouping by levels, one of his most inspired innovations.
'You will be able to form three classes in your school', he
recommended, 'and choose for the little ABC children the one
that will be right for them'. The number of boarders, very
variable at St Nicolas, alarmed the sisters, but Fourier soon

calmed them down: 'While you have them, teach them well, as you are doing. But if they go, accept this as coming from God' (C. 1, 28). For the problems encountered – firewood and foodstuffs are dear, corn is in short supply – he gave them the true remedy: 'I will show you a great fountain full of all good things, wherein you need only dip your bucket', it is called 'trust in God', through which 'you shall lack nothing' (C. 1, 14).

CHAPTER SEVEN

God can bring good out of evil

> It seems that Our Lord wants to bring our Congregation forward
> through honour and dishonour . . . I pray to him who knows how
> to bring good out of evil that he may turn all this to our profit.
>
> Letter of Pierre Fourier to the sisters of Nancy
> 11 December 1606 (*C.* 1, 23)

Our Lady's Cloister

After three successful years it was obvious that the little school
in the Rue St Julien was too small. This was a real problem and
Alix worried about it. It would be better, she thought, to find a
new house that would be more suitable – an impossible dream,
as she knew very well. In Nancy, where speculation was raging,
building sites and houses were very dear and the sisters did not
have a penny. Used as she was to confiding all her various
anxieties to the Virgin Mary, she received from her a message
that gave her confidence. 'One evening, asleep', she wrote, 'I
saw Our Lady upon an old wall and she complained to me,
saying that she was being allowed to fall down there. I woke up
at that and thought as to where we could find a house; I heard
a voice telling me that it was already built' (*Rel.* 49). A good
omen, indeed, that Mary should take on Alix's concern to the
point of declaring herself distressed that her work was being
allowed to fall, while it ought to be built up, or at least she
should be lodged in a house that was already built. 'Next day',
continued Alix, 'my lord Primate came to tell us that the
Cloister of Our Lady in Old Nancy was for sale because my

lord Cardinal was turning out the religious of that house because they had rejected the reform he wanted to give them'.

Alix's 'my lord Cardinal' was Charles of Lorraine who had brought the sisters to Nancy in 1603 and in the same year had granted the Congregation its first official approval. The 'Primate' who visited Alix in 1606 was Antoine de Lenoncourt, who a year later became primate when the cardinal died. At that time he was only grand dean of the primatial chapter, and it was as such that he invited the young Superior to buy the Cloister of Our Lady. The buildings, also known as the priory, were in fact a disused monastery where only the church had kept its original function, becoming a parish church. The Benedictines, settled there in the eleventh century, had just moved out, and Alix reported the facts correctly: because they refused to accept the reform ordered by the Council of Trent, the cardinal of Lorraine, their commendatory abbot, had expelled them and given their premises to the canons of the primatial chapter, who were preparing to sell them.

Alix, strong in the support of the Virgin Mary, won Pierre Fourier to her cause. He sent the cardinal a petition which is one of his finest defences of the education of girl children (*C.* 1, 19–22). Listing all those who did not think it was beneath them to teach little girls, such as St Jerome, 'schoolmaster to little Paula', and those too who had supported the actions of nuns, such as St Germain protecting Geneviève and St Jolain[85] who founded the Benedictine nunnery at Bouxières, Fourier hoped to revive the practice of the early church by instituting women who, performing the holy office and the duties of nuns, would work for their neighbours' salvation by teaching, not from church pulpits but in schools. From Aristotle he borrowed this assumption: that the more a good thing (here, education for the young) becomes general, the closer it comes to the

divine. To this he added the compelling argument: 'If half the
people in a large town are women and girls, as Aristotle says in
his *Politics*, and if care is taken to educate the other half, the
men and boys, there is no less reason to educate the girls'. The
cunning petitioner ended his request by promising the cardinal
that God would reward him for giving a home to the sisters,
who are 'poor volunteers, Our Lord's own poor'. He also asked
the prelate to sell the property at a reasonable price, less than its
value, to be paid in part cash down and part at a later date.
Alix bought the Cloister of Our Lady for 6,000 francs and
acknowledged that she had been able to do so thanks to divine
Providence. Her business sense and her trust in God encouraged
her to buy the gardens and adjacent buildings as well, to avoid
future neighbourhood problems and to give room for extension.
But this further purchase, costing 14,000 francs, provoked
much criticism in her circle. Gante, helping Claude Chauvenel
deal with debts at Saint Nicolas, and Isabelle de Louvroir,
confronting those at Pont-à-Mousson, did not approve of this
expenditure. In Nancy itself there were murmurs that this was
madness, against all common sense, unspeakable rashness. Alix
smiled and declared that God would see to it, because 'his purse
is big enough to do it all'. And very soon gifts came pouring
in. We are told that the noble ladies and girls of the city
spontaneously offered to pawn their plate and their pearls to
meet the promised payment, to get the Mother out of her
trouble, even beyond what was needed'.[86] A neighbour, however, who may have wanted the property himself, tried to
oppose the sale, and began to discuss it with Alix. She let the
gentleman express his anger, told him how sorry she was to
disagree with him, and serenely stood firm. To the sisters,
alarmed by his shouting, she foretold that he would be one of
their best friends, very attached to the congregation, to which

those pre-Revolutionary days in France children were often abandoned and it was not until 1638 that St Vincent de Paul by beginning the care of foundlings was able to help these 'little creatures' whose unhappiness is unbearable. In the secret hope that some kindly hand would pick up their baby, mothers would put them down usually near a church and in Nancy it was not uncommon for passers-by to gather up a baby at the entrance to the Cloister of Our Lady. One morning such a child was found, and the finders, full of ill will towards the teachers, made up a story alleging that Alix had given birth to this infant and thrown it out into the gutter to hide her shame. The rumour grew as it spread round the town, so that she could not go out without being shouted at and insulted. She showed no sign of anger or distress but endured these attacks for more than three months 'with such patience and sweetness,' says the chronicle, 'that it did much to confirm the good opinion people had of her'.[92]

Setbacks and squalls

An early problem of expansion burst upon the Congregation in 1606, one that is not easy to follow from the surviving reports, some too concise, others too partisan. Comparing these witnesses however, we can come to some conclusions.

The most credible source is naturally Alix's own *Relation*. After a passage covering the years 1613–15 she reverts suddenly to an earlier period and writes:

I forgot to say here that in the seventh or eighth year of our vocation I was troubled with impatience and with lack of trust that our plans would succeed, as until then I had always had good hope that they would, but now there came many small disturbances and disagreements, stirred up as much by

the devil as by our lack of experience. I then doubted whether
I ought to persevere in the hope of ending my days here. And
as our good Father confessor knew all about it, I told him
when I was very upset that I wanted to pray to God and the
Virgin to tell me what it was they wanted, because he himself
was not giving me any decision. One day when I was more
upset than usual about this, a white ghost appeared in front
of me. I made the sign of the cross; it disappeared at once,
and I had an inward message that this was the spirit tempting
me to mistrust and impatience, masked with fine pretexts. I
felt at the same moment my spirit strengthened with new
hope and encouraged to end my days there. (*Rel.* 57)

Alix describes frankly the impatience and mistrust which
overcame her when confronted by the obstacles to what she
called 'our plans', that is to say the founding of a Congregation
in which she would be able to consecrate her life to God
according to her chosen ideal. In the passage just before the one
quoted above she recorded in the same words the 'disagreements'
and 'disturbances' during her stay in Verdun, a recollection
which reminded her of earlier but similar events which she had
forgotten to mention under their own date. Charitably she
blames the devil and the sisters' inexperience for the 'small
disturbances' and 'disagreements' which in 1606–1607 affected
their original plan to the point where she doubted whether it
could succeed. She does not tell us what sort of troubles these
were, but reveals their effect upon herself: the hope she cherished
of creating a new form of religious life gave way to mistrust.
The question was one she felt she should ask her confessor
Father Baccarat: Did God and the Virgin want her to go on
with her plans? The priest did not know what to say, and
left Alix at the mercy of her confusion. Then how are we to

understand the appearance of the white ghost, sufficiently alarming for her to dismiss it with the sign of the cross? It seems to have represented the 'fine pretexts' which for a moment justified abandoning the project, for once the ghost had gone Alix recovered her strength and courage and gained 'a new hope' that she would end her days in the way of life she had chosen. The crisis affected her personally, bringing home to her the insecurity of a new order so as to make her anxious about her own future. But she put it well, it was the project common to all the sisters that was threatened, and by the same token herself as its foundress.

The letters Pierre Fourier sent now to the communities make clear some of the details of this event, especially the one he wrote on 11 December 1606. He addressed it as he always did to all his beloved sisters in Our Lord at Nancy and not just to Alix, as some biographers have claimed. He did certainly use the same words that she must have used when telling him of her anxiety, and we find them again in her *Relation*. He wrote: 'Do not, I beg, distress yourself so much for all these little dis-agreements which come one upon another. All this happens with the permission of God who seeks our advancement and greater good [...] If a few Maries leave us, he will raise up others who will come and take the empty places' (*C.* 1, 22). This allusion is clear and refers to the departure of certain nuns such as the Superior at Saint-Mihiel, Marie de Saint-Nicolas. To these defections was added the refusal of some families to give their daughters to an institution which was not enclosed and had no regular commitment. The sisters themselves passionately wanted to be 'nuns and schoolteachers' as Fourier had told the cardinal in his first petition but were impatient to have some official ratification of their double vocation. In establishing a difficult balance between prayer and mission, opinions differed, minds clashed and discord sprang up in their communities. To the Saint-Mihiel sisters (*C.* 1, 27) and those of Pont-à-Mousson (*C.* 1, 25) Fourier preached mutual support and charity. He hoped for fine weather after these 'small troublesome clouds' *(C.* 1, 24), but squalls were getting up, the wind was rising and the storm broke.

One episode in this drama comes to us in the *Life* of Pierre Fourier written by Jean Bedel, a man who greatly admired Gante and liked to decry Alix.[93] His assertion that Alix, needing a director always 'at her elbow', had made a vow of obedience to her Nancy confessor which alienated her from Fourier is scarcely credible. How could Alix, whose frankness is clear in every line of her *Relation*, have failed to record such an important detail? On the other hand it is an undisputed fact that differences between Fourier and his daughters were such as to necessitate a joint meeting. Other contemporaries confirm this but none of them say what these differences were, so that we can only guess. Ought the schools to be given up and some monastic rule installed? Should they accept enclosure? How far should they turn to a variety of confessors rather than to Fourier, who already had too much pastoral work on his hands? As for the meeting itself, Bedel gave an account of this which Mother Louis de Gonzague refused to include in her biography of Alix Le Clerc,[94] so disparaging, she said, were the terms used of her heroine. Such reticence is understandable in this nun of Lunéville who, like most hagiographers of past days, thought it best to record only her subject's virtues and keep any weaknesses hidden. Modern historians, however, see things differently and strive to show how divine grace can transform sinners and turn them into saints, sometimes at the cost of a long process of purification. Monseigneur Blanchet, in his panegyric of Alix Le Clerc during her beatification in Rome, used the famous meeting at Nancy to show that Blessed Alix had not achieved holiness without a long struggle. After expounding a masterly comparison of the founder and the foundress, the speaker did not hesitate to describe the conflict that broke out between them. He wrote:

'For some time Mother Alix, under the influence of an unwise confessor, seemed to be distancing herself from the common task. Pierre Fourier called the Superiors to a meeting and going straight to the difficulty but cloaking his severity in mock humility he declared: "I am only a poor village priest; while you were my parishioners I was perhaps good enough to instruct you in your duties. Now you have become more learned by reading good books and conversing with learned men. I see therefore that I am coarse, too coarse to lead you to that delicate spirituality and eminent perfection to which you aspire. That being so, I ask you to leave me and to take on someone else who is more capable and has more leisure." Mother Alix did not take this lying down, she rose to his ironic attack and to the amazement of all replied calmly, "Certainly your parish business gives you quite enough to do. I will find the best I can." '

Here the orator broke off to express his astonishment:

'Mother Alix, after so many years of inner struggle, is the proud girl of Remiremont still so much alive that she can blaze out so suddenly?'

Then he picks up his thread and goes on:

'This was quite momentary. Mother Gante stood up and affirmed their faithfulness to them all, energetic, indignant, moved almost to fainting. Already Alix was controlling herself, asked forgiveness for her attitude and discovered the true line of her life. But what an indication of the heroic work she had to do to reach that self abnegation which we shall see her achieve! She did not model herself all at once on some code of virtue to which she could easily conform. It was a battle she had to fight under the direction of her Mattaincourt parish priest, and she did it with her whole soul.'[95]

And so in Alix's soul the crisis of 1606 ended in her certainty that God would ensure the congregation's future and her own part in it. She knew too that Fourier would not abandon her. This hope would shine like a ray of light in the difficulties which were to mark the end of her stay in the Cloister of Our Lady.

CHAPTER EIGHT

The mystical path

Preludes

In 1618 at the request of her confessor, Father Guéret, Alix began to write down the acts of grace with which God had favoured her. She would record, she said, everything she remembered 'rather unusual' sent by God 'for the good of [her soul] and vocation' (*Rel.* 1). This was a work of mysticism, using the word in its sixteenth and seventeenth century sense as referring to an exceptional condition in the life of faith, attainable only in the higher levels of contemplation. On the content of the expression Alix is in complete agreement with Teresa of Avila, but it is a word neither of these women used. Teresa spoke of supernatural states of prayer – 'I give the name supernatural to that which we could not achieve by our own hard work and our own efforts, however great they might be'.[96] Using this definition, Alix's mystical journey is undeniable, as she records in her Relation several direct and passive experiences of the presence of God which for a period suspended the natural activity of her senses and broke off all communication with the outside world. She was then in an ecstasy. But her extreme discretion and humility in describing such favours make the task of a biographer difficult, dealing as one must with only scattered and usually undated fragments in order to follow like an explorer a road which through patches of light and dark will reach the shining summits.

No one can say exactly when her mystical journey began. An

ecstasy is mentioned by those close to her when she was living in the Cloister of Our Lady (1606–1609) but God's breaking into her life must go back to her conversion or better still to her baptism. If God did indeed grant her the grace of mystic union in her thirtieth year, we have to say that she was then wonderfully well qualified to receive it. The asceticism of her religious life, her longing for penance and hatred of her sins had prepared her to delight in the presence of God in a purified heart. And she had accustomed herself to encountering this beloved God in her neighbour and in the practice of charity within her community and outside it. Her liking for recollection, peace and silence had made her attentive to the least breath of the Spirit. Knowledge of her worthlessness and trust in God's mercy ensured that she never took any credit to herself for these favours. Finally, her good judgment enabled her to distinguish between truth and falsity when the devil tried to trick her. Already at the start of her vocation, when she saw visions of the Virgin Mary, Fourier had introduced her to the discernment of spirits and warned her of the danger of 'illusions'. It is evident that in a few years she had moved forward on the mystical path.

The visitations of God

Unlike Teresa of Avila or the Ursuline nun Mary of the Incarnation, Alix speaks so briefly of the gifts of mystical grace that it is not easy to describe them. None the less, the little that she does say is so profound that we are out of our depth. Paragraph 33 of her *Relation* is the most helpful here, as it comes straight after an account of several unusual events, presents a synthesis of these and fully describes the progress of the mystic experience. She wrote:

In these raptures, ecstasies and trances that I have mentioned and others which have sometimes come to me, a light spreads out in my soul, making me desire and long for divine perfections, sometimes one in particular, at others for the holy humanity of Jesus Christ. They are not very frequent and I hold it a great goodness and kindness of God that no one has yet noticed them, so far as I know. They come to me suddenly without my foreseeing or expecting them; they do not last long and during this time I do not know whether I have my eyes open, but I do not see or hear or know where I am. I remain on my knees or in the position I was when this happened to me. Once recovered, I cannot help sighing for a long time afterwards, even when I am busy, working, eating or waking up at night'. (*Rel.* 33)

Alix did not bother much with subtle distinctions of mystical vocabulary. Her companions talk in the 1666 biography of 'ecstasies' and 'ravishments' but she uses the words *attractions* and *évanouissements*.[97] However, she describes the visitations of God as clearly as Teresa of Avila, whose writings she certainly knew. Like the Carmelite saint, she distinguishes between two unequal elements of the ecstasy. What is essential is the infused grace of light and love God gives to the soul. Secondary is the suspension of bodily faculties, an accidental result of their inability to register so intense a grace. Alix takes careful note of the effects of the ecstasy on her whole person; immobilised as if from a sudden shock her body holds its position but she does not hear or see anything, does not even know whether her eyes are open. 'I do not know where I am', she said, because strictly speaking she is not there, she is somewhere else, immersed in God as God in her. Once she allows us to see clear glimpses perceived in the light that floods her – able for a brief moment

to share the vision seen by the blessed, she is left with an
intense thirst for it, a thirst which makes her, she says, 'yearn
and sigh for divine perfection'. For her these words mean
something quite other than the solemn and abstract formulae
of our old catechisms which define God as 'a pure spirit,
infinitely perfect, omnipotent, eternal and sovereign master of
all things'. In the brightness of mystic union Alix contemplated
divine perfection, sometimes one aspect sometimes another, or
the glory as a whole, with the same enthusiasm as did the
inspired author who sang the praises of Wisdom – 'Within
her is a spirit intelligent, holy, unique, manifold, subtle, active,
incisive, unsullied, lucid, invulnerable, benevolent, sharp,
irresistible, beneficent, loving to man' (Wisdom 7, 22–3).
Contemplation of the transcendent God brought her to that of
the holy humanity of Jesus Christ, because for her as for Teresa
of Avila, 'even the greatest saint who has reached the summit of
contemplation must go by way of the humanity of Jesus, the
only bridge between God and men'.[98] Alix does not speak of
the infused revelation which was granted her, and as if fearing
to have said too much, tries to minimise her ecstasies. They
were quite infrequent, she said, as intense as they were short,
sudden, unexpected. Nobody noticed them, she thought, and
she was glad of this. In two words she describes her return to
normality but then emphasises her subsequent condition which
lasted 'for a long time afterwards'. As in the ecstasy but without
the suspension of awareness, she would keep sighing, mindful
day and night of her beloved God and ready to let him take
hold of her once more. But she did her tasks, worked and ate
with her sisters. How could these sisters fail to be anxious about
her sighs, which seemed to express an obvious dissatisfaction?
She had to provide an explanation. 'Our sisters', she wrote,
'think that this comes from illness or some trouble of the

mind; sometimes I give them trivial reasons. It seems to me that it would be very shocking for them, seeing me so full of wretchedness and imperfections, to have such things' (*Rel.* 33). Although there was no risk whatever that the sisters would see her take pride in God's gifts and be shocked, Alix preferred to let them misunderstand her sighs, even if it meant she sometimes told them 'trivial reasons'. Perhaps she would then share with them one of the 'very high things in the knowledge of God', while assuring them that no one could know more than 'a tiny part'[99] of his greatness. But of herself she said nothing, and the sisters later bore witness: 'She was so reserved in speaking of the extraordinary graces that we could discover nothing about herself on this subject'.[100] Alix, understanding her own character, declared herself astonished – in the true sense of the word, thunderstruck – to see the wonders the Lord did for her. Far from being shocked, she, like the Virgin Mary, gloried in them and proclaimed that he, being infinitely good and full of mercy, 'wanted to support her weakness and lukewarmness by his visits' (*Rel.* 33).

One day the truth at last broke out. It was, says the chronicle, while Alix was living in the Cloister of Our Lady in Nancy.

She then had a trance so long that the sisters being unable to bring her to herself, one of them thought that there could very well be something more in this event than they under- stood and they should send for her confessor to see her in this state. This was Father Baccarat of the Company of Jesus. He came, together with the parish priest of Our Lady, Monsieur Sébastien Soury, a very capable and spiritual man, and they at once judged what it was. [...] The Mother came back to herself gently. She was so surprised to see these good Fathers and the others around her that she did not know where to put herself for embarrassment. She made them great apologies for the trouble they had had for nothing, said two or three words to them in a low voice, and they went away. Afterwards she begged the sisters never to raise such alarms again, they must have a little patience when she did this, and it would pass at once.[101]

The sisters' lack of experience contrasts with the competence of the two priests. But they learnt their lesson and afterwards were able to recognise the physical effects of Alix's ecstasies. And it tells us an important point, that these experiences were part of her daily life in the Cloister of Our Lady. Soon there was no member of the community who was fooled by the skill with which Alix disguised her ecstasies 'with the excuse of her normal illnesses and infirmities'. And the sisters noticed that God's action lasted well beyond the encounters themselves. Shrewdly they described what François de Sales called 'the ecstasy of work and life' or sometimes 'the ecstasy of action and activity'.[102] 'She was so busy', they noted, 'with God that you could say her prayer was almost continual, and that besides the union of mind and will that she always had with him, she was often drawn out of herself by divine attraction, just as she notes it in her *Relation*, not only at times of prayer but in the ordinary activity of the whole day. She received through God's communications so much light and grace that no one noticed in her anything but acts of goodness and holiness'.[103] We can admire the tact of the sisters who did not try to intrude into the closeness between Alix and her Lord; all we need to do is delight in the resulting radiance. Less admirable are the confidences broadcast by Mademoiselle Langlois, who had a room next to that of Alix in the Cloister of Our Lady and used to spend the nights watching 'to see and hear what she did' and would then tell the sisters about the mystical utterances she had, she said, managed to catch.[104]

'She spoke of God with a heart on fire'.

Alix's teaching vocation now led her into a new mission. A privileged witness of God's love, she became its ardent apostle. Her community was the first to benefit from her spiritual knowledge but soon it shone out beyond the cloister walls. Pious people wanting to find a director came to her, and for two or three hours together she would talk to them about the love of God 'with joys and delights' which could be seen in her face, said the sisters.[105] We know little of what was said, but we are told about the wonders which accompanied them. Alix mentioned them out of loyalty to the purpose of her *Relation*, and the sisters repeated them, often tempted to expand them, because in those days extraordinary phenomena were thought to be a guarantee of holiness. The first of these scenes took place one Easter day in the Cloister. Alix and a 'very devout and spiritual lady', were talking about our Lord's resurrection, both of them no doubt much moved by the day's liturgy. Together they were fervently meditating on the meaning of the feast when suddenly they saw a burning torch which moved all round the parlour and then vanished. They reassured themselves by making the sign of the cross. To this the chronicle adds that Alix later told a nun that 'the torch having vanished, it left her with quite extraordinary feelings of the love of God and of his constant presence throughout eight days'.[106] But in her *Relation*, Alix, a humble woman, did not posit a relationship of cause and effect between the good feelings of the two people talking and the presence of God, indicated by an unusual event. Using the conditional voice, she suggested without asserting that 'if we had wanted to rely on the good feelings which this left us, we would have said that this was a mark of Our Lord's power' (*Rel.* 66).

The second scene, more disturbing, comes to us indirectly. The same lady told it to the same nun, who had confirmation of it from Alix herself. The two friends were in the parlour that day, talking about 'the purity of heart God requires from perfect souls'. They exchanged their ideas on this subject and Alix concluded the conversation with the beatitude dear to mystics, 'Blessed are the pure in heart for they shall see God.' These are, she said, the infallible promises of eternal Truth'.[107]

Scarcely had she said this when they both heard an angry voice clearly saying, 'Blessed are those who are in a state of mortal sin for they shall see the devil'. A sign of the cross restored calm and the nun and her guest took up their talk again.

The devil's intrusion

This intervention on the part of the devil is significant. Father of lies, he used words from Scripture and in falsifying them he showed his tactics, that is to say, by mimicking God's action in the soul. In paragraph 35 of her *Relation* Alix records the most striking of his counterfeits, an exact reversal of the mystic experience described in paragraph 33. She wrote:

I will also say here that I sometimes have visions of evil spirits which want to frighten me, but I am not afraid of them because I believe that they have no power but through the will of God. At first they sometimes wanted to give me false trances, making them come upon me bit by bit and making me feel them in the distance, so as to get me to welcome them out of curiosity, which God always gave me the grace to recognise by the fact that these withdrawals left nothing but darkness in the soul. And I turned towards Our Lord asking him not to let me be deceived and [telling him] that I felt myself to be more worthy of hell than of that which was only right for the saints.

This text gives us the key to other passages. For a more certain attack upon Alix the devil summoned his assistants and mobilised a horde of evil spirits who tried to alarm her by presenting terrifying visions to her imagination. To these she responded with scorn. 'I am not afraid of them,' she said. Her faith and trust supported her because she knew that Christ had conquered sin and the devils could only torment her in so far as God wanted her to be tested. The evil spirits, thinking Alix was at the start of her mystic travels and would be hungry for unknown delights, tried to arouse her curiosity and excite her spiritual greed. With a clearness of thought given her, she said, by God, she at once recognised their contrivances, so different from the actions of God. Divine visitations were swift, sudden and unforeseeable, but these false trances began with prolonged attempts at seduction and left behind them effects which betrayed their origin. 'These withdrawals left nothing but darkness in the soul', unlike true ecstasies which, as she knew, filled the soul with long lasting light. Alix, lover of light and enemy of lies and ignorance, turned – a significant word – towards Our Lord, 'asking him not to let [her] be deceived'. Most certainly her prayer was answered, and she must now, we think, acknowledge the favours she receives from God. No, not at all. In a brief phrase she thrusts aside the obvious conclusion, thinking herself, she said, 'more worthy of hell than of that which is only right for the saints'. A humble avowal, of which we can take the last words and apply them to their author – Alix was indeed walking on the mystical road towards sainthood.

The evil spirits, annoyed by their defeat, kept up a fierce attack. They changed shape and tried to terrify her in frightful forms which she confronted every time with calm courage. If they were 'ugly and misshapen men' she banished them with the sign of the cross (*Rel.* 36). If they turned into hands which moved about and tried to touch her, she grasped them, threw them down and cursed them 'in the name of God' (*Rel.* 36). Often her first reaction was alarm, but she always overcame it. One moonlit night, for instance, just as she was about to go down a stairway in the little house in the Rue St-Julien at Nancy, she saw below her 'a black phantom in the shape of a man'. 'At first I shivered a little with fear', she wrote, 'but at once I reassured myself with the sign of the cross and decided to pass him and putting my hand on his head in the name of Jesus Christ, he fled' (*Rel.* 38). Another night she admits that she was frightened 'to begin with' because 'not thinking of anything of the kind', she saw moving towards her 'as it were a great globe of fire ready to devour me in its flames' (*Rel.* 37). Did this ball of fire come from the very mouth of hell? So too, perhaps, came the wild beast she mentions on another occasion. It had 'large ears, sparkling eyes and wonderfully large paws', flung itself at Alix in fury, but as soon as she made the sign of the cross, it vanished (*Rel.* 37). Alix knew that this monster was an 'illusion', that is to say a phenomenon produced by the devil to control her imagination and her feelings. But she was all powerful against the forces of evil. Like the disciples who received the gift from Christ, she could expel demons. As soon as she brandished the arms of the Church – the name of Jesus, the sign of the cross, the laying on of hands – they disappeared.

The episode of the furious beast reminded Alix of two other 'illusions'. One dates from the earliest period of what she called 'our' vocation, at the beginning of the sisters' communal life. 'It happened to me,' she wrote, 'that by illusion I could not move myself, I felt the evil spirit close to me' (*Rel.* 37). Another memory evokes actual demonic possession, when the evil spirit attempted to control not only her senses but her whole body. 'He wanted to pierce my mouth with an iron hook and make me swallow it. Another time he pulled at my hands with this hook, and I said in my mind that I was very willing to endure this for the love of Our Lord' (*Rel.* 37). Alix had already, when tempted to blasphemy and mistrust, offered to God her body 'to be crushed into a thousand pieces' in expiation (*Rel.* 10). Here too, when the devil sought to overcome her, she used prayer to win the battle. In prayer she took refuge in a place where the enemy could not come. All the suffering the evil spirit caused her, she accepted, she told Our Lord, for the sake of his love. Thus she defeated the devil twice over: on the one hand she triumphed over his attack by her clear sight in thwarting his traps and by the immunity she apparently enjoyed through her humility and her trust in God; on the other, the worst satanic torments became for her so many opportunities for showing God how dearly she loved him. Infuriated by her resistance, the devil hated her twice as much.

CHAPTER NINE

Alix in distress

An alarming episode

As the community was ending its night prayers with an examination of conscience, Alix saw through the windows of Our Lady's Cloister 'four big men wearing black' who were about to come in, all holding burning torches. The sight startled her, but then suddenly they vanished, leaving the building 'apparently all on fire, as if burning in tall flames'. The sisters were all alarmed and wanted to get help to put the fire out. Here Alix pauses for a moment in her account: 'Coming back to myself a little', she wrote, 'I thought that this could be an illusion'. The sisters took comfort and resumed their prayers and 'the great fires' died down and gathered into 'a great ball of fire' which they watched as it 'rolled along the cloister passages' and 'fell with a loud noise into the lavatories'[108] (*Rel.* 28). Alix artistically maintained the suspense till the end of the story, but gave enough hints for us to see the truth behind the 'illusion'.[109] These four men, were they policemen on their rounds? Were they lantern-bearers who had just lit up their cressets, or is lightning flashing from a thunderous sky? It does not matter. What does matter is that Alix goes back over this event of paragraph 28, dating it to 'sometime before' the temptations she described in paragraph 27. The two are connected.

Most striking in this episode of 'the four big men wearing black' is Alix's emotional readiness to fear the worst at 'seeing men coming so late' to the sisters. Indeed, the times were dangerous, and Our Lady's Cloister had no high walls to protect the nuns. Afraid of men, Alix was also afraid of fire, a normal enough emotion at that period. More serious than this habitual anxiety was her instant fear of succumbing to an 'illusion'. She had second thoughts and saw her mistake, but although the word 'illusion' is enough by itself to indicate a demonic presence, we may wonder whether in making this record, she did not intend to flag up a new tactic on the enemy's part. On to the accustomed scene – nightfall, devouring flames, the fireball – come new actors, 'four big men wearing black', who succeed in distressing Alix but are disappointed that they have been dismissed as 'illusions'. They will come back and torment her. So they did, but she knew them at once, they were 'four devils in human shape'.

'Hell fire in the flesh'

The devil had already tried to stir Alix's imagination by taking on the appearance of 'ugly and misshapen men' (*Rel.* 36) or that of 'a black phantom in the shape of a man' (*Rel.* 38). The device, intended to terrify her, failed. With increased venom the devil would then try to arouse her physical senses by appearing to her as a male partner seeking a guilty pleasure. How would Alix defend herself?

Considering the times in which she lived and what we know of her youth, it seems probable that she was not well prepared for this battle. The rigour of Catholic reform cannot have failed to develop in her a pathological sense of guilt, which her confessors would have done nothing to lessen, as they repeatedly told her that 'there is no vice which drags so many souls down to hell as the sin of impurity'.[110] But is excessive fear of a danger the best way to counter it? And her refusal to accept subjection to a husband, did this perhaps only keep suitors away during

some crisis of independence? And there was her sudden conversion, involving a resolution to avoid the company of young
people, seen as servants of the devil – was this intended to last
for a long time? Was not the vow of chastity, made without
seeking advice, a vow very difficult to keep? To all these
questions Alix gives an absolute negative in her trust and
perfect loyalty. She wrote:

> I will speak too of the help I experienced from the Virgin
> Mary in a great temptation which traversed my soul. [...] For,
> being greatly oppressed by the imaginations and illusions of
> the hell fire of the flesh, there even one night appeared before
> me four devils in human shape who by their illusions deprived
> me of physical strength and of my voice to shout with, Our
> Lord permitting this in order to teach me that it is he who
> fights our enemies when he knows our good will. These evil
> spirits, showing themselves in a dirty and horrible way, ready
> to execute wicked actions against my person – and I, not able
> to do anything to defend myself except raise my thoughts to
> heaven, begging Our Lord and his holy Mother to protect me
> from them – and at once I felt divine assistance. For, these
> devils, unable to accomplish their purposes, took me by my
> feet and arms, pulling me from side to side. I was quite
> content that they should treat my body in this way, to avenge
> myself on it. During this time my mind was so confused,
> humbled and full of mistrust that I did not dare lift the eyes
> of my thought towards God. (*Rel.* 27)

The establishment of this text needs comment, for since the
Evreux manuscript was found in 1937 we know that it is very
probably identical to the original which Alix gave to her confessor. Earlier readers did not have this good fortune, as ever
since the first biography of their foundress appeared in 1666,

the sisters have altered the passage. Softening phrases they found too direct, they make Alix say: 'The evil spirits seemed the more horrible in that they threatened me with some dirty attack'.[111] Two hundred years later Count Gantelet found the expression displeasing and suppressed it in his 1882 edition of Alix Le Clerc's writings, declaring that 'girls educated in nineteenth century boarding schools were not used to hearing the language one might have used in the seventeenth century'.[112] At the request of teachers fearing enquiries from their pupils on a delicate subject, he also omitted the expression 'illusions of the flesh'. Finally, making it clear that these were 'completely insignificant changes', he made Alix say that she was 'greatly oppressed by imaginations of hellish flames with which the demons were trying to consume her'. Never mind the deplorable tampering with the text or the policy of silence on a risky subject – a teaching technique which confuses ignorance with innocence – and let us concentrate on Alix. Anxious to be 'restored and counselled' by her confessor, as she stated at the beginning of her *Relation,* she spoke frankly about a subject which prudish centuries – as we have just seen – thought taboo. In doing so she gives us testimony which is all the more important because it is apparently unique among mystics of her period and calibre. As for our own century which acknowledges no restriction on discussion of sex, we now can only approve the freedom with which Alix reveals her own case. Astonishingly modern in her avowal of temptations, she shows how they can be defeated.

But there is no word of triumph in the account just quoted. On the contrary, she stresses her weakness, saying as did St Paul, 'I shall be very happy to make my weaknesses my special boast so that the power of Christ may stay over me' (2 Cor. 12:9). Keeping her innermost spirit free, she frustrated the manoeuvres of the four devilish men who had robbed her of strength and voice so that they could abuse her. In this enforced paralysis she saw one way permitted by Our Lord to teach her 'to know that it was he who fights our enemies'. And she went on praying, demanding divine assistance which she at once received, for in the fresh torment devised by the four devils she saw only a kind of martyrdom which would avenge her on her body. Thus once again the demons' traps were sprung and the distress they caused her was transformed into expiatory sacrifice.

None the less the struggle exhausted her. Beset by lascivious images, she was afraid of taking pleasure in them; struck by vertigo, her will seemed to abandon her and to be plunging her into an abyss of sin. While the flames she detested raged in her body, shame overcame her, then came self disgust, then helpless despair made her long for death. In this descent into hell, nothing but the Virgin Mary any longer connected her to life. Since the day she adopted her for her confidant and protectress, a tender intimacy bound her to Our Lady and in every need it was to her she turned. Her plea here is more poignant than any others. She wrote: 'And when I could do no more and despair came, I turned to the holy Virgin, mother of the afflicted, imploring her that as I had put myself under her protection, she would beg for me the merits of her Son to wash my soul and adorn it with his grace' (*Rel.* 27). Her metaphors are not mere stylistic flourishes. They illustrate an exact theology. Mary is seen as a mediator who obtains from her Son the grace of forgiveness. And just as the evil spirits made ready to perform their 'dirty and horrible' deeds, so the sin of impurity is comparable to a material substance which befouls the soul. Nor does any image better express the grace and merits of Christ than that of water, the purifying waters of baptism or the living water of the Spirit which dwells in the reborn soul.

In spite of the Virgin Mary's helpful intervention, temptations continued to harass Alix, who, resolutely faithful, noted events down. 'I could often smell', she wrote, 'very bad odours around me, such as sulphur and other hellish mixtures, as I suppose', filth which, as she later realised, warned her of a coming 'temptation or affliction' (*Rel.* 29). Too weak to utter the prescribed prayers, she simply repeated the penitential psalms, saying with the psalmist, 'God, create a clean heart in me, put into me a new and constant spirit' (Ps. 51:10). What exhausted her was that she could never feel sure that she had not sinned, could not determine where she stood between fascination and disgust for the pleasures which attacked her senses.

'Opposition from good people'

In all this distress, Alix experienced another test which she described in the *Relation* she wrote for Father Guéret: 'To increase my difficulties, Our Lord allowed your fathers [the Jesuits] to begin to doubt my spirit, fearing there might be something hidden in my soul which I refused to reveal, which I did not notice. None the less I became doubtful with them – perhaps I was possessed, or something still worse which I did not understand' (*Rel.* 29). This 'opposition from good people' as Teresa of Avila called it, is not surprising. Those around her now knew about the mystic gifts of grace she received, and knew too about the contrary manifestations contrived by the devil to discredit her. At that period a 'tide of satanism' was sweeping through Lorraine and churchmen were talking a good deal about the devil and the illusions he created in the imagination, especially in the minds of women, more fragile. Alix's confessor, Father Baccarat, taking note of one of her ecstasies, needed to consult his Jesuit colleagues, and it may have been they who inspired his doubts – was his penitent not perhaps a false mystic, clever enough to dupe her public?

Alix was appalled. She had faithfully told her confessor what
happened to her, hiding nothing, so that he could help her
discern the truth. If now the men she consulted, pious and
learned, saw in her the action of the devil, she humbly accepted
the verdict. Perhaps she was possessed by the devil, or something
still worse, or a witch endowed with demonic powers. This was
not the last time her confessors caused her distress.

An unhappy event

After the sisters moved to Our Lady's Cloister they stopped
going for confession to the Jesuits whose monastery was at the
far end of the New Town, a long way away. Pierre Fourier
wanted them to avoid being seen out in the streets; they should
as far as possible keep to the enclosed existence which was then
considered an essential sign of monastic life. They were not to
go oftener than once a month to the Jesuits who directed their
consciences, and otherwise would go to 'a good secular priest'
who lived nearer them. This is how Alix described him: 'He was
known to be a good man and very capable, one who took great
care of the devout women he directed. But although pious he
did not have all the discernment and other qualities [I needed]
in my spiritual necessities. He embarrassed me very much and
made me very anxious with the excuse that he wanted to help
me in my temptations' (*Rel.* 30). Poor Alix, for whom the
unveiling of her conscience must have required heroic courage,
the sacrament of forgiveness brought her nothing but trouble
and uncertainty. With her characteristic wish to see clearly, she
spoke about it to Father Baccarat, confessor extraordinary to
the community.[113] He declared that this priest was not suitable
for work with nuns, as he was 'too free and too familiar'. Alix
left him at once, but could not avoid 'often' encountering him,
when she would have to deal with his annoyance and anger and

'sometimes indiscreet and indecent words'. 'However hard I tried to get rid of him', she wrote, 'I could not avoid meeting him'. Now this evildoer took the place of the tempting devil in an 'illusion' which was all the more plausible because it made use of a known image with which Alix was constantly struggling. 'Through the fear I had of him', she wrote, 'or by God's permission to test me more, it happened that in the violence of my temptations he appeared often in my imagination, which put me into very great torments of conscience' (*Rel.* 30). First despair, now madness lay in wait for her. 'Unable to bear the apprehension', she wrote, 'I was really afraid of losing my mind'. She described her condition exactly: 'I could not and did not dare sleep because of so many bad illusions; I had no appetite for food and became skin and bone. I could not believe my confessors who told me I was not offending God'. And so, like a sick person who rejects the doctor's diagnosis, Alix made her trouble worse and insisted on prescribing her own cure. She intended, she said, to keep her memory and her reason constantly alert so as to counter shameful suggestions by ceaseless vigilance. But she did not succeed, and hence arose the endless scruples and the darkness which overshadowed her mind.

Weakened by her bad health and this painful struggle, Alix did not lose her clarity of mind or her freedom of decision. Looking at it coolly, she judged the situation: on the one hand, her serious condition; on the other, the impossibility of finding the help she needed in Nancy. She now wrote several letters to Fourier, genuine calls for help because she knew, as she had known once before in the convent at Ormes, that she was 'in danger'. But how to express it? Something that is hard to say is not necessarily easy to write. Although the community in Our Lady's Cloister was not bound by any canon law enclosure, she asked the founder for permission to leave Nancy and go to Mattaincourt. But he did not reply. Alix took action – 'I decided to go and see him myself', she wrote, 'and tell him the state I was in' (*Rel.* 30).

Painful though it was, the episode of the priest who was 'too free' cannot be passed over in silence, for it completely explains Alix's decision. The 1666 edition of the *Vie* did not suppress it but distorted its meaning, providing all later biographers of Alix Le Clerc with a toned down but inaccurate text. Prudish persons had no shocking words to suppress and the book could be put into anyone's hands. But the discovery of the Evreux manuscript has shown what distortions were made. In her opening lines Alix listed this among other temptations, writing: 'A great trouble came to me because of a confessor and this was one of the most distressing traps the devil set for me to afflict my mind'. The printed version reads: 'My troubles increased through an occasion which showed how important it is for afflicted souls to meet a good confessor'.[114] Then everything which stresses the priest's guilt is omitted, as are the renewed temptations which attacked Alix. The anger of the confessor, displeased to see his penitent leaving him, is transformed into a case of conscience for Alix: she is 'in danger of sinning in this', she is 'the cause of his disturbance', she thinks. It is this that leads to her 'tormented conscience' and her decision to go to see Fourier to ask for 'a more powerful remedy'.

Hélène Derréal, discoverer of the Evreux manuscript, was the first to point out these mistakenly altered passages in the 1666 edition. 'Is there any need', she asks, 'to say more about the significance of this rewriting? Alix is exposed to annoyance from a priest, one who was at least too free in his ways, as so many unfortunately were in those lax days, and the distress caused to her virgin soul by this painful situation better explains why she, normally so obedient, left her convent without permission'.[115]

The lives of saints are disconcerting. One would expect Pierre Fourier, who had been Alix's director since her conversion, to take pity on her distress and give her the supernatural comfort and friendship she needed. No document makes any such mention, but we may suppose it happened none the less. We have only to look at the lines he sent to the sisters at Nancy on 11 December 1606 to appreciate the kindness of his heart: 'You write in the last line of your letters that you are a little distressed, and yet you do not say how or why. Please tell us this in your next letters so that we can help you bear this trouble' (*C.* 1, 23). However that may have been, Alix's condition was too serious for hope of a rapid recovery. Her health was already shaken by excessive penances and could offer only weak resistance to the despair which now overwhelmed her. Psychiatrists would talk of depression, phantasms, anorexia, or a suicidal crisis. More simply she wrote: 'Sometimes I said to myself that if Our Lord had allowed us to kill ourselves, I would do that much more readily than be as I am now, and would gladly and whole-heartedly have accepted any kind of death if it had pleased God to give me the choice' (*Rel.* 31). This feeling of worthlessness which drove her to long for death in order to be free of it was not self pity or narcissism. It is the 'evil state' linked to the condition of the sinner who is drawn to the evil which he challenges. The time would come when Alix would accept this condition, because, she said, from the depths of her nothingness God's greatness seemed to her so much the greater. For the present, the weight of her misery was crushing her. She used what strength was left her to pray, and this prayer saved her. She tells us herself how she was healed.

How the Virgin Mary freed Alix from temptation

Alix's encounters with the Virgin Mary never happened in ordinary situations. The chosen places were perhaps dedicated to Our Lady, such as the church at Remiremont and the chapel at Poussay. The special days were liturgical feasts when Alix's devotion was more fervent, the Purification on 2 February or her Nativity, as it happened on 8 September 1609 (*Rel.* 23).

It was a feast day at Mattaincourt and the sisters were singing vespers in the church. The liturgy gave Alix the words of her prayer and their savour sank into her like a balm. *Ave maris stella*, Hail, star of the sea . . . The words of the hymn and cry of help from Alix, storm tossed but trusting in Mary's all powerful intercession, rang together. 'I lifted my soul and my hope to the holy Virgin, begging her to ask her Son that I should never offend him in this temptation'. Much moved, she recalled the advice of St Bernard, commenting on the *Ave maris stella*: 'When rough winds blow temptations upon you, when you are heading straight for reefs of adversity, look at the star, call to Mary! When desires of the flesh shake the barque of your soul, look towards Mary!'[116] Like him, 'the Virgin's singer', she placed Mary between men and God, mediatrix, full of compassion, of divine grace. For Alix, Mary was a living presence, acting in different ways as the needs of the moment required. Yesterday she appeared as a mother giving Alix her child to bring up, initiating her in her calling as a teacher; today she appeared to her as the purest of women, *virgo singularis*, her incomparable virginity a gift of God. Alix, deep in prayer, contemplated 'the woman who, ever since her immaculate conception, most perfectly reflected the beauty of God'. In her, 'sanctuary of the Holy Spirit, shone the splendour of the new creature'.[117] Alix, enraptured, could not tire of praising the Lord for this splendour, now praising him for his choice of Mary, now thanking her for her obedience to the holy Word which was made flesh in her. The devil, ready to take advantage of Alix's distress to defeat her, was on the watch. She was all but defeated, he called in his reinforcements – but as the nuns sang the praises of Mary, all four demons lost heart and fled, 'completely' releasing Alix from the temptation that attacked her. From then on with each decade of her rosary she invoked Mary as *Virgo singularis*, delighted that she had found in her the model of consecrated virgins.

CHAPTER TEN

Mattaincourt and Pont-à-Mousson
1609 – 1610 – 1612

Sister Alix

After leaving Nancy on 20 February 1609, Alix arrived in Mattaincourt, but we do not know whether or not she received the reassuring welcome that she needed. Pierre Fourier was immobilised in his presbytery after injuring his leg in a fall from his horse. He wrote to the sisters at Pont-à-Mousson on 5 March to tell them the news: 'Sister Alix made an excursion here some fortnight ago. I don't know whether God may not have allowed this so that she will stay some time' (*C.* 1, 36). Accustomed to recognise God's hand in events, he saw a providential purpose in this journey. In fact Alix's stay there, lasting until 1610, was useful, but her condition did not improve and her healing, won for her by the Virgin Mary, did not take place until 8 September 1609. Always valiant, in spite of her distress she shared in the life of the community where she was no longer the Superior from Nancy or the leading nun in the congregation but simply Sister Alix. This position suited her, for the duty of obedience gave her life a direction which her own stumbling will was no longer strong enough to provide. The chronicle insists at length on her unquestioning submission and to glorify this still further stresses the authority, cruel to say the least, of a Superior who was 'the most uncouth and boorish girl one could ever see, although good and virtuous'.[118] So ill that every quarter of an hour brought her fresh suffering, Alix could not ask for a rest or a little water to drink without a rough answer. The other sisters were indignant to see her treated so harshly, but her perfect obedience made others copy her, and it was said that her example eased relations between the community and this Superior, 'forever scolding'. It was said too that Fourier 'took pleasure' in exercising Alix's obedience. One day, for example, when Alix was at the bedside of her mother who had come to end her days in Mattaincourt and was now ready to die, he ordered her to leave her mother and go urgently to prepare the church for an imminent ceremony. Often too he would send her 'begging from door to door round Mattaincourt, sometimes asking for bread, sometimes for a little soup, to the astonishment of people who did not understand such mortification'. At this period, in fact, the custom of begging continued in convents where it was not possible to live the impoverished life of the mendicant orders. What amazed people was to see Mademoiselle Le Clerc, once so smart, dressed like a beggar-woman 'with old leather soles stitched onto her shoes'.[119] Here too, as in Nancy the year before, she wanted to know by experience what it was to be society's reject. Are we to conclude, with Edmond Renard, that 'the good Father was a very poor nurse'?[120] No, we can say more accurately that he used methods which we find inhuman but to him were simply supernatural. He judged that obedience sets the will free and opens a way for a greater gift of the Spirit. It was at any rate he who set Alix on the way to recovery by putting her in charge of the sick poor of the parish. In the depths of his heart the priest of Mattaincourt had concern for the poor, and he entrusted his helpers, preferably women, with the distribution of assistance. Alix now therefore became the nursing sister, a task she undertook with careful tact.

She had everything the sick might need prepared by the sisters, at their expense, according to the little they could do. She cooked their *potages* (soup/stew) made ready their helpings of roast or boiled, sent them fresh eggs and other small appetising dishes that she could make for them, took care that there was always sugar in the infirmary, as well as almonds, liquorice for hot drinks and jams to comfort the poor sick people. There were even beds, coverlets, pillows and linen kept especially for the use of the very poor who did not have these things.[121]

With the same charity Alix took care of the sisters when they were ill and forgot her own suffering in trying to relieve theirs. During an epidemic which left none of the sisters on her feet except the cook and the mistress of the boarders, she dealt with the situation day and night, even taking the place of a sick nurse who was sleeping too heavily to hear a dying woman calling for her. No care disgusted her, no pestilential wound kept her away from the sick.

> One anecdote shows Alix's preference for 'the most neglected and most despised' poor. The author sets this in a location which linked Alix's two fields of mission, within the convent and outside it. Through her window she saw a scene which horrified her. A poor boy, a typical village simpleton, was begging from door to door, and although the law had released him and declared him innocent, he was everywhere driven away 'with loud shouts and mockery'. Overcome with pity and urged to justify her emotion, Alix explained that in the shape of this poor wretch she had seen that of the Lord Jesus, who had been treated in that way.[122]

In Mattaincourt Alix accomplished deeds of 'burning charity' while keeping her attention fixed on the Son of God, an attitude she was soon to teach all the sisters.[123] Day by day she was able to shape the spirit of the new institution, earnestly doing for the

REMIREMONT: Land of Saints

Alix liked to visit the saints in the chapels on the Holy Mountain – Menne, Romary, Amé, Sabine and Magdalene.

Photos: J. Couchouron

Georges de la Tour: *The Penitent Magdalene*

Magdalene is shown with a type of still-life known as *vanitas* or vanities.

In love with the absolute, Alix meditates on the emptiness of worldly life. 'My soul was very sad among the vanities.' (*Rel.* 5)

Photo: RMN

Notre-Dame du Trésor, Remiremont

In the abbey church at Remiremont Alix regularly prayed before the ancient statue of Our Lady of the Treasure, 'safeguard against any fall or any sin.'
Photo: D.R.

Gospel cover, Poussay

This tenth century Gospel belonged to the canonesses of Poussay. In the centre of its pure gold cover, studded with rubies and emeralds, is an ivory plaque with an image of the Virgin and Child, surrounded by four motifs: Christ in majesty, St Peter, St Andrew and St Menne, the abbey's patron saint.
Photo: BNF

Demon, sixteenth century

In periods when the Church most strongly denounced the actions of the devil, artists sought to explore the depths of sin by representing its many faces. In this early sixteenth century gradual of St Dié the devil is shown as a hybrid monster with two faces, one of them human. Both exert a similar perverse fascination.

Photo: IRHT

Below:

St Francesca Romana, Roman fresco

Frescoes on the wall of the small convent of Tor de' Specchi in Rome depicting the life of St Francesca Romana show the real kinship between this Italian nun and Alix Le Clerc. Both had heavenly visions both received the Child Jesus in their arms and both resisted evil spirits with invincible courage. When such spirits confronted Alix 'as ugly and misshapen men', she used the sign of the cross to drive them away.

Photo: D.R

Virgin and Child, church of Poussay

'Our Lady appeared to me holding her little son, and she gave him to me, telling me to feed him till he is grown, meaning that I should seek his glory.' Photo: Inventaire général

Below:
Juan del Castillo: The Holy Family

Contemplating the workshop in Nazareth where Mary, Joseph and Jesus were working, Alix said, 'I watch them, I listen to them, I marvel at them.'   Photo: RMN

Below right:
Ligier Richier: Christ on the road to Calvary

'I begged Our Lord urgently that he would always imprint his Passion and the example of his holy Life upon my mind.'
Photo: Inventaire général

Her models of Holiness
St Augustine

'All time is wasted that is not used to love God.' St Augustine.

Photo: CND, Karlskron

Pierre Fourier

'Let everything, prosperity or loss, be for you a way to go straight to God.' St Pierre Fourier.

Photo: CND, Karlskron

Claude Deruet: *Portrait of Alix Le Clerc, 1622*

'She had a sweet and helpful nature, a pleasant manner, modesty which surprised one, together with a certain gravity, grace and gentleness, was very quiet and thoughtful in what she said, and of a calm and always pleasing temperament.'

Photo: Arch. CND

The school at Poussay

The opening of the little school at Poussay marks a date in the history of education: in 1598 girls had for the first time a right to free education.

Photo: M.-P. Dubart

The Virgin and St Anne, Church of Poussay

Like St Anne, the new teachers taught small girls to read, and like Mary, the children ran their finger along the lines in the book.

Photo: Inventaire général

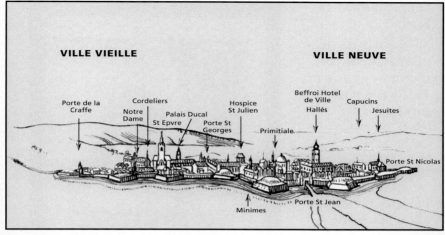

Plan of Nancy

So many children came flocking to the school in Nancy that the Sisters of Our Lady needed new buildings in 1603, 1606 and 1616.

Alix teaching, **stained glass at Saint-Etienne-les-Remiremont**

'Poor children must be accepted and treated there just like rich ones and this must cost no one anything; and as well as doctrine each girl must be able to learn to read, write and work at good tasks that will help earn a living.' Constitutions of 1640.

Photo: J. Couchouron

Icon, 'a window into heaven'

Alix shows us the little school at Poussay, first of so many yet to come. The Mother of God gives Alix her Son, who blesses the foundress and her work.

Photo: Marie-Joseph Moulin

The school of Madre Alix at Juazeiro do Norte-Cearà in Brazil

The school welcomes its pupils from the neighbouring *favelas*.

Photo: D.R.

love of God everything possible to help the neighbour. The most important result of her time there was that the two founders were able to work together on the constitution which would provide a body for this spirit. At that period they not only needed to establish the details of the text but also to win the protection of the prelates of Lorraine who would send this dossier on its way to Rome. Monseigneur de La Vallée and Cardinal Charles of Lorraine had both died in 1607, and this task now fell to their successors, Monseigneur de Maillane, the new bishop of Toul, and Monseigneur de Lenoncourt, now primate of Lorraine. Although the statutes written while Alix was in Mattaincourt are now lost, or did not lead to anything,[124] we can make a guess at their content, as a fresh text, sent to Monseigneur de Lenoncourt in 1611, takes up their ideas. Amongst them some seem very likely to have come from Alix. The two founders did certainly have the same purpose but their temperaments were different, Alix as a woman, intuitive and self-willed, Fourier as a man not less daring than she but with a positive mind, one that knew the law and its limitations.

Now Pierre and Alix had to modify their plans, as Pius V had ordered the closure of newly formed congregations.[125] In order to obey canon law but not surrender the schools, they created two sorts of houses, one in which cloistered nuns made solemn vows, and also 'not enclosed' houses where 'poor but talented girls' would be admitted, without dowry, would practise a 'moderate' form of enclosure and, bound only by a simple promise, would devote themselves to teaching in small mission posts. These determined ventures certainly seem to bear Alix's stamp. Indeed, despite her irresistible inspiration to 'make a new house for girls so as to do all possible good there' (*Rel.* 15), it was she who was the most determined to create various forms of mission, both in Mattaincourt and Nancy, before any cloistered convents were built. Later it would be she who struggled hardest to keep the unenclosed houses. And as for the idea, unheard of at that time, of accepting nuns with no fortune, we find that expressed among the memories of Alix recorded by her companions. 'She was much distressed', they said, 'at refusing girls suited to the religious life because they had not enough property for the dowry, and said flatly that if it depended only on her, she would accept them, trusting that God would not fail them'. Not long before her death she advised the sisters in Nancy to accept girls 'for the love of God, provided that they had a true calling and were suitable for their Institute'.[126]

The plan, the *Sommaire du dessein des Filles de la Congrégation de la bienheureuse Vierge Marie*, seemed too venturesome to Monseigneur de Lenoncourt, who did not forward it to Rome. But for us it is one of the most interesting of such texts, for it makes clear the founders' plan in all its original sincerity. In avoiding the difficulties of enclosure by establishing external teaching posts served by a mobile teaching staff, Pierre and Alix anticipated the future and created apostolic nuns such as would later be recognised by the Council of Vatican II. And the model for these nuns would be Alix Le Clerc, a woman led by a single desire towards Christ and to the poor.

Alliance with lay personnel

The earliest *Life of Alix*, published in 1666, gives us some dates not mentioned in the *Relation*. Alix joined Fourier at the beginning of 1609 and stayed almost a year and a half, 'the first seven or eight months in great distress'. Towards the end of 1610 Fourier sent her, we are told, 'to manage the house at Pont'.[127] Sensibly he did not send her back to Nancy, where she might have fallen ill again. When Isabeau de Louvroir, Superior at Pont-à-Mousson since 1606, had to go away to deal with business matters, Alix took her place. It was a wise choice – now fit and healthy, she took up her life again and could cope with serious problems.

Like the other foundations, victims of their success, the house at Pont grew, needed to buy land, put up buildings and therefore to borrow money and guarantee repayment. But what guarantee could be offered by nuns who were not acknowledged by the Church? Alix stepped in as the woman of the moment, businesslike, strong minded, in the Biblical tradition. Fourier created a kind of management committee for her and with his gift of organisation settled its membership and function in his letter of 17 January 1611. The matter was urgent, for Alix, determined and energetic, was already talking of 'setting up a noviciate in Pont' and the consequent need to buy new premises. Fourier in alarm pointed out the risks of these transactions but also, in his usual way, did not forbid them. 'I would much prefer you to follow someone else's opinion rather than mine', he wrote to the sisters, as he pointed out to them the way they should go. First of all they must pray and get the pupils and friends to pray too, and above all must offer some good masses for the Jesuits. Then the three heads of the household must meet – Sister Alix, her helper Sister Sybille and Aunt Marie, who was a lay bursar or manager who lived with the sisters and took care of the practical needs of the house. The title 'aunt' given to these devout widows whom we find named in the foundations' early years shows clearly that they were part of the family, much more than administrators; they were part of the life of the congregation and shared in its spirituality. The three must discuss the day's business 'as a family, pleasantly and diligently'. Then, with 'all three present and not one without the others', there would be a second and full meeting. Two other lay persons would be there, Madame Jenon and Madame Anne, and to these five women Fourier added one or two men: the sisters' almoner, and if necessary his Jesuit colleague, Father Lambert. Finally, when everyone's ideas had been 'examined and thoroughly considered', it was the duty of the two ladies Anne and Jenon to settle matters, if necessary. Jenon was even asked to offer the opinions of her brother and her husband on the matter under discussion, but the sisters were asked 'not to put forward any of their individual preferences'. They must above all 'well and faithfully make clear [their] debts and the condition of the house'. Fourier repeated his instructions: 'Do not rush into anything at all and remember that we have very many debts, and do not rely on your own individual judgment'.

Considering the important role Fourier gave to lay persons in the management of the house at Pont, it has been suggested that he distrusted what Edmond Renard called the 'mysticality' (*mysticité*) of Alix. We must note that in order to disentangle very complicated matters to do with finance and house property, Alix needed training, and that she was doing well at getting this training on the job. As she had done at the Cloister of Our Lady, she stimulated donors' generosity. The abbot of St Marie made them a gift of 900 *francs barrois*'.[128] And when the sisters at Nancy refused to guarantee the loans which were to pay the debts at Pont, she said nothing about this to friends who might have been shocked and refused to help the sisters. The founder did regularly co-operate with lay people, and we should consider this. His natural ability to create links, his deep sense of friend-ship and the way he never did anything without first taking advice all do more to explain his frequent recourse to lay persons than does his interest in them. As a priest he had much to offer, and being exceptionally well informed on legal matters, he was very well able to discuss secular topics. His collaboration with

Alix the foundress is also worth studying. Her liveliness was much tried by his slow caution. 'Think about this a little at leisure, there is no need for haste', he wrote on 9 March 1611, adding direct criticism to this advice. 'I did not find it good that when it was a question of suggesting to this lady [a possible purchaser] something that mattered so much to us, you [two] should have gone ahead on your own (Alix and tante Marie), you should take Sister Sybille or your co-adjutrix with you. Do not hurry into decisions such as this'. Clearly Alix was always one or two decisions ahead of Fourier and sometimes hundreds of years ahead of the Church. The noviciate she dreamed of was certainly a general one, a place where novices from different houses would come to complete their initial training.[129] The Congregation of Our Lady had to wait to realise this ambition until it had a centralised government in the twentieth century. In Alix's time, we must remember, each convent was auto-nomous and trained its own novices. But Fourier had good reason to restrain Alix's creative drive, for not only was she heavily in debt but he thought it pointless to plan for a new noviciate until they knew how the business of the Congregation would prosper in Rome. On 28 February 1611 he met Mon-seigneur de Lenoncourt in Nancy and told him of the sisters' unanimous wish to choose him for their protector. At once the prelate poured forth promises – his credit, his time, his money, he would use all these on their behalf – but a year had passed and nothing had happened.

To understand Alix's behaviour at Pont we must look at evidence from Fourier himself. On 17 March 1611, very dis-appointed by the situation in Mattaincourt where money and community were going to rack and ruin, he finished a letter to the sisters at Pont with the words, 'How badly we would need Sister Sybille or another just as shrewd!' He did not mention

Alix by name, no doubt out of consideration for her humility, but everything points to her as the shrewd sister he felt was wanted. A year later, on 19 March, he sent an approving review to the sisters in Pont: 'I have been much solaced and very pleased by your letters, both for the spiritual, seeing that you are so peaceful and contented together and with the Fathers, and for the temporal which consists in so much grain for the year, so much corn, so much bacon in the barns and chimneys of your houses, God be praised!'

Scenes of daily life

A few examples of convent life in Pont give us glimpses of Alix. For example Fourier declared that if Sister Claude was 'troublesome and a nuisance' she must be sent back to Mattaincourt (*C. 1, 47*); it was for Alix to decide. Another day he asked, 'At Pont, could they do without Sister Anne, who teaches lacemaking?' (*C. 1, 44.*) The request shows that the houses stood by each other and that Alix certainly approved of this mutual usefulness. The kindness of Sister Bastienne was appreciated by the pupils she taught in the top class, but it would be necessary to think 'whether she had the necessary capacity' (*C. 1, 50*). When it came to running the schools, Alix took on the responsibilities of a principal. In order to deal with the influx of pupils, she saw that they would need to enlarge the day girls' house, and considered a purchase which Fourier approved in every way – situation, neighbourhood, and the dates of payment (*C. 1, 52*). After Alix left, he told Isabeau de Louvroir and Gante André to conclude the bargain. But running the boarding house brought serious difficulties which Fourier discovered by chance. He described them in detail in his letter of 12 June 1611. It was like this – little Marie, boarder at Pont and niece of Aunt Méline, had just arrived in Mattaincourt, granted exceptional leave to help nurse her uncle. It was a good opportunity for Fourier to find out how the boarding house was doing. When she was questioned, the child would not say anything, but after a while made some admissions. Six or eight strong-minded girls had got themselves into a clique and were encouraging each other and making a lot of noise because they were so glad they would be leaving the boarding house on 24 June and never coming back. 'And why is this?' Fourier asked Marie, who tumbled out the reasons pell-mell. 'In class,' she said, 'we start too many new things; our good mistresses who used to treat us more kindly have gone; and now we eat dry bread because no one gives us anything for our snack'. The child also said that Sister Marie was unhappy because Sister Alix shouted at her all over the house. Fourier did not exaggerate or minimise what he had heard but made his report to the sisters, saying tactfully that they had perhaps not heard anything about 'all these little grumbles which come and go without your knowledge'. He asked the teachers to see together how they could re-establish order, and told them what methods to use – they should calm the two older girls who had been whipped (an extreme punishment it seems he would not have authorised for 'I hardly know for what'); inform the clique in revolt that the sisters had decided to treat them more gently; every day give the boarders 'some cherries, which are not dear, or some other food, for their snack'; and finally to take care that discipline should be maintained without making the children unhappy, as it was essential 'that they should live joyfully and very happily'. In her zeal as a young principal, had Alix been too harsh? She refused to admit that one of the mistresses, Sister Marie, had supported the pupils in their revolt, thus affecting the unity of the teaching team.

In the aura of a saint

Wherever Alix lived, extraordinary things happened. They gave rise to marvellous accounts in which it seems that her circle, more open than ourselves to the supernatural, sought to focus the brilliance of her holiness. We must look at these as fair and shining images in which history and legend join.

On an icy evening in February, half blinded by wind and fog, one of the women servants from the convent and a lady were making their way from Dieulouart[130] to Pont. It was better to go on, they thought, rather than struggle among the meadows and streams, but the dark made it hard to see where they were going, they could hear wolves in the distance, and they knew they were lost. Then it occurred to them to ask Alix to pray for them – they were sure God listened to her. Day dawned at last and they were safe. They reached the convent and were welcomed by Alix herself who warmed them and washed their feet. Not allowing them to describe the terrors of the journey, it was she who described it to them, adding with a laugh, 'My poor children, what a strange night you have had! I saw you in my mind. Quickly now, go and rest'.[131]

Another story comes from a road in Lorraine, the one from Pont-à-Mousson to Nancy. Alix and Madame Claude de Condé were travelling together. They got down from their carriage to walk in the country, and as they walked, a leper came towards them holding out his hand.[132] Not content with giving him a silver coin, Alix knelt down and reverently kissed his hands. Once he had gone, she sank into such deep recollection that Madame Claude kept quiet, but when they were back at Pont she could not wait to tell the sisters that the leper had been Christ himself. The sisters were sure that this had been the Lord showing Alix how pleased he was with her kindness to poor people.[133] As we know, the episode of the kissed leper occurs in several hagiographies ever since St Francis of Assisi. In the life of Alix the scene bears witness that her mysticism was not only heavenly but ran alongside effective service to the poor.

CHAPTER ELEVEN

Verdun, 1612–1615

The union shaken

The house at Verdun, opened in 1608, was the first foundation in which the earliest sisters of the congregation were not closely involved. Alix became its Superior in 1612 and remained there for three years during which she contended with serious problems. Worst of all was the disastrous financial position which affected all the houses. These formed a solid and increasing network in which the condition of the most heavily indebted houses affected all the rest. This was not all, for some houses were not well managed, so that fraternal life deteriorated and dissension crept in. Fourier's letters from this period contain long lamentations in which he could find no words strong enough to bemoan these 'irksome and wretched' debts, whether at Nancy or Saint-Nicolas or Mattaincourt. He wrote, for example, to the sisters at Verdun on 13 December 1612: 'You would not believe the nuisance, the neglected duties, the annoyances, distractions, journeys, expense, the waste of time these debts at Nancy are causing us'. He described the exhausting approaches Sister Isabeau was making, now away at Mirecourt and Epinal trying to raise funds, the unpleasantness of creditors who pursued Madame Jeanne Méline to the very door of the convent, she having stood surety for the sisters (*C.* 1, 74). He bewailed 'the wickedness of this world and the trouble poor people have in finding money in it' because of the exorbitant cost of borrowing (*C.* 1, 65). And then when the sisters at Nancy were annoyed because the help sent to them was not, they thought, enough, and asked for more, he gave vent to his feelings: 'There is no end, no satisfaction, no rest, no improvement, no keeping of the rules in these debts. They gnaw, they ruin, they disgust everyone. For the honour of God, let there be no more, if nothing else' (*C.* 1, 66).

No new debts, not till the old ones are paid off, the sisters had already decided this together at a meeting in Saint-Mihiel early in August 1612. This was therefore not a good time for Alix, always enterprising, to ask for permission to buy a house in Verdun and there install her community which was at present living in rented property. The young Superior now took charge of operations, advised, it is true, by influential friends, Messieurs d'Issoncourt, Regnault, Gilles, and other well-wishers who thought this was a magnificent chance which should not be missed. Fourier himself, if he followed 'his own inclination, would be tempted this time once again to leave something to holy Providence' (*C.* 1, 56). Cautiously he blocked Alix with a refusal, pointing out the probable annoyance of 'all the rest of the Congregation at this new extra debt'. Besides, he added, this purchase is only 'advised' (*de conseil*) and 'you know that works of obligation must always take precedence of works of devotion'. Paying one's debts was for him an obligation of conscience, to neglect them was sin. Then he piles on other objections – the situation of the building, the incompatible temperament of the postulant from whose inheritance Alix was hoping to receive a bequest, and so forth. Amongst his arguments, let us note this one: 'You tell me of all the usefulness and the hope you have for this house at Verdun, and indeed convincingly, but if you, Sister Alix, left there one day to go to one of our other houses, perhaps all this would go topsy-turvy and the poor girls (*les pauvrettes*) left there would not be able to pay the required rent' (*C.* 1, 66). In other words, while Alix managed affairs, the budget held good, with her gone, they risked bankruptcy. This had certainly happened after she left Nancy. 'Have a little patience', he told her again (*C.* 1, 67). Obediently she resolved to live patiently for a while, as long ago', he told her, 'the great saint Paul lived in Rome, that is, in a rented house' (*C.* 1, 65). But she got her way in the end. On 19 November 1614 a house was bought, larger and more convenient than the first one. And on the feast of the Presentation of Mary in 1618 the sisters moved in (*C.* 1, 134).

The stubbornness Alix displayed in such matters as the purchase of a house in Verdun was well understood by her companions, who saw it as a proof of her trust in God and not at all as a sign of overconfidence in herself. Their comment is interesting because it shows her when she had succeeded in the difficult conversion of a dynamic temperament to one of serene wisdom based on her faith in God. Here is the text:

When she was busy about affairs in obedience, or when she had undertaken them upon advice, whatever obstacles arose, she would thrust them aside, saying that she felt a firm inner certainty which allowed her no doubt of success. [...] If matters dragged on and were hindered by great difficulties, she would bear these bravely without dismay, her spirit remaining always calm and equable among the frustrations. She used to be surprised that anyone could be troubled or anxious about the outcome of any matters once they had been put into God's hands, saying that one must wish impartially for whatever it should please his goodness to ordain or permit, and that the great secret was to abandon them to his divine direction, making the care of them over to him and for our part doing what little we could, because it

often happened that by being anxious to do too much ourselves we would spoil everything and obstruct the good results
which his providence would bring.[134]

Unity is built

Alix was reluctant to speak of her own life but Pierre Fourier's
letters are an indispensable source of information. Parish priest
of Mattaincourt, always busy in his parish or at the annual
synod or receiving a visit from his bishop, he visited his nuns
less frequently but instead wrote them long letters, excellent
reports which allow us to understand the communities. We can
see not only events as they occur and the sisters' reactions
to them but also those of the founder, never indifferent to
the smallest piece of news, always ready to deliver blame or
encouragement to any who needed it. Among the letters we still
have from his vast correspondence, those he sent to Verdun
between April 1612 and March 1615 number a good twenty.
They are unusual in that although they are as always addressed
to 'his good and well beloved sisters in Our Lord', they are
clearly meant for Alix. This is obvious for those dealing with the
purchase of the house at Verdun, and so too for letters discussing
questions which were of interest to the whole congregation, its
unity and its future. Reading them, one seems at times to hear
Fourier sharing with Alix the news, so often disastrous, from
the different houses. In them he expressed his overburdened
heart, his grief, discouragement and indignation. But although
Alix became his chief confidant, he never refers to her as
foundress of the movement. This would have been against his
principles, based on the collegiality which gave each sister her
place in the making of decisions. Alix in fact ranks alongside
Isabeau, Jeanne, Gante and Claude; we must think of them as a
founding team. Affairs were then serious enough for Fourier to

ask the Superiors to meet for discussion together in groups we can call 'chapters'. These took place on similar dates in the different convents, August 1612 in Saint-Mihiel, October 1613 in Nancy and October 1614 in Verdun. We note that meanwhile it was Alix whom he told of the significant changes he was planning. One example is the letter of 19 October 1612 about the pitiable condition of the community in Nancy. He wrote: 'It would be expedient to search among ourselves and put into practice all the right and possible methods by which we can bring some relief, and among others that every house should consider in heart and affection how they can contribute in charity as much as they can, over a period during which the place would be cleansed of all the poor feeble ones who are dying in there because they are not living and then it would be restocked with other stronger girls'. Then follow the names of the sisters he thinks suitable for this 'restocking' and a direct request to Alix: 'Write and tell me what you think about all this if you have the time'. Fourier refers to Alix at other times too. For example he asks her to read the letters he wrote to Messieurs d'Issoncourt and Regnault telling them why the sisters had decided 'not to acquire new houses, even though they were suitable for doing something great in them'. It would be different, he added, if a rich benefactor were to offer the house – and at once his imagination leaps ahead to view the wide and glorious future of the convent . . . Fourier took pleasure in sharing with Alix this wonderful vision which we must not overlook: 'It would be different', he said, 'if some good person inspired by God, and recognising that this building was sought for Our Lord himself, to house the servants of His Majesty, his daughters and spouses, to train a thousand and a thousand souls in perfect observance of his holy commandments, to offer his precious body in the holy sacrifice of the mass, to serve him night and day in all perfection, to sing his praises there during many hundred future years and there to do ten thousand other good things – if such a one should wish for these and similar reasons to buy it for the Daughters, or to give them money to do this themselves' (*C.* 1, 61).

Life in Verdun

In the Verdun community Alix worked day by day to achieve the perfect way of life which she and Fourier wanted for their Congregation. She was given permission to reserve the holy sacrament in the convent's small chapel, and the Jesuit fathers, who ran a large college in the town, provided the sisters with spiritual help. Young Father Le Brun (1585–1656) performed this ministry with a 'charity, modesty, prudence and goodwill' which pleased Fourier (*C.* 1. 63). Fourier was astonished but delighted that Alix should have introduced the *Spiritual Exercises* of St Ignatius to the community. 'Is it possible', he wrote, 'that this divine treasure, the Spiritual Exercises of these holy Fathers, should be used with girls! Write to me I beg you, write at length and tell me everything the Reverend Father said to you about this, and how it can be done for girls' (*C.* 1, 66). Here too Alix was ahead of her time concerning the place of women in the Church. 'It is really noteworthy', remarked Louis Châtellier, 'that in 1612 the sisters of the Congregation should be among the first persons outside the Company, and certainly the first women, to use the Spiritual Exercises.[135]

Various items of news from the convent Alix was directing reach us by chance. Day pupils were numerous but there were only nine boarders. The teaching was so good that Fourier sent Sister Anne to be taught at Verdun by Sister Catherine, so as to take her place with the boarding pupils. Bushels[136] of wheat were heaped up in the loft, and far sighted Alix had been right, for as Fourier said, 'a store of this is better than money, especially when it can be bought at a good price, as now, God be thanked. Do buy it then, and store it where it will be quite safe from thieves and other nuisances' (C. 1, 63). He did not know how well he had spoken – Alix tells us what happened:

> Being in Verdun, having made a good provision of wheat for our year, weevils came to it in such numbers that there was no human remedy. I felt moved in devotion by the names of Jesus and Mary and of their servant St Ignatius, trusting in his credit, I told the servant woman to spread the wheat out in layers and to mark these three names on it. By this remedy all the creatures were lost, so that nobody saw a single one again during the whole year. (*Rel.* 64)

More difficult for Alix than these domestic problems was the rivalry that arose between the sisters of Our Lady and those of the Dominicans, known in Verdun as *Filles de Saint-Jacques* (the Daughters of St James).[137] Relationships worsened, and Fourier, told of this by Alix, sent the sisters his advice on 15 August 1612: 'Praise them, respect them, serve them, do not take away their role, moderate your zeal'. On 3 December he struck a loftier note: 'Let them get on with it. Don't say anything at all against them. Live as if you did not know what they are saying and doing against you. Try to outdo them [...] in diligently and faithfully teaching your little ones the piety and other exercises which belong to your vocation. If this is of God, then we must be very pleased that he should raise up several to do that work which you, with God, have chosen as being most needed in this world'. Taking Fourier's advice, Alix learnt to establish friendly relations with other female congregations. He wanted them to make only rare visits to the Poor Clares, 'so that you don't overwhelm them but on the contrary leave them hoping to see you again'. And he felt strongly about the image the sisters of Our Lady offered to people who could not see an uncloistered nun as genuine. From this sprang his prohibitions: 'Do not be inquisitive or gadabouts, not even for going to churches, to pardons, exhortations or spiritual visits. Let the good and holy Jesuit Fathers be enough for you' (*C. 1, 55*). Nothing escaped his notice and on 15 August 1612 he wrote, 'It seems to me that you, Sister Alix, and you, Sister Catherine, should wear your veils a little lower over the forehead so that your hair does not show, as it has been doing recently'. As Alix's role became more important in Verdun and in the congregation, and as too her holiness became more apparent, so Fourier strove to exercise her humility, wanting this to become perfect. She for her part was gaining in confidence and was now in the habit of signing her letters, as she did legal documents, with a great flourish. Fourier perceived self assertion in this, and told her so in a personal letter dated 12 December 1612. Here is the opening:

> Sister Alix, if it is yourself you are seeking, always write your personal name boldly in fine large letters at the foot of the missives you send here and there, as I find it written on those I have most recently had from you. If it is purely and simply Our Lord and the good of the Congregation you are seeking, follow the common form used by your companions and in your statutes, which is this: "Your very humble servants in God, the daughters of the Congregation of Our Lady in Verdun." Self love is dangerous and subtle, and clings easily to the fingers of those who take up writing.

Later when Fourier was writing the *Constitutions de 1640*, he remembered that a mother Superior could be tempted, as Alix was in 1612, to act in her own name rather than in that of her sisters. The rule he laid down for her then is no different from the one he prescribed for the mother Superior at Verdun. Here it is: "In treating business matters with others, whether in writing or speech, she will remain within the bounds of modesty and humility and will not speak as if for herself alone, saying for example: "I will do, I will receive, I cannot . . . " but rather: "Our Mothers, or Our sisters or Our Community will do, receive, consider, refuse, cannot . . . "[138]

Alix was well taught and Fourier's lessons did not go to waste. Later, praising humility, she as it were echoed his letter, writing: 'It is a great mistake to feel an empty satisfaction with our work. If we consider that it is God who gives us grace and strength to do it, should we not rather be afraid of not doing it as perfectly as he wishes and not measuring up to the light he gives us?'[139] Without Fourier, would Alix be the saint we love? A strong personality indeed, but humbly sweet and how attractive in her simplicity.

Business with Rome

It was Alix who thought of entrusting the Congregation's business to Canon Jean Xandrin, who was about to travel to Rome. Much respected in the see of Verdun and also in the Vatican, he was approved of by Fourier too, who in a letter of 20 January 1613 confided that it was exactly fifteen years since on St Sebastian's day 1598 he had first been inspired to establish a concept which should serve the sisters now and in the future. He thought the anniversary was a good omen. Alix shared his enthusiasm for one who seemed 'heaven sent', and tried to organise his activities. She was not pleased that the new petition on its way to Rome did not mention the 'unenclosed houses' which were deemed too venturesome. She therefore thought up another expedient: these should be waiting houses, situated in small humble towns where a convent could not be placed. After ten or twelve years the sisters, not cloistered, who taught there would be eligible for reception in the convents and could there make their vows. Unfortunately her letter reached the Mattaincourt pastor on a Saturday of frantic activity and the carter who brought it wanted a reply. Impossible, grumbled Fourier, 'in two or three hours to discuss, conclude, write about so many points which touched the glory of God and the advancement of his service and other people too besides yourself and me'. Conclusion: 'Let us change nothing of our first resolutions' (*C.* 1, 69–71). Let Monsieur Xandrin suggest any emendations, continued Fourier, and then let Alix discuss these with all interested parties. This was his habitual method, with the added feature here that he entrusted this general consultation to Alix. He wrote to her: 'You will take the trouble to give me a word of information by letter, and from this to communicate the whole to the great and holy Fathers in Nancy, in Pont and Verdun [the Jesuits], also to our sisters who would otherwise be shocked if they knew that you and I had come to a decision on something without going through these channels which until now have been our normal ones' (*C.* 1, 68). After this pronouncement he himself travelled to all the houses, taking with him a doll which the sisters at Verdun had dressed in the religious habit later adopted by them all.[140] He asked for letters of recommendation from highly placed persons and obtained them without delay. His Highness Duke Henri II, his wife the duchess Margherita di Gonzaga, Madame de Lorraine,[141] and Monseigneur de Maillane, all these had nothing but praise for the sisters who exercised 'in a most praiseworthy way so many virtues and taught girl pupils with such good results' (*C.* 1, 71). On 15 April 1613 Monsieur Xandrin took the great dossier to Rome. On 30 May Fourier told Alix to consult the Jesuit

Fathers as to the sum of money he should receive. Bad news came on 10 October and was forwarded at once by Fourier to the five houses (*C.* 1, 75), 'They cannot see in Rome', he wrote, 'that it is possible to teach and to maintain enclosure'. The pope had referred the dossier to the Congregation of Regulars, which Xandrin called 'the Congregation of Nothing or of Eternity, because once any business goes there, it becomes immortal'. But the brave canon said he was prepared, if necessary, 'to die in the struggle' and in order to be sure of getting schools for day pupils, he would first ask that a building should be erected for a cloistered convent, then for permission to teach boarders and finally to be allowed to take day pupils. Fourier objected, because this procedure was the opposite of the principle he had long held, before declaring it on 17 September 1627 when a fresh approach was made to Rome, and he said, 'I have always thought it necessary to say that primarily they were teachers and that in order to be closer together and stronger they have wanted, asked to be and insisted on becoming nuns, lest anyone should think that they were nuns first of all and had then asked for schools'. However, not wanting to break off the negotiations with Rome, he suggested they should put their request aside for the present and consider the matter more maturely whilst awaiting 'some other, better and more favourable time'.

Alix says no

But the sisters were getting impatient and thought they had seen a way out of the impasse. There is no documentary evidence to prove it, but it seems likely to have been Isabeau de Louvroir who took the initiative. What is certain is the energy shown by them all to get their business settled, and also the wide margin of liberty Fourier allowed them. There was an encouraging precedent, for at the dawn of the canonical revolution (a phrase used by Hélène Derréal), with its explosion of teaching congregations, the Company of Mary Our Lady, was the first in France to receive official status. In 1607 its foundress Jeanne de Lestonnac had obtained, with the help of Cardinal de Sourdis, archbishop of Bordeaux, permission to open schools for day pupils inside enclosed convents. The brief, signed by Paul V, specified that permission depended on the pope's good pleasure and on two conditions: enclosure, and a link to be formed to one of the great orders. They could choose from four foundations, those of the saints Anthony, Basil, Augustine and Benedict. The foundress and the archbishop opted for Benedict, although this did not mean that a teaching congregation devoted to the spirituality of Ignatius would show any marked signs of a 'Benedictine' observance. The example of Bordeaux established the law and encouraged the sisters of Our Lady to try the same approach. In attaching their institute to the Order of St Benedict, the sisters had every reason to hope that the Roman curia would authorise it. Monseigneur de Maillane undertook to request the brief from Rome, relying on the letters patent already granted in 1603 by the cardinal of Lorraine.

The opinion of the sisters was still to be heard. A meeting was held in Nancy in October 1613 and a vote taken. Fourier did not speak, so as not to sway their decision, and the sisters put forward their arguments. Since the Rule of St Benedict is not incompatible with the free teaching of children, said some of them, and so that they could at last be acknowledged as nuns, said others, they requested the brief. All were agreed but one. This was Alix, who, says the chronicle, being 'very thoughtful and gentle', did not oppose the fervour of the others but turned to Fourier. Let him speak, she begged, for nothing in this debate had persuaded her to change the decisions maturely

considered and recognised as being the will of God. At the end
she asked for postponement and that they should pray to God
'in all leisure' before making a decision.[142]

Fourier agreed with her and the meeting ended without a
decision. Yet on 12 December he wrote to Xandrin to apply for
the brief in question, 'as brief as possible' he added, perhaps
hiding in this word play his wish to interpret it more freely. He
himself did not specify the rule chosen or the town where the
convent should be placed. He did however remind Xandrin of
the sisters' wishes – 'These devout women [...] cannot bring
themselves to accept bulls or briefs based on the petition (a copy
of which they have seen) because they do not want to be
cloistered without there being schools for day pupils'. Here
Fourier was certainly venturing one last attempt at negotiation,
but his letter missed Xandrin, who had already left, and nothing
more was heard of the brief. Fourier took this patiently and
exhorted the sisters at Saint-Mihiel and Verdun not to lose
heart. 'He who is the author of your devotions', he wrote to
them, 'has in the treasures of his omnipotence plenty of other
ways to establish you, when he shall find you deserve it. Try to
make this be soon' (*C.* 1, 78).

Both Alix and Fourier felt perfectly certain that their institute
would have a future. Both had the same trust in God that
together they expressed, even and indeed especially after such
checks as they had had from Rome. Alix's description of the
matter of the brief in her *Relation* displays the same burning
confidence. After speaking of the temptations which attacked
her at Verdun, she went on to mention other troubles.

There were certain disagreements which seemed to bring
trouble to our Congregation. Letters of institution had been
obtained from Monseigneur de Toul, and these placed us

under the rule of St Benedict, which I did not think suitable for our vocation. I recommended the matter very warmly to Our Lord and received inwardly the reply that the matter would not be decided like this but in another way which would content me. This I repeated to the Reverend Father Le Brun. And it happened just as had been told me, by the grace of God. (*Rel.* 56)

There spoke the true Alix. Always sensitive to fraternal bonds, she was upset by disagreements among the sisters, even slight differences which can cause division. It was painful to her to oppose her sisters, but she stood firm because she knew she was right: St Benedict was a good patron for contemplatives but not for teaching nuns who lead a 'mixed life'.[143] In this situation she turned to prayer. The inner response she had from God bears witness to the intensity of her mystical life. Humbled and astonished by this instant divine message, she spoke of it to her confessor, Father Le Brun, who showed no surprise because every day he was encountering the actions of God in his penitent. Another characteristic of Alix is her use of under-statement, a classical technique where less means more. Thus when she wrote, 'I thought the Rule of St Benedict was not suitable for our vocation', we should understand, 'I thought the Rule of St Augustine better suited to our vocation'. It is a pity she did not tell us why she thought this, but we can easily supply this want and understand her choice. It was through Fourier that she had learnt to know St Augustine. He, Fourier, as we know had not hesitated to join the Augustinian Canons Regular, then in extreme decline, so strongly was he drawn to Augustine's ideal of a life of brotherly union, of communal prayer and apostolic work. Unable to reform his brothers, he was to found a new Order of Canons under the name of the Congregation of Our Saviour and hoped that these two congregations, one for men and one for women, would have the same spirit and the same rule. So here, at the head of the earliest Constitution, obtained by the sisters in 1617, stand the ten short chapters of the Rule of St Augustine. As did Fourier, who wrote fervent comments on these articles, Alix perceived the richness and the apostolic inspiration which gives life to the text. Like him, she saw there the model of religious life she would set before the sisters, 'an apostolic life in both senses of the word, the life of the apostles with Jesus and the sharing in his mission'. A life 'in the service of God, of the public and of the whole Church'.[144] She in her turn would teach her nuns how 'in outward activity to keep the intention and the spirit raised to God, working for the salvation of souls, one of which', she wrote, 'is more before God than the whole world, for he said, "Who shall do and teach shall be great in the kingdom of heaven'.[145] In choosing St Augustine for their patron, Alix, with Fourier, gave the initial impetus to the apostolic drive which was to carry the Congregation's work across continents and down the centuries.

CHAPTER TWELVE

Foundation in France – Châlons 1613

Inner conflict

The letters written by Pierre Fourier during Alix's time as Superior at Verdun give to the most physical realities – the purchase of a house, the signing of a letter – their spiritual dimension, sometimes as advice, sometimes even reprimands. But the text of the *Relation*, dealing with this period, allows us to see more deeply, as Alix is here recording what we may call the story of her soul. The battles she fought against evil spirits in the years 1612–1615 hold a significant place in it, because she was faithfully following her plan of describing to her confessor the temptations that attacked her, safe in the knowledge that acknowledgment of her wretchedness would open to her the fountain of God's mercy. A prophetic dream in which she saw the town of Verdun lying asleep was enough to tell her that she would there have to endure 'something that would last long' (*Rel.* 52). Through similar predictions the Lord traced the stages which would mark her journey.

In dealing with recollections from this period Alix obeyed the rules of narrative and made brief note of the time, place and situation. She wrote: 'I spent half a year at Verdun in great calmness of mind, because the Reverend Father Le Brun had settled for me several things which had troubled me in previous years' (*Rel.* 53). The Jesuit fathers of Verdun must have a special mention here, as it was they who had brought the sisters to the city, or at least had acted as go-between for the inhabitants in getting Fourier to provide schoolteachers for the girls.[146] They ran a large school there for boys, of which Father Le Brun was spiritual director before he became provincial head of the Order in Champagne. He was chaplain to the sisters' community and Alix's confessor. She found him a perceptive director of conscience, since he had as she said 'settled' her past difficulties, that is to say had freed her by producing effective solutions to her problems. After six months his helpfulness came to an end, and, as had happened before in Nancy and in Mattaincourt a storm arose within Alix's soul. This is how she described it:

> All of a sudden I was tormented by my great temptations which began again more violently than ever, that of sensuality and the other of despair. They always come together in order to hurt me more. My soul was so hard pressed that I felt suddenly that I would go out of my mind, so that these extremes caused me a severe illness which lasted a very long time. (*Rel.* 53)

Only the context of this passage betrays the presence of the demon which Alix does not name here, but she was far enough advanced along the spiritual path to know that it was there. The shock attack, the power of perverse suggestions, the destructive effects, they all reveal the power of its assault. She emerged from it broken, 'crushed', she said, on the brink of madness and despair. Her experience made her say, as other mystics have done, that sensuality and despair go hand in hand. As a commentator said of Alix's contemporary, Catherine of St Augustine, 'sensuality impregnates every part of an individual, so that when an attack takes place, that person feels threatened in his or her whole being; if it is an extreme attack, despair invades, so great is the struggle to overcome this formidable emotion'.[147] Alix indeed used all her strength to fight, and fell ill. This fact enables us to place here two other passages among accounts of similar 'illusions'. Here is the first of them:

> While I was Superior at Verdun, during the Juliers wars,[148] many troops used to pass by, often causing alarms of an attack on the town. I prayed God urgently that he should be pleased to save and calm his anger. It was shown to me that the poor peasants would suffer much but that the town would be saved. (*Rel.* 39)

The Verdun house was certainly not inward-looking, as the echo of events outside resounded in it. How could it be otherwise, when the town was threatened by the appalling calamities of passing armies? Ever since the duke of Juliers, Jean Guillaume, died without an heir in 1609 the neighbouring princes had been quarrelling over his succession. Catholics and Protestants took up arms against each other and the intervention of great powers which had an interest there, France, the Empire, Austria, Spain and the Netherlands, threatened to turn every incident into an international war. Tension was high in 1614 and the two sides gathered new allies. Reinforcements on one side were driven out by those on the other in confrontations which cost Lorraine dear, standing as she did between the two opponents, whose troops fought on her soil. Alix understood the position, and when it was proclaimed that siege would be laid to Verdun she prayed fervently to God, begging him to save the town and calm his anger. She knew from the many examples in the Bible that the horrors of war were the result of human sin which stirred God to wrath and deserved punishment, but she also knew that God's mercy would prevail over his justice. Knowing that her intercession would be heard, her confidence gave her knowledge of the future. The inhabitants of Verdun would be spared. As for the unhappy peasants, they would have much to endure. Their distress touched Alix, and this brief allusion throws a shaft of light on her charity. She certainly knew more than she says here of conditions of life in the Lorraine countryside. We have to admit that whole areas of her personality remain hidden from us. In using the expression, 'It was shown to me', she says nothing of the means of communication between herself and God, but we can see that his reply reached her as a kind of silent film, a series of images she could interpret. The message was received: her trust was not misplaced, military operations moved away from Verdun. The treaty of Xanten, 12 November 1614, put an end to the war of Juliers.

The second passage, following straight on from the one above, deals with same events in a more narrative tone:

> One morning, being in bed in the infirmary, very ill, it seemed to me that a citizen of the town had come into the bedroom, very frightened, pulling the curtain suddenly aside, he said to me, 'The town is taken, the enemy are within'. While he was speaking I saw a great ball of fire thrown on to me in the bed. It was an illusion. (*Rel.* 39)

Alix was then very ill. Her illness, a combination of moral distress and chronic debility, reached a crisis which events raised to a paroxysm. The recurring discussions on the identity of the sisterhood, cloistered or not cloistered?, the negotiations about house purchase while the congregation's funds were at their lowest, the ravaging armies drawing ever nearer, the alarms and outcries that the soldiers are at the gates, the obsessive temptations infesting her – there was more than enough here to heighten the fever which was undermining her and open the door to delirium. In front of her rose a nightmare image which she knew was imaginary, for she introduced it with the words,

'It seemed to me . . .' The citizen left his signature, 'a great ball of fire', flung on to Alix's body in her bed. So far the suspense was complete. Alix did not name the demon but she recognised it and said simply, 'It was an illusion'. The calmness of the text here is remarkable, because it is only the contrast between these two successive passages that reveals their significance. The demon, never short of tricks, was disguised. Making use of Alix's delirium, it could increase her terror at will, throwing her into panic with a false item of news. Through this lie he meant to shake her confidence; she had asked God to spare the town but he, the demon, tells her that her prayer is not heard. As Antoine Vergote said, 'the tempter is one who causes us to doubt God, God as radically transcending man'.[149] But his attack failed. The sick woman is calmed, as trust banishes fear. The town was saved and we can surely say that Alix's prayer did its part.

An exercise in discernment: Châlons, yes or no?

When the authorities in Rome were finding it so difficult to accept the originality of the work, was it wise to try to increase it? The question became urgent in 1613 because the bishop of Châlons-en-Champagne, Monseigneur Cosme Clausse, wanted some of the nuns of Our Lady to go to his episcopal city. His request was supported by Father Fleurant Boulangier, who had once wanted to send Alix and her companions to the Poor Clares in Verdun and who now, admiring their mission work, wanted them to open a school in Châlons. Father Le Brun, the Jesuit, joined him in this request, and the suggestion reached Fourier. Undecided, and wishing to consult the sisters before making up his mind, Fourier wrote them a long letter on 12 December 1613, in which, like a good rhetorician, he weighed the pros and cons of making a new foundation. The

small number of sisters who were good teachers, the risk of
ruining one school by taking members of its staff away to
promote another, the uncertainty of success, the unreliability of
promised support – there were plenty of reasons against the
idea. Reasons for it were weighty. The first, said Fourier, was
the apostolic zeal of the sisters, which he defined as 'the pious
and fervent desire you have to keep on advancing in the land
to the greater glory of God'. Then there would be the new
vocations which the dynamism of the Congregation could not
fail to arouse. And above all 'the weight which the name of
Châlons, joined to those of Toul and Verdun, would give to
your petitions and memorials if there is any question of sub-
mitting new petitions to Rome'. Last of all came the decisive
argument – it was an opportunity to get into France. As
Georges Viard rightly points out, 'a Lorrainer to his fingertips,
passionately attached to the independence of the duchies as also
to the ducal house, the parish priest of Mattaincourt saw that
the Congregation now taking shape must cross frontiers if it
was to advance for the greater glory of God'.[150] 'But you risk
losing this chance', Fourier explained to the sisters, 'for there are
other Daughters hard on your heels, all of them already nuns,
who are trying to take it from you', a reference to the Ursulines,
now swarming into Champagne and Burgundy.[151] Clearly he
was in favour of the foundation at Châlons, but expressed one
last anxiety: 'Think how many Daughters can be taken from
your Congregation without inconvenience, and which ones;
where are they?' He let the sisters make the final decision 'as
long as there is unanimous agreement'. Then, well informed
and 'having seriously thought it over with God', they all
approved the project and prepared to follow their founder's
instructions.

He planned a journey of inspection which he organised as

follows: 'Let the Mother be Sister Isabeau, if she is well and content to go there; let her assistant and travelling companion be Sister Alix; let the daughters they take with them be Sister Marie d'Epinal and Sister Marguerite Gaillot, as long they are both content to go, and furthermore some of the young boarders from Saint-Mihiel or Verdun, whom Sister Isabeau will choose, and they are to come back with Sister Alix'. What admirable instructions, where authority is tempered by tact! Devoted as he was to the very soil of Lorraine, the good Father understood that to go into France was a kind of exile. He also knew that at this period the frontier is a reality which political events and war have strongly reinforced'.[152] Fearing disorientation for the sisters, he only sent volunteers. Alix received special instructions: 'Let Sister Alix return as soon as the decision has been taken, whether to stay or not, and let her there and while travelling obey Sister Isabeau and address her as Mother and defer to her in every way she can so as to give authority and a good opinion to our said Sister Isabeau to the greater glory of God'. The obstinate one sidedness of some biographers who accuse Fourier of deliberately underestimating Alix has prevented them understanding these words with which Fourier had in fact been entrusting Alix with a delicate task, one he knew she would perform perfectly. In those few days Alix was to establish Isabeau's authority. In Lorraine Isabeau did certainly enjoy the respect her qualities and the tasks she performed deserved – she was made mistress of the novices at Mattaincourt in 1602, from 1604 to 1611 was Superior at Pont-à-Mousson and in 1612 she rescued the house of St Nicolas. But no one knew her in Châlons and only the deference shown her by Alix would establish her position. The protective role given to the Superior of Verdun was in no way humiliating for her but illustrates the kind of charity which Fourier connects with that function, expressed in his *Rule of 1640*: 'After Our Lord and the blessed Virgin Mary, and with them and for love of them, the Mother Superior of the convent, as it were their lieutenant, will be in her own way the Mother of mercies, the Mother of solace, to all her sisters who need it'.[153] Isabeau did indeed need Alix, and barely six months passed before she turned to her again.

One of the group who travelled to Châlons was the novice Angélique Milly, who would play an important part in Alix's life. Born in the same year as the Congregation itself, 1597, this child, Martine, very early gave proof of such a lively mind and true piety that Father Fleurant Boulangier destined her for the Poor Clares. Until she should be old enough to enter the noviciate she was sent to board at Verdun, where from the example of her mistresses she discovered the beauty of the teaching vocation. Although her parents did not like the fact that the Congregation was not officially recognised, they allowed her to follow this call and at fifteen she entered the noviciate at Verdun. Angélique was a delightful creature, well brought up, friendly, helpful, highly intelligent and gifted with sound judgment. Taught by Alix, she soon became her trusted confidant, and an exceptional friendship arose between them.

To Châlons

On Monday 30 December 1613 seven women and girls climbed into a wretched hired carriage. They were Alix Le Clerc, Isabeau de Louvroir, Nicole Médreville (Sister Claire of the Resurrection), Marie d'Epinal (or of Verdun), Marguerite Gaillot, Angélique Milly and a servant. It was unusually cold and the vehicle made slow progress on the icy roads. In this wintry setting, with the black woodlands of the Argonne now white with snow, Alix fought an inner battle which she had first begun in Verdun. She wrote: 'The evil spirit chiefly began to repeat his attempts when I went to take the sisters to Châlons, for it seemed to me as we left the gates of Verdun that a cloud of demons flung itself upon my soul, and all along the road, suffering their furious attack, to resist and defeat them I sang hymns and devout songs' (*Rel.* 53). This short account expresses the condition of any Christian who asks God not to let him yield to temptation but to deliver him from evil. The seventeenth century setting emphasises the essential aspects of the struggle. The words 'it seemed' are no more than an oratorical signal to the reader by which Alix warns him that she is here dealing with invisible realities which have no equivalent in the visible world. The enemy, instantly recognised, is called 'the evil spirit'. Together with 'a cloud of demons' he makes ever stronger attempts to fling himself upon her soul. Using military terminology, Alix describes their 'furious attack' which she will 'resist' and in the end 'defeat'. There is no triumphalism in this victory, quietly noted, for Alix knew that her strength came from God, as it was the singing of hymns and holy songs that made the demons flee. Her devotion to the holy office and to choral song is recorded by her earliest biographers,[154] and here let us do no more than point out that she knew by heart the songs of the Church which nourished her prayers and came spontaneously to her lips to combat temptation.

More detailed accounts tell us about the rest of the journey. The improvised choruses, sung by them all as they travelled 'all along the road' helped them ignore the discomfort of the journey. But as they were going through the gorges between Clermont and Ste-Menehould, the cold intensified and Nicole lost consciousness. What alarm then in the carriage – rubbing and warming her, they brought her back to life and wrapped her in a wolfskin, laughing as they said, 'It's a marvel that this poor lamb (so they called Nicole, for her sweet nature) should

be saved by the hide of a wolf!'[155] When on the second day
the town of Châlons could be seen on the horizon, Alix realised
that she had already seen it in a dream, from a high point in
Verdun as she recalled in her *Relation*: 'I was taken to a high
place near St-Vanne,[156] there I was shown a large town in
France that we must go to, it was situated in a plain and a very
long way from Verdun; this was Châlons. When I went there
some years later,[157] I saw that it was the same town; in fact I
thought in surprise that I had seen it from Verdun and could
not understand how we could see so far' (*Rel.* 52). Alix's surprise
is very reasonable if we remember the many obstacles which
formed an almost unbreakable barrier between Lorraine
and France. She was cautious and even doubtful about her
premonitory dreams, as she says: 'In sleeping, often things that
are to happen are shown to me, both about myself and those
that affect the Congregation. It disturbs me, for fear of some
deceit, although I never trust them at all'. She had to admit,
though, that her foreknowledge was often correct. Knowledge
of the future then became for her an opportunity to entrust
what was to come to Our Lord in the most absolute act of
abandonment: 'Let him do with it as he shall please'. Then she
concludes, 'Things usually happen as I have seen them' (*Rel.* 44).

When they were still some leagues from Châlons, the travellers
found a man lying in the snow at the side of the road, half dead
with cold. Alix had the carriage stopped and they went to his
help. A little wine and the invaluable wolfskin restored him.
The man was certainly not some needy person but a citizen of
Châlons who had been overtaken by the blizzard, had fallen
and could not get to his feet.[158] Full of gratitude to the sisters
who had saved him, he invited them to his own house before
taking them into Châlons to the hostelry of Petit-St-Menge
where a welcoming group of clerics and devout women was

waiting for them. A certain Madame Braux put them up, and very soon the sisters opened a school, which was rapidly filled up with little girls. After a fortnight Alix and the faithful Angélique set off for Verdun.

Return Journey

Several sources provide us with accounts of the return journey, all written from different points of view. Alix concentrated on the inner battle she was fighting against the demon and so makes little mention of external circumstances. Her short closely written page is best read all of a piece, but it will be useful to consider the various episodes in detail, partly to clarify an allusion which she explains elsewhere, and partly to include in their appropriate places the events of the journey which the biographers took care to include, using them to introduce edifying and at times even marvellous stories.

Although Alix never laid claims to literary merit, her text shows real talent. Here is the passage in question:

> They (the demons) caught me up with terrifying violence. The first night of the return journey – because we were lodged in a hostelry where there was only one bed, I made my companion take it and lay on the floor, because of a vow I had made never to sleep with another person – just as I was thinking of sleeping, look, there were devils in the shape of men who by charms took away my speech and began to do villainous things, trying to touch me. I felt hell fire in my flesh as if in a brazier. I had nothing free but my mind, which was still very wearied in resisting the temptation; I fixed it hard upon Jesus and his holy Mother, telling them that since they were allowing me to lose everything except my mind, they should strengthen it and act for me so that I should not

offend them. I was battered like this all night long without the demons ever getting the power to touch me. The landlady was taken very ill, people were going to and fro through the house; a candle was brought into the bedroom and that released me from the illusion. (*Rel.* 54)

Alix struck directly into the heart of her subject: the antagonism between herself and the demons is posited and the action is begun. They were pursuing her (Alix does not say this, does not need to) and they catch her up. Now what will happen? The author of the chronicle writes in more detail and tells us about their arrival at the inn. As darkness was falling, the coach driver got lost. Anxious about the poor state of the roads which ran along the edge of precipices, he halted the vehicle, and while Alix called upon the Virgin Mary a lad came out of some woodland and guided them to the next village. The inn here was a mere hovel and the room offered them was a cowshed, from which a cow and some calves were hastily turned out. Angélique said that they should find a better place to stay and not risk a bad night. Alix replied with a laugh that the Kings (it was in the octave of Epiphany) found the baby Jesus in a stable and not in Bethlehem's best hotel. What's more, she said, 'If we were offered a better choice, we should do without it for love of him'. She refused to share with her companion the only bed brought to them, and as the chronicle does not tell us why, we must go to Alix herself to find out when and why she made the vow of sleeping alone. Not having mentioned this at its appropriate date, she repaired the omission a little after the account of the journey, as follows:

While I was still living in my father's house at the beginning of my vocation, in bed one night, fully clothed, with another girl, quite suddenly as I was talking to her about things of salvation, a stench as of hell took me by such vehement surprise that I had to get out of the bed, and yet the girl smelt nothing. And as long as the garment I was wearing lasted, something of that stench clung to it. It came at once into my mind that Our Lord wanted me to sleep alone. I made the vow there and then. Often I perceive something of these foul smells when I am bound to suffer some great distress; and they sometimes come before my great temptations. (*Rel.* 62)

This return to the past is interesting because it shows that Alix was attacked as early as 1597 by the enmity of the devil, who could foresee that she would be an apostle well able to speak of 'things of salvation'. Although in recalling this memory she does not give 'the evil spirit' a name, she could fathom his deceitful ploys: a foul stench indicating his presence and an obscene collusion between the two meanings of 'to sleep with', meaning either to share a bed or 'to have sexual relations with' someone. Alix was no dupe; the very idea of this double meaning disgusted her. Not a woman for half measures, she got straight out of the bed where her companion was lying beside her and at once made her vow to sleep alone. In those days it was not uncommon to take a vow, because that in itself made the deed more meritorious, although it also made the sin of failure worse. She saw it above all as a response to the Lord's purpose for her, and as a way of telling him again of her love for him, by renewing her vow of chastity. The demon did not admit defeat and pursued her with his 'hellish stench' long after this event.

On the return from Châlons in January 1614 the devil had every reason to redouble his violence against Alix, much more so than at the beginning of her vocation. In attacking her he aimed at the Congregation as a whole, which with its new foundation had entered France and from there would shine out far and wide. And in the wretched inn where there was only one bed he took revenge for the vow she had made, even to the point of trying to make the place of the holy promise one of unrestrained debauch.

The account in the *Relation* shows this clearly. With remarkable clarity Alix analyses the different stages of the temptation, distinguishing the way it affected her body and left her mind free. On this occasion too the devils took the form of men, an imaginary appearance but essential as indicating the role they assumed. Seeking to possess her virginal body to make her commit 'villainous actions', they began by depriving her of all movement and speech through the use of 'charms'. For Alix this word meant powerful enchantments in which she recognised the demon's tactics, but it does not here make explicit reference to magic or sorcery.[159] Rejecting the embrace of the demons who were trying to touch her, she felt her flesh burn with a hellish fire, as if in a brazier, a strong image of hell very common in the iconography of the period. Free only in her mind, her spirit, she resisted, prayed, forced her attention to Jesus and Mary as one bends a bow the better to attain the mark. It was for them, she told them, to strengthen her only point of resistance, as they had allowed her to be tempted. Only one thing mattered to her: that she should not offend them. The struggle lasted all night but day dawned with victory: these powerful demons were defeated, they had not been able to touch her. In a few lines Alix concluded the episode – the landlady fell violently ill, there was alarm and confusion in the house, someone brought a candle into Alix's room and the light, she said, freed her from 'this illusion'.

The matter of fact description in the *Relation* did not satisfy Alix's contemporaries, who took five long pages to do justice to this tragic night.[160] They do not mention the demon's actions, but the end of the episode is expanded, as we shall see.

Shivering with fever, stretched on bundles of hemp on the ground, Alix struggled and prayed. At about three in the morning appalling shrieks were heard. Loud in the dark night they filled the room and maddened Alix who thought they were the screams of one possessed. Unable to bear it, she woke her companion and said that they must leave the inn at once. Angélique found a candle, whose flame restored reality to the room, shabby indeed but now well enough lit to dispel demoniac illusions. Forgetting their disarray, the two nuns went to the hostess' bed and found her struggling in intolerable pain. Alix, weak as she was, gave her comfort. Her knowledge of souls helped her see that the violent illness she was suffering stemmed from an inner moral evil. She asked for the date of her last confession; it had been Easter. Had that confession been sacrilegious? What had happened since? Alix instructed her 'with great sweetness', made her ask God to forgive her sins and promised that next day she should receive the sacrament of pardon. On her knees at the foot of the bed she prayed with the sick woman and did not leave her without giving her an *Agnus Dei* and some relics which, if she wore them, would protect her from the demon. This was not superstition, it was devotion to pious objects which reveal the presence of the sacred and transmit divine grace. Fourier called such things 'precious drugs' which comfort the sick, 'a sort of medicine' which helps them back to health.[161] The woman became calmer, and before dawn the two travellers made haste to leave the inn. But in the carriage Alix was overwhelmed, sad and silent.

Back again in Verdun she fell ill, rejecting all offers of relief, till her anxious companions asked advice from Father Le Brun.

He put a stop to the passion for penance which was ravaging Alix by putting her under obedience. From now on, he ordered, in everything that concerned her health she was to consult the youngest of the sisters, Angélique. She performed this task with tact and was horrified to discover her friend's inner conflicts, for Alix continued to be tormented by the same temptations. She reveals this herself in the *Relation*, adding immediately after the description of that night:

> These shapes of evil spirits have appeared to me several times, applying some sort of charms to my feet, and it seemed as if I felt as it were shivers, until the fire in the flesh was blazing so hard that I could not restrain outward movements of the body. And it is chiefly in this that my scruples lie. Sometimes when I wanted to throw myself out of the bed some shape of a man would appear to keep me there. (*Rel.* 55) These temptations lasted two full years in Verdun. (*Rel.* 56)[162]

In this way God subjected Alix to a singularly painful experience which gave her entry to the mystery of weakness. The best comment on her 'great temptations' comes from St Paul, who with the same clarity wrote, 'I was given a thorn in the flesh, an angel of Satan to beat me and stop me from getting too proud! About this thing, I have pleaded with the Lord three times for it to leave me, but he has said, "My grace is enough for you: my power is at its best in weakness". So I shall be very happy to make my weaknesses my special boast so that the power of Christ may stay over me'. (2 Cor. 12:7–9)

CHAPTER THIRTEEN

Fresh openings – Paris 1615

Temptation of Isabeau de Louvroir

Isabeau de Louvroir, just as determined a character as Alix, was suffering from not being anything more than a 'secular member of a congregation' because the institute to which she belonged was still not recognised by the Church authorities. We do not know what steps she took in this connection because the documents are either silent or contradictory, and she herself left no record of her dilemma. Several historians[163] have identified her as the woman who at the gathering of October 1613 suggested putting the congregation under the Rule of St Benedict in the hope of accelerating procedures in Rome and obtaining a brief like that won by Jeanne de Lestonnac in 1607. But this suggestion does not hold good, as the scholar Hélène Derréal has shown.[164] A different source has Isabeau ready to abandon the Congregation, not for the Benedictines but for the reformed Poor Clares.[165] She was encouraged in this by the Recollects who were directors of the sisters after they went to Châlons, and seemed to welcome their persuasions because she despaired of seeing her own institute ever becoming a regular order. One day, tired of hesitation, she decided to go, and said as much to Jean Jennin, priest of the parish of Saint-Eloi where the sisters' school was situated. He passed this news on to the archdeacon, Nicolas Itam, telling him bluntly, 'You have no Daughters of the Congregation of Our Lady in Châlons any more'. The two churchmen, anxious not to lose the sisters, united their efforts to keep them. Jennin preached patience to Isabeau and deployed strong arguments: difficulties with Rome were nothing new, all founders of orders had them, especially recently; worldly opposition showed what great benefit would result from this new work, and so on, and on. Nicolas Itam, knowing the generous spirit Isabeau had and aware that her longing for penance would be fulfilled with the Poor Clares, took a different approach: 'Is it not true that in God's eyes work as exhausting as the constant toil of sisters who teach the young is equivalent to the most austere life? One can find anywhere young women who practise the greatest austerities in the cloister but there are few who sacrifice themselves with as much courage as you do to bring up children at no charge in the fear of the Lord and in the activities that are right for their age'. Jean Jennin, who had refused to undertake the direction of the sisters because of his age, he being not yet thirty, did in the end accept it, after making a retreat with the Jesuits at Verdun. Under his firm guidance, Isabeau gave up all thought of leaving and courageously confronted the usual problems of a foundation. Difficulties were made for months together about the renting of the Maison Sainte-Marie. She achieved this, but when she wanted to buy the place the mistresses of the school, thinking their pupils would leave them, did their best to prevent the sale. In order to have at her disposal a competent body of teaching staff, she asked that Sister Catherine should join them from Verdun, and Sister Barbe from St Nicolas would take her place. Fourier disagreed, because children become fond of their teachers, and 'these little people', he wrote on 13 March 1614, 'behave according to liking. I feel', he added, 'that this sudden removal of those who are considered the best (perhaps for wrong reasons) would be damaging, would lose you your day pupils, your boarders and the affection of your well wishers and people'.

Difficulties piled up. In the hope of resolving them, he spent
five weeks in Châlons, from where on 12 June he sent a postscript to Verdun: 'Sister Alix, after my letters were written and
closed, our Sister Isabeau told me that she would very much
wish that you might spend three or four days here to satisfy
her'. We know nothing of the visit from Alix but may suppose
that it had a calming effect on Isabeau, to judge by the events
that followed. Returning from Châlons, Fourier visited the
different houses, and on 9 September 1614 he sent news from
Pont to the sisters at Verdun:

> I found our Sister Isabeau at Saint Mihiel, where before
> mass and my departure she made in the presence of our
> sisters a promise to remain all her life in the Congregation
> and to be obedient there according to the constitution, so
> that I am reassured by my hope that this bond will serve to
> keep her more easily within the limits of her duty and in the
> good and very resolute disposition that I have recognised in
> these past days, not only in her words and looks but also in
> the depths of her soul and of her intentions, as it seems to
> me. This promise was not acknowledged and given without
> examination and pertinent reasons.[166]

References to Isabeau's temptation are discreet. Did she stage
a revolt and draw in one or more sisters? We do not know, but
the affair must have been lively. At any rate we find her a few
weeks later Superior at Châlons in a thriving house. When
Fourier wrote on 10 November it was to pour out heartfelt
thanks because, he said, the lord bishop, the parish priest, the
archdeacon, the Jesuits and the benefactors were all delighted to
have the sisters at Châlons. Crowds of small girls attended the
schools. In future the money they brought for their school fees
would not be accepted.[167] Fourier was anxious too about the

sisters' wellbeing: 'Who feeds you? Is there not something you need?' (*C.* 1, 88.) There was just one shadow darkening the picture – the House of St Mary was not yet bought. A month later on 13 December he told the sisters of St Nicolas more news: 'My lord the Primate wants your place and the house you have in the town of Nancy to be sold in order to buy one in the New Town opposite him and to build you a convent there, otherwise he does not wish to give the income he has promised, it is said. We need prayers and special help from God about this'.

Monseigneur Antoine de Lenoncourt

Fourier was no simpleton, he could see straight. The prelate was authoritarian and he liked a good bargain. He had nothing to lose, but what did he in fact have to gain? His interests undoubtedly coincided with the policy of the duke of Lorraine, Charles III (1545–1608). Neither this duke nor his predecessors had succeeded in getting Nancy elevated to episcopal status, owing to opposition from France and from the archbishop of Trèves, metropolitan of the sees of Metz, Toul and Verdun. To make up for this the duke had founded a collegiate church in Nancy dedicated to Our Lady, and the pope, wanting to please him, had granted its principal dignitary the title of primate of Lorraine. The first to enjoy this honour together with a kind of episcopal jurisdiction had been the cardinal Charles of Lorraine. When he died in 1607 he was succeeded by Antoine de Lenoncourt who became an active collaborator in ducal politics. Just as eager as Charles III to turn Nancy into an important capital city, the primate was also an evangelist, and wanted the town to become a centre of reform through wholehearted implementation of the decrees of the Council of Trent. The support he gave to the sisters of Our Lady fits exactly into this picture.

As yet he had taken no decisive step. In 1606 as dean of the primatial church, he negotiated the sale of the Cloister of Our Lady where the sisters took up residence in Nancy-la-Vieille, Old Nancy. Then in 1611, needing help from some powerful person in their applications to Rome, the sisters chose him as their protector. Fourier, despite some reservations, told the primate of their request, and knowing that he was about to leave for Trèves to meet the nuncio of Germany, he gave him the description of their plans, the *Sommaire du dessein des Filles de la Congrégation*. But Lenoncourt had his own business to see to and the sisters' request came to nothing. In 1614 the increasing success of the Congregation's houses, especially at Verdun and Châlons, rekindled his zeal and he decided that he himself would undertake the task of asking for a bull of approbation. As he felt it was important to locate the head of the new Congregation in the capital of Lorraine, he planned to establish in Nancy a principal convent which would be a model for all the others. He would be its founder, would commit himself to endowing it with an annual income of 1,000 francs, and it would be built near his future primatial church. He insisted therefore that Our Lady's Cloister should be sold, although the debts for its purchase had not yet been paid. After much discussion the sisters who gathered at Verdun in October 1614 complied with the wishes of the primate, who held stubbornly to his plans and was single-handedly conducting his business in Rome. Without troubling to consult Fourier or the communities about the applications his representative was taking to the Vatican and without any reference to earlier petitions, he presented a new dossier, and in record time obtained from Pope Paul V a bull dated 1 February 1615.[168]

The bull exactly fulfilled all his requests. The pope granted to him and to the 'dear Daughters of the Congregation of the

blessed Virgin Mary established in Nancy' permission to found
there 'a true convent of the Order of St Augustine' and to
practise there 'the same perpetual enclosure, the same rule, the
same 'usages, customs and statutes'. The primate was satisfied
but Fourier could not contain his anger. Only the convent in
Nancy was mentioned and not the group of houses united as a
Congregation. There was no word of teaching, still less of schools
for day pupils. 'The Reverend Father', says the chronicle, 'would
have preferred them [the sisters] to stay in their residences
uncloistered, as they had done in the past, rather than give up
the free schooling of day pupils, because of the wonderful and
successful results seen everywhere, and because both rich and
poor could benefit from this'.[169] Fifteen years later in a letter of
4 February 1630, Fourier's pen still shook with indignation,
when he wrote, 'This double omission, nothing said about
the schools in the first bull, which did not represent the Congregation as a whole but only one convent, is the principle, the
cause, the origin, the source, the fountain of all the present
difficulties', and those yet to come. He rejected the bull and
opposed any purchase of land or the start of building for the
new convent. The primate took offence and when Alix went to
see him as a messenger of peace he received her brusquely, said
he would have nothing to do with it any more and would make
no further application to Rome. While he was giving vent to his
anger, important guests were announced. Alix withdrew and
prayed fervently to the Virgin Mary, asking her to ask God to
calm the primate. A little later he went to her, listened kindly to
her ideas, promised he would never abandon the sisters and
prepared to write to Rome 'to complete their business'.

Fourier then felt it was necessary to gather the sisters in Nancy
in mid-February. The summons reached Châlons when Alix
was again with Isabeau, but the latter did not attend the reunion

because on that day Father Gilles Gauthier was to preach in the cathedral to ask for funds to help the sisters. 'You were much missed and needed in our discussion, Sister Isabeau', Fourier wrote to her on 7 March. Hoping that the new steps taken by Monseigneur de Lenoncourt would put the disappointment over the bull behind them, the assembly confirmed some important decisions: in accordance with the primate's wish, Alix would spend time with the Ursulines in Paris to study their teaching methods and the pattern of their religious life. When she came back she would undertake the direction of the convent in Nancy.

The journey to Paris

At the thought of Alix and other sisters setting off for Paris, Fourier issued utopian commands. The nuns must not enter a carriage in which there were men. They must only travel accompanied by a lady whom they knew. 'Do not behave in a friendly way to any man at all, not even to a saint who performs miracles', he ordered (*C.* 1. 90). The rest of the story shows that at this period (and is it any better now?) there were real dangers threatening women who travelled alone in a public vehicle. Armed with all the protections of heaven, Alix and Angélique Milly left Verdun. They went by way of Châlons to pick up Nicole Médreville, whom the primate wanted to have in Nancy because she was nobly born and a successful teacher. Expecting 'tears and sobbing' from the sisters at Châlons, Fourier offered them Martine, or Angélique, she being 'very worthy, very capable, very holy'. In the event Nicole was ill and could not travel, and it was Angélique who went to Paris and on her return would be appointed to Nancy. Isabeau de Louvroir and a woman friend accompanied the two nuns and then returned to Châlons.

On Saturday 14 March 1615 the four women got on the coach. At the first stop five coarse and vulgar men climbed aboard. Annoyed by the women's downcast eyes and closed lips, they made all kinds of more and more unpleasant jokes at their expense. Next day, Sunday, they got the postillion to set off at dawn so that the pious women could not hear mass. But in the village of Vauchamps the bell was ringing for the service and the delighted women went to attend, telling themselves that they would rejoin the coach when it stopped for the meal at Montmirail. And the sermon went on and on and it was a long road under the bright March sun. But, oh surprise, the coach was there. Fresh horses were put to, replacing the ones which had caused a three hour delay when, without obvious reason, they had refused to go on.

The visit to the Ursulines

Although strict observance of silence and enclosure required that the Ursulines of Paris should receive no strangers, Alix and Angéline were welcomed as sisters on 15 March 1615. When in Nancy Father Gontery, one of the eminent Jesuit directors of the Paris house, had arranged this visit in agreement with Monseigneur de Lenoncourt, and the two months spent in Paris by the Lorraine women was for them a real immersion in a new form of religious life, one that was practised by the Ursulines some years before it was known to the sisters of Our Lady.

When the two travellers reached the convent in the Faubourg Saint-Jacques, it had already reconciled the various foundations on which it was built. Traces were still visible from this rich past and Alix examined them with interest because any initiative could be useful in a time when new orders for women were springing up. The earliest Ursulines were those whom Angela Merici (1474–1540) placed under the protection of St Ursula

when she created a secular order, before its time, consisting of girls who were consecrated to God but lived in the world. They took up different works of evangelisation, and these very soon included the teaching of girls. In 1581 the cardinal archbishop of Milan, Carlo Borromeo (1538–1584), gave them a Rule which profoundly modified the primitive *Regula* by restricting their activities solely to the teaching of Christian doctrine. But soon, radically new, there appeared informal groups of devout girls who, although without any formal bonds but their piety and their charitable work, adopted the Rules of the Ursulines. From the Comtat-Venaissin, their first establishment outside Italy, they moved into France in 1600. By 1607 they were in Paris.

This was the period when Madame Acarie (1566–1618) was working to recruit future Carmelites for the houses of this Order which were being founded in France, following the example of those in Spain. Amongst those she gathered for the contemplative life were some whom she did not think suited to it, and these she set to teaching girl children in their neighbourhood. Then it occurred to her to turn them into Ursulines. Her cousin Madame de Sainte-Beuve agreed to be foundress of the new community, to which she would devote her life and her wealth. She installed them in 1607 in a mansion in the Faubourg Saint-Jacques and in 1608 asked Françoise de Bermond to join them there. At that time Françoise was managing groups of Ursulines according to the original Rule of St Angela in Avignon, in L'Isle-sur-Sorgues and then at Aix. When this pioneer from Provence left Paris in 1610, a significant change was on its way: Madame de Sainte-Beuve wanted her secular members of a congregation to pronounce solemn vows and to adopt enclosure. With this end in view she obtained one after another letters patent from the king, the elevation into a convent of the Parisian

house which later became the Great Convent, and in 1612
a papal bull with planned Constitution attached. Alix,
remembering the 'disagreements' which had split the sisters in
Lorraine over their choice of religious identity, was anxious to
know how the group in Paris had accepted the changes imposed
by this transformation. She was not in the least surprised to be
told of the reactions that had followed – some few hostile, but
above all a profound longing for a monastic life. Cloistered
existence seemed to these secular women to be a more perfect
way, and more in keeping with the desire for abstinence and
mortification which Madame Acarie had encouraged in them
when recruiting them to the Carmelites. Madame de Sainte-
Beuve, moreover, a lover of austerity and uncompromising
regularity, wanted the Paris bull to compel her seculars to be
taught monastic life by nuns of one of the great Orders. Four
Cistercians nuns therefore went to the Faubourg from St
Stephen's abbey in Soissons. Their presence made possible
the opening of a canonical noviciate, followed by religious
ceremonies – nine novices took the veil on 11 November 1612;
professions were made in 1614. While the sisters from Lorraine
were in Paris, two of the Cistercian nuns were still there and
Alix had long conversations with one of them, Mother Marie
de Villiers de Saint-Paul, 'of the Incarnation', who had agreed
to spend some time as prioress of the Paris Ursulines and
superintendent of the boarding pupils.

Fourier had given Alix and Angélique a detailed plan of the
enquiries they were to make in the Paris convent so as to provide
him with information which would help him draw up the
Constitution of this Congregation (*C.* 1, 91–93). They were to
observe everything, note everything – the Rule, spirituality,
food, clothing, teaching, liturgy, and so forth. Comparing the
life the sisters of Our Lady would soon be leading with that of

the Ursulines in Paris, the one looks very like a model for the other, its almost exact copy, so great are the resemblances. In fact, despite the similarities arising from the pronouncements of the Council of Trent, which left little room for variation, we should take note of the very many shades of difference, especially in teaching methods, so strong was the influence of Fourier's charismatic personality, evident in the tiniest regulation. We shall do better to look at some points which will have interested Alix and her companion more than others.[170]

When Madame de Sainte-Beuve and her advisers, especially Monsieur de Marillac, a legal expert, applied for the 1612 bull, they did not mention the education of day pupils, a suggestion which would have threatened the whole enterprise. But if they enclosed the Ursulines behind the grilles of a convent, they were in no danger of seeing them taken for contemplative nuns. In fact a fourth vow guaranteed the nuns their mission, and the fact that no details were laid down as to how it should be performed gave them a certain latitude. Fourier did not overlook this useful thought, and included a vow of teaching in his 1617 Rule.

Originally both founders, Alix and Fourier, had wanted to create an institution based entirely on poverty. But after some years of attempting this, they had to change. Too much poverty results in disorder.[171] The example of Paris confirmed this decision. When Madame de Sainte-Beuve signed the act of foundation in 1610 she guaranteed an income to the convent, as she did not think that nuns could live by the work of their hands if they had been teaching children all day long. This dependent poverty, limiting the number of nuns and of pupils, together with the increase in dowries required from novices, as well as the founders' generosity and well wishers' unreliable donations – all this seemed to Alix more problematic than harsh poverty. But she realised that the change in the Ursulines' status had encouraged the court and nobility to be more open handed, as they saw that the houses would in future be more stable. Certainly the establishment of the Ursulines in the capital city had its effect on the convent's way of life.

Alix's friendship with Madame de Villers Saint-Paul opened her eyes to the influence of the Cistercians from Soissons, who, without meaning to do so, made changes to the original spirit of the Ursulines. The novices filling the house were mostly from simple homes whereas the nuns of the abbey in Soissons were from the nobility or the upper burgess class and were addressed as Madame. They were also canonesses and it was therefore their duty to sing the Roman office in the choir daily. Naturally they tried to introduce the Ursulines to a liturgy which was advanced, yet suitable for their evangelical function. Thus in order to protect their voices the teaching nuns said, not sang, the lesser office of Our Lady, and those who were employed to teach the pupils recited it privately. Alix, who enjoyed remembering Madame d'Apremont's teaching about rubrics, and the canonesses at Poussay singing the services, liked sharing the Ursulines' worship. One day, perhaps a Sunday or a feast day when solemn vespers were sung, she experienced an ecstasy which she describes as follows:

> When I was with the Ursulines of the Faubourg Saint-Jacques, being one day in the choir with the nuns, I felt strongly urged by a wish to know what I could do that would be most pleasing to Our Lord, and prayed to him about this. It was said to me, I being out of my senses, that inwardly and outwardly I should find out whether all my actions were always purely done for the love of God. (*Rel.* 67)

Are we to suppose that care for her own perfection led her

away from the task Fourier had given her? No, certainly not, for
he too had this heartfelt desire for perfection. When he wrote to
Châlons on 7 March 1615 he described exactly the purpose of
the sisters' visit to Paris, 'to see exactly,' he wrote, 'to learn, keep
and bring back to Lorraine the practice and method of all that
is happening there, so that if we perceive in their statutes,
behaviour and way of proceeding anything nobler, higher, more
perfect than in our Congregation, we can in holiness do the
same'. This search for the best, for the most perfect, it was what
Fourier wanted for his institute, it was Alix's own personal rule
of behaviour, but both drew it from the same source and
attained the same summit. They did not aim at perfection as in
a performance of personal efforts and abstract intentions. They
were led to it by God's love through the all powerful mediation
of Christ Jesus, himself the Way.

   While the founder and foundress were going forward in
harmony on the 'path of perfection', a new road was opening
up before them: the understanding between the Ursulines and
sisters from Lorraine seemed so close that people thought of
uniting the two congregations. This idea was put forward at a
time when the Ursulines were founding new houses and trying
to have them all recognised together in a single bull. Perhaps all
the foundations could be united as dependencies of the Paris
convent with Madame de Villers Saint-Paul as Superior of the
order. Then why should the congregations in Lorraine not
simply unite under the Rule of the Ursulines, rather than
pursuing their chancy hopes in Rome? We can guess that Alix
refused – in similar circumstances she had always held firm to
the hope of 'a new house' from which would come all possible
good. In 1600 she and her comrades had blocked Father
Fleurant's endeavour to take them all to join the Poor Clares in
Verdun. When it was suggested at the gathering in Nancy in

1613 that the congregation should adopt St Benedict as their patron, she opposed this, being afraid that it would lead to integration into a contemplative Order and the permanent abandonment of the 'unenclosed houses' which were so important to her. And moreover the 1612 bull had put Madame de Sainte-Beuve's Ursulines under the authority of the arch-bishop of Paris, who in his turn had put them under the close direction of three ecclesiastics who would draw up their statutes, manage their property and appoint their officials – all these being tasks which Alix knew very well belonged to no one but Fourier. She understood the value of having one and one only spiritual leader in the creation of a religious order, and concluded that it was here that lay the difference between the Congregation of Our Lady and the Ursulines who had had several different leaders in the course of their development.

As in the past, Alix's sweet nature and her prayer were her best weapons. In humility she consulted Pierre de Bérulle (1575–1629) whose shining holiness had impressed her when he visited the convent in the Faubourg Saint-Jacques. He was not yet a cardinal but in those early days of the seventeenth century he was one of the most significant personalities, known and admired both as a reformer of religious orders, as a spiritual director, a politician and a diplomat. He was a cousin of Madame Acarie and wholeheartedly engaged in setting up the Carmelites in France. In 1604 he settled Spanish and French nuns in Paris. Other Carmelite houses followed, totalling thirty-two by 1623. Meanwhile in 1611 he also founded the Oratory, a congregation of priests with the intention that they should rediscover the purpose and the methods of their mission. This meeting between Alix and Bérulle – does it allow us to think that it was here she first learnt her spiritual doctrine, totally centred on Jesus Christ and the mystery of the Incarnation? It seems probable. The passionate devotion of both to the Word incarnate was a good basis for their meeting and they agreed in asking for time for prayer. Unlike the Jesuits, Bérulle did not much approve of this sort of union between convents, and what is more, he understood the problems that could arise from the tense political situation between France and Lorraine. One such was the deadlock now affecting the Benedictine reforms – the Congregation of Saint-Vanne encompassed the convents of Lorraine while Saint-Maur gathered those of France. Too sensible to send Alix and her sisters down such a road, Bérulle advised against the union. But in Nancy the primate took fright. Fearing he would see the Congregation of Our Lady vanishing in favour of the Ursulines in Paris, he recalled Alix and Angélique to Lorraine.

The return to Nancy

Back in the capital of the duchy, Alix found Monseigneur de Lenoncourt urgently wanting to build 'his' convent, while the sisters were waiting hopefully for a second bull to correct the first. At last it came, dated 6 October 1616, and offered more disappointment. The extra conditions obtained were ringed about with restrictions. Yes, boarding pupils could be taught, but the instruction of day pupils was only allowed provisionally, at the pleasure of the Holy See. More depressing still was the fact that this bull, like the first, only concerned the house in Nancy. Only there was teaching authorised, on the grounds of the approbation of this convent. There might be objections – and Rome would not fail to provide them – asserting that the other convents, approved too like that in Nancy, could not legally take advantage of this authorisation. It would have been better if the primate had broadened his interest to include the whole congregation and not simply the convent in Nancy.

Alix returned to Nancy at the end of May or early in June 1615, but not with an easy mind. She describes this simply in her *Relation*:

> When I had the message from Verdun telling me to go back to Nancy, I found it very difficult to make that decision, because of some chance which put me in fear of temptation. But seeing that I had to go there, I told Our Lord that he would have to take care of me there as I was going there for love of him, and not intending to stay there if he did not grant me this grace. I spent two and a half years there, very peacefully on that score. (*Rel.* 58)

Keeping the same honest intention, Alix did not change her attitude. In Paris she had made it her rule to try to act 'always and only for the love of God'. In Nancy she used the same words 'for love of him' to express her desire to be where God wanted her to be. None the less she did not abandon her intention of leaving Nancy if she was again subjected to exhausting temptations. Straightforwardly familiar, she bargained with the Lord: it was for him to dispense grace and for her to obey. In fact Alix scarcely stirred from Nancy during the rest of her life and encountered fresh temptations there, but the bargain was not broken. Had not the Lord told her, 'When I am with you, that must be enough for you'? (*Rel.* 25)

CHAPTER FOURTEEN

The teaching nuns cloistered

The spiritual foundations

As the spiritual building matters more than the one made of stone, it is important to determine a convent's rules before it is built. Monseigneur de Lenoncourt gave this task to Fourier who, in obedience, settled down to it. If it had not been for the primate's order he might well have postponed undertaking it, saying that it was beyond him. But when he declared that the best rules are those dictated by experience, he was told that this objection was not now valid, as the sisters had been practising the religious life for twenty years. He had plenty of material to work from – the *Provisional Rule* of 1598, the articles approved by the cardinal of Lorraine in 1603, the Rule of St Augustine, comments from the sisters and the observations Alix had brought back from Paris. All he had to do was to codify what had been in practice for so long. By the end of February 1617 he had finished the task.

After a short introduction he makes three demands of the sisters: they are to work 'for the greatest love and glory of God, for their own salvation and perfection, and to give bodily as well as spiritual help to their neighbour'.[172] Then in a dozen short pages, well structured, he develops his great ideas, divided into six sections. The first deals with the instruction of young people, the institute's main purpose. The second contains what relates closely to the glory of God, towards which this instruction must be directed. The third lists the best methods by which nuns can learn to practise their state of perfection. The fourth discusses the help they can give their neighbour. The fifth explains the monastic system of government and the sixth speaks of novices and the qualities needed by those who are admitted to profession.

The historical context explains the importance Fourier attached to the education of the young, especially of the day pupils whom Rome had accepted with reservations. Aware that there could well be legal difficulties ahead, he insisted on the details of enclosure, for instance in the very specific regulations for entering and leaving the classes. Besides this, he tried to recover what had been omitted from the bulls, enshrining in the Rule the fact that there were two sorts of houses, cloistered and not cloistered, and therefore two sorts of nuns, those who were cloistered and made solemn vows, and those who were not and made simple vows, but all of them living the same life and sharing the same work. The teaching vow, the fourth, which would become official in the bull of 1628, is already present here, formulated as article five in part one: 'And in order that this way of teaching young girls, both boarders and day pupils, so necessary, important and fruitful, is not in the course of time lost or neglected in these houses, the nuns when actually making their profession shall solemnly promise God that they will always maintain and continue to his glory the practice of teaching the young'. An Augustinian tone is heard with each mention of the question of unity – that of sisters who form only 'one heart and one soul', the community of goods and the agreement of all in important decisions. Although the sober style of a convent's Rule does not lend itself to flights of mystical prose, Fourier could not restrain his pen and in some passages, later to be developed in his *Constitutions de 1640*, he allowed his own voice to be heard in speaking of spirituality. Superlatives enabled him to reach the highest generosity, tempered by a calming note of humility. 'These nuns', he wrote, 'will try to apply there [in teaching the young] the main part of their studies, and will do this with the most care, diligence and faithfulness possible, and under the best observances and methods which they can find'. The same enthusiasm is found in the prayer 'to be instruments more appropriate and capable, so that they can better, more efficaciously and with more success serve God in this pious exercise [teaching the young], they will endeavour', he wrote, 'to praise and glorify his holy Majesty'. When he mentions obedience to the Superior, who holds 'the place of God here', he recommends that this be done 'with spiritual cheerfulness', another dominant theme in his spirituality.

The voice of Alix, who was always in search of the greatest perfection, is clearly heard in this text which she and Fourier worked on together. Here and there a feminine note comes through, as for instance in the choice of material for the sisters' habits. They must 'never use silk, lace, velvet, cambric, nor starch or any other ornament or daintiness repugnant to poverty'. In another place it is the episode of the confessor who was 'too free and too familiar' which comes to mind as we read that there must be care taken 'that no familiarity or excessive affection should be engendered or nourished between one [of the confessors] and another [of the nuns]'. So evident was Alix's hand in the text that she was invited to accompany Fourier on his visit to the bishop of Toul to request his approval. The text had already been checked by the primate and four Jesuits. But Monseigneur de Maillane asked Alix for her opinion on various points and showed interest in the religious habit in which she had dressed the doll she brought him. On 6 March 1617 the prelate approved the text, to be known in future as the *Rule of 1617* or the *Little Constitutions of 1617*, to distinguish them from those of 1640, known as the *Great Constitutions*. These are fuller and more complete than the earlier text but inspired by

the same spirit. Fourier returned to Nancy from Toul, exclaiming
to anyone who would listen, '*Benedictus Deus! Benedictus Deus!*
As for the sisters, they sang out their gratitude to God in a
fervent *Te Deum.*

Nancy, the first cloistered convent

The prediction was fulfilled: on the land Alix had pointed
out to Claude Chauvenel in 1603 rose the convent buildings.
Primate de Lenoncourt, in command of the work, had had it
started before the authorisation was granted and before the
sisters had sold the Cloister of Our Lady. On 4 July 1616
Mauléon de la Bastide, official of Toul, went to check that the
assurances given in the 1615 bull were kept: the building site
purchased for 1,000 crowns and the endowment guaranteed by
Lenoncourt with a sum of 14,000 francs bringing in an annual
and perpetual income of 1,000 *livres*. The primate even undertook to pay this capital out 'day by day' so that the sisters would
be able to pay the contractors without delay. But in spite of his
generosity, as Hélène Derréal observes, the erection of the first
convent was still a burden.

It was placed in a magnificent setting in the ever more
splendid New Town. The great gates of St Nicolas and St
George stood at the ends of the straight highways which defined
the town. Protected as it was by its network of bastions and
ramparts, many religious had come to settle on the wide terrain,
Minims in 1613 and then Jesuits in 1615, ready to welcome
250 students to their new college. But the area richest in
ecclesiastics was that of the primatial church in the east of the
New Town. The large church dreamt of by Duke Charles III
did not yet exist, except as drawings, but a temporary, a
provisional primatial church stood close to the future site.[173]
The primate already had a fine palace there, surrounded by

houses where his dean and canons lived. Not far away rose the new hospital of St Julian and the Grey Sisters' convent. Between the hospital and the ramparts lay a considerable stretch of ground, not yet allocated. There had been a suggestion that the Jesuit college should go there, but the primate decided that this would be the ideal location to put the convent of the Congregation. The sisters, protected from the bustle of the town by the hospital buildings and only separated from the fields and meadows by one single rampart, should have their protector himself next door.

The primate now thought about nothing but getting the buildings finished. He haunted the area and went to and fro among the workmen to encourage them. Alix too kept a close eye on the works which were to meet the demands imposed by the Church on teaching and cloistered nuns. The enclosing wall bordered a new street, Congregation Street, crossed St George Street and turned off at St Julian Street. Inside the precincts were separate buildings – the chapel, the convent itself where the sisters lived, the boarders' house and classes for day-pupils, all these linked by gardens, a cloister, a cemetery and a vegetable garden. The whole work was going well and Alix approved of the well built, solid constructions, free from useless decoration. She made sure that each worker was paid and when at the end of a week the cash box looked empty, she prayed to God with such fervour that they never ran short of money.[174]

Her encounters on the way to the New Town include episodes which reveal her holiness. When for instance she came out of the Our Lady's Cloister, there was a man there who watched her offensively and used to follow her. He was one of those who spread the ridiculous story about the baby abandoned at the cloister door. One day a lady to whom he had passed on this vile accusation went to Alix and begged her to have the calumny silenced. The response she had from Alix was simply, 'Ah Madame, if God abandoned me, I would do much worse'. Unscathed, this malicious individual now hounded Alix, so much so that Angélique asked her, 'Do you know that man who is walking after us?' 'Only by name', came the answer. 'He is a bad man. I pray for him every day'. And then it happened that he fell ill with a fatal disease and Alix's prayers were granted, for he repented and made a good end.[175] Another chance meeting bears witness to her holy intuitions. One day, happening to see the wife of the duke's chief secretary and her two daughters, elegant and rather snobbish girls, she said to Angélique, 'One of those will become a nun with us'. Five or six years later the elder girl entered the noviciate.

Meanwhile in Nancy building went ahead fast and furious so as to get the work done quickly; in fifteen months' time it was finished. The same activity was buzzing in Saint Mihiel where there was nothing to prevent enclosure. Gante André, the Superior, was at work there with her usual energy, moving 'stones, heaven and earth'. She had received an unexpected legacy which enabled her to transform the house into a regular convent, and as well as this she had the support of the bishop of Verdun, Monseigneur Charles de Lorraine-Chaligny. Fourier was sure this enterprise would succeed. 'But', he wrote to the sisters at Châlons on 14 June 1616, 'the primate is against it, he is determined to have his [convent] at Nancy established first'. In fact this wish to be first masks a more ambitious desire, to make the Nancy convent the principal one, where from the very start all the sisters should take the habit, make their profession and remain there throughout the period of their noviciate. Fourier, faithful to his principle of making no decision without consulting the sisters, put these questions to the vote. Gante was against the common investiture, because the sisters at Pont-à-Mousson, Saint-Nicolas, Verdun and Mattaincourt were unable to take the habit as their houses could not quickly be enclosed. She also felt strongly about the delay imposed on the enclosing of her own convent, although it was the oldest. But for the sake of peace she gave in and went to Nancy with two of the novices from Saint-Mihiel. In the same way Isabeau de Louvroir was accompanied by two sisters from Châlons, but after the ceremony they all returned to their own communities. Including the seven from Nancy, only recently settled in their new homes, there were thirteen who took the habit on 21 November 1617. Fourier had taught them about the virtues of religious life. Now, he told them, the time is come to put in practice your earliest wish, 'to do all you can that is most holy and most perfect for the glory and service of God'.[176]

The event was splendidly celebrated in the collegiate church of St George where there were such crowds that people flocking to the entrances could not get in. After celebrating mass, the primate gave each of the sisters her religious habit, but the chronicle records that it was Fourier who placed the veil and crown on the head of Gante, a gesture which some historians saw as a sign of preference. The words of the ceremonial resonated deep in Alix's heart, and she could in all sincerity sing, 'I have despised the pomp and glory of the world for the love of my Lord Jesus Christ whom mine eyes have seen, to whom I have given my love, my faith and my tenderness'.[177] She chose the name Teresa of Jesus as her name in religion, making clear her desire to follow the Spanish saint along the mystical path that led to Christ. The ceremony done, the primate led the procession which guided the sisters to their new convent and with his own hands shut the gates which cloistered them and promised excommunication to any who should break that law.

Disputes about unity

The common ceremony of investiture was done, but the problem of uniting the convents remained a burning one. Brains were racked to find a solution, but discussions about means of reaching agreement can too easily bring disagreement.

The actors in the drama shaped the development. Gante led the opposition. For the sake of peace she went to Nancy to take the habit, but she refused to stay there for noviciate and profession. With perhaps too much courage she acted as she had done before when obtaining for Fourier the jurisdiction questioned by the priest of Saint-Mihiel, and placed the matter before the bishop of Verdun. He agreed with her, no one would go to Nancy, and he enclosed her convent on 4 March 1618. In the same way Isabeau de Louvroir returned to Châlons, where Monseigneur Cosme Clausse established enclosure. During this time the primate Lenoncourt was working in the duchy's capital to provide the Congregation with a centralised structure. The idea of a mother house is not in itself one to reject out of hand, and that of a general noviciate appealed to Alix. As for the Visitor, his role as a federator was useful and after Fourier's creation of the Canons of Our Saviour, he was to give this task to one of them. But all these projects were undermined at the start, for it became more and more clear that Lenoncourt was organising the centralisation of the house in favour of Nancy. Gante had seen this and told Fourier of her suspicions. He, prisoner of his habits, could only ask for immediate prayers and leave the decisions to the sisters. The victory here belonged to Gante, for Alix, Superior at Nancy, could not easily stand up to the primate, and in any case she did not like confrontations. From 1618 onwards Fourier was named 'visitor', a title which in no way changed his role of founder. As he had in the past, he visited the sisters, preparing those of Verdun to accept enclosure on 20 September 1620 and encouraging those of Pont-à-Mousson to be patient until 1623. The canonical approbation of the Nancy convent gave the communities fresh impetus. New foundations came fast, Bar-le-Duc in 1618, Mirecourt in 1619, Epinal in 1620, Dieuze and Châtel-sur-Moselle in 1621, Metz and La Mothe in 1623. Monastic life seemed so attractive that the two sisters at Mattaincourt wanted to join 'a closed house' or establish a convent in the village, but Fourier saw 'very little hope' for this. 'They would need', he wrote on 11 September 1621, ' to buy premises, which are as dear and dearer than in a really large town, to build, rent, find girls, confessors, and so much else which is not easy in a village'.[178] Meanwhile progress was being made in France: Soissons in 1621, Vitry-le-François in 1623, Laon and Sainte-Menehould in 1626, and Troyes not until 1628.

The increasing number of convents made it the more imperative that they should be united and duly instituted. Fourier was asked to work on this in Nancy with the Jesuit Fathers, but in spite of his admiration for them, his situation was not easy. How could he tell them that 'the Daughters of the other houses seem suspicious of everything which is to be written there'? Ought he to admit that they suspected the primate or one Daughter or just two (does he mean Alix and Angélique?) of contributing 'to the resolutions which are being formed in the said place'? (*C.* 1, 229) In collaboration with Father Tiphaine, rector of the college at Pont-à-Mousson, he worked out a plan which he submitted to Gante on 6 September 1620: 'There would be', he wrote, 'one Mother Administrator over the whole Congregation, to remain in charge for three years only, and to be chosen from each of the convents in turn'. 'One cannot shift the primacy from house to house, diocese to

diocese, in a mechanical game of precedence, without election',
as an historian truthfully pointed out.[179]

The pressures on Fourier became stronger. As he was slow
in drawing up the rules for office-bearers and the monastic
customs which were needed to complete the *Constitutions de
1617*, the primate gave this task to Father Guéret and asserted
that he was compelling the founder to accept the minor role of
humble assistant. Fourier felt that he was repudiated by some
among the sisters 'who did not want to see this done in Nancy'
(*C. 1, 247*). Nevertheless he obeyed, and when the text was
finished and checked he gave it to Gante, telling her to send it
to the sisters to obtain their comments. But this came to
nothing, owing no doubt to the lack of enthusiasm on the part
of both Gante and the sisters.

A few months later Gante is again seen centre stage. The
Jesuits, friends of Lenoncourt, were steering girls with vocations
towards Nancy, including among others a Mademoiselle
Gervaise whom Father Fagot sent to that house rather than to
the one in Saint-Mihiel, although this town was her home.
Fourier, an impartial judge, looked into the affair and found the
sub-text. Certainly he attached great importance to confession,
but he insisted that it should be free of all constraints. But
Gante had systematically excluded Jesuit confessors from her
convent, especially Father Fagot. In a letter of 6 March 1621 he
openly reproached her for this and told her of three ways in
which she could put the matter right.

Incidents like this invite us to consider the increasing importance of Gante in these years when Alix did not intervene.
We recall the occasion when Alix in a fit of annoyance told
Fourier that his ministry in Mattaincourt gave him quite
enough to do and his daughters would have recourse to others,
not to him. At these words the indignant Gante came close to

fainting, and Fourier promised that he would never abandon the Congregation. And Bedel concluded, 'On this chance event [Fourier] based the proposition that without Gante, there would be no Congregation. And in fact, attaching themselves in this way to different directors, one black, another grey,[180] [the sisters] would have chosen minds of all colours and would never have been able to meet together in that unity which was essential for the creation of a body which could endure in future centuries. And thus the Congregation was lost and dispersed'.[181] This conclusion is certainly exaggerated but takes on a new interest in the context of Lenoncourt's stranglehold on the Nancy convent. By resisting all interference from the primate, Gante stirred up ill feeling and rendered impossible the forms of centralisation which Rome might not have accepted, but she blocked the external influences, even from the Jesuits, which could have altered the original spirit of the congregation. At that period the power of the churchmen who directed these houses was such that they could quite naturally take command of them. In this way Father Lebrun was inclined to make the convent in Verdun a thing of his own, even during Fourier's lifetime, and once Fourier was dead it was Lebrun who drew up the Rules, the first to be approved by Pope Urban VIII, in 1643.[182] We can understand that when Nicolas Itam, protector of Châlons, died in October 1618 Fourier checked Isabeau's urgent attempts to find a successor. We can forgive Edmond Renard for attributing to the founder such thoughts as, 'What mind can have conceived the idea of this parasite? It is quite enough to have a protector in Nancy without providing them everywhere'. [183] Not until 1640, the year of his death, was Fourier able to produce the definitive Constitution for his congregation. But by then political circumstances – war and exile – did not allow him to gather opinions from all the sisters and several convents refused to acknowledge the text as his. This time it was Nancy that led the opposition. Unable to establish union between all the convents, owing to the dependent situation of one of them, he would insist on the interdependence between all the sisters created by 'the holy bond of charity'.[184]

Isabeau de Louvroir, just as enterprising as Gante but more tactful, strove to promote understanding in these years after the debates about union. When Fourier visited Châlons she discussed with him a plan for a seminary for poor girls. Young girls, drawn to the religious life but unable to provide a dowry, would be trained as teachers in a kind of college to be paid for by the communities. Once trained, they would be sent to this or that convent or unenclosed house. But the plan was dead in the water, as on the one hand the sisters opposed the very idea of a common seminary, no one but themselves should receive and train their novices, and on the other when Fourier examined the idea, he saw insurmountable material difficulties (*C.* 1, 240). Isabeau did not give up and produced an alternative. She founded the *Establishment of Secular Daughters of Châlons*, for which Fourier provided rules which clearly show how original a creation this was.[185] She set up an association which offered all the advantages of a club for former pupils, of a group seeking a spiritual life, and of a movement for Catholic action. The initiative spread from Châlons to other convents and developed into a company of young women, associates of the sisters, taught and trained by them so as to extend their activity to areas where enclosure now forbade them to go themselves. One such woman was St Marguerite Bourgeoys (1620–1700), who before she took ship for Nouvelle France belonged to an external congregation attached to the convent of Troyes.[186] In establishing the earliest school in the new colony of Ville-Marie and in founding the Congrégation de Notre-Dame de

Montréal, she bore witness to the fact that Pierre Fourier's work, thanks to its remarkable adaptability, could travel far beyond the walls of a cloister.

Although Alix left no indication of her ideas as to how union between convents was to be established, it seems likely that she would have approved the setting up of a general ruling body. She glimpsed such a solution, claims Hélène Derréal, 'with all the spontaneity of her woman's intuition, more apt to bypass problems than to consider them'.[187] Pierre Fourier saw the problem from a legal point of view, aware of difficulties. A centralised system of command exactly suited Monseigneur de Lenoncourt; the headquarters would be in Nancy and Alix at the helm. She, seeing that the primate was exceeding his powers and ignoring the wishes of the founder and the unanimous agreement of the sisters required by the Constitution, kept quiet and allowed events to overtake plans. In this way she avoided schism without any hardening of positions. She did her best to keep the Nancy sisters and those of the other communities 'in perfect unity and understanding between each other, using, helping and communicating their affairs by letters and other means, as if they had all come from the same house'.[188] This remark by Angélique Milly, the probable author of the 1666 biography, tells us, perhaps with a touch of nostalgia, that the general noviciate had failed, but also that the 'good harmony' of minds would not be lost.[189] The German-speaking federation was constituted in 1961, and in 1963 joined to form a single body with the Union of Jupille-sur-Meuse and the Roman Union.

At the service of the Congregation

On 1 May 1620 Alix accompanied by Claude Chauvenel went to Saint-Nicolas to accomplish a double task. The convent was to be cloistered two days later and the eleven novices taking the

habit wanted Alix to be there as a living model at the start of
their life in religion, and Fourier was counting on her to settle
Claude Chauvenel in her new post as Superior, replacing Jeanne
de Louvroir. Rightly or wrongly the Saint-Nicolas sisters had
asked for this change, against the will of the founder, who
exclaimed, 'God send that all goes well!' In fact all went badly,
as the new Superior did not have the gift of governance. Alix fell
ill and spent the three months of her stay in the infirmary. 'I am
very ill here', she wrote to the sisters at Mirecourt on 4 June.[190]
Fever ravaged her, temptations tormented her, and she turned
as she always did to Mary who in answer to her prayer came
with the Child Jesus to visit her. She does not mention this
vision in the *Relation*. The account is one of the contributions
gathered for the first biography of the foundress, for it was she
who, breaking her usual reticence, told one of the sisters what
had happened.

Speaking one day to one of the nuns, about the trust one
must have when invoking the help of Our Lady, she told her
that in 1620 when she was at Saint-Nicolas for its cloistering,
she fell ill with a very violent unremitting fever, and that when
she was in the extremity of this distress it pleased God to afflict
her still further with her ordinary temptations, but to such a
point that she could no longer think what she should do.
Immediately she remembered that she could turn to her dear
protector, the holy Mother of God, praying and imploring her
with all the strength and affection of her heart to help her in
this extreme and urgent need. At that very moment the mother
of consolation appeared to her in the infirmary, close to her
bed. She was as if in a cloud, in wonderful majesty, shining with
light and her robe all full of stars brighter than the sun. She was
holding the Child Jesus in her arms, and coming close to the
sick woman she said to her, 'My daughter, be comforted. I

bring you my dear Son to assure you that he has granted the prayer I made him for you'. And holding towards her her divine Child's feet, she made her kiss them. Then with this vision gone, the Mother was completely freed from this temptation and was not made anxious by it any more during this illness.[191]

Even though Alix did not write this passage, we can be sure that it reports the event faithfully, so closely does it echo her style. She would perhaps have been less wordy, although the phrases do in fact reinforce the tragedy of the situation. Struck down by pain and anguish she addresses herself to Mary, 'Mother of consolation', who with motherly tenderness and a nurse's care comes to the sick woman's bedside, a closeness mentioned twice, and brings her the remedy. Now the tone changes and a liturgical celebration begins. Mary appeared in a cloud, not in the rack of clouds in which painters set celestial beings to show that they have left the earth, but like the Christ transfigured in a cloud, a sign of the presence of God. Clad in the sun, her robe bright with stars, she appeared to Alix like the woman John described in the Apocalypse, 'a great sign appeared in heaven' (Rev. 12:1). She was also the figure of the Church which in her sufferings engenders the Christ in the faithful. All-powerful mediatrix, she did not merely transmit Alix's prayer to her Son but added her own to it and as a reply brought to her the Child himself. The queen of 'wonderful majesty' is now no more than a tender mother with a baby in her arms. But this baby is God the Saviour. Alix believes in the saving power which Mary passes to her in holding the Child out to her. With the passionate love of the woman who kissed Christ's feet at dinner in the house of Simon, with the reverence of devotees kissing the feet of statues, Alix pledges allegiance to her Lord who frees her 'completely' from the assault of the devil.

This vision more than any of the others, often similar in

many respects, shows the depth of Alix's mysticism. Well accustomed to meditating on the mystery of the Incarnation, she gave proof here of great accuracy in theology, perceiving without sentimental familiarity and in an exact scriptural context the ambivalences – the woman Mary, Mother of God, and Jesus, God who became a child.

When Alix returned to Nancy, Fourier did not have the heart to send her back to put things right at Saint-Nicolas, where matters did not improve. Confined to her convent by ill health, she could no longer rush off to restore order and energy where they were lacking. None the less we know that until the last months of her life she was working in the service of the Congregation. Now it was the house at Epinal that needed to be rescued, because Fourier had put her in charge of it from the start. It began like this – in 1619 the primate had seized the chance of establishing a convent dependent on the one in Nancy, and had demanded that Fourier should go to Epinal to sign for the purchase of a house which was 'very small and inconvenient'. The founder did as he was told, although afraid that the sisters of the other houses would find 'strange and ill to digest' a plan of which they had been told nothing. He had made just one condition, told to Alix in a letter of 29 October, 'Your house will have to be responsible for supplying 'everything needed' by the Nancy sisters who have been sent to Epinal, 'who will find themselves in difficulties for some time'. Needs were not slow in appearing, and the trouble all fell upon Alix – sisters badly housed, lack of income, a Superior who ought to be replaced . . . Fourier, fully occupied in his parish and immobilised by a serious leg injury, did not say a word. In any case, why should he worry? He had every confidence in Alix. She tactfully let the primate know of the lamentable state of his foundation. Off he went to Epinal, bought a building site and had a convent built. Gifts flowed in, and so did postulants. By what prayers, by what sacrifices did Alix obtain these miracles? By the time the house at Epinal, now prospering, was enclosed on 9 October 1622, Alix had left this world.

At the same time as she was busy with the affairs of Epinal, Alix was working to open a house at Dieuze. Neither she nor Fourier had chosen this. It was the wish of the De la Ruelle family, who offered a building together with such guarantees that no one dreamt of refusing it. The act of foundation, dated 22 May 1621 was signed by Mother Alix Le Clerc, 'Superior of the first Monastery of the Congregation, established in New Nancy, Mother Angélique Milly, her assistant, and the whole community, before the gates of New Nancy'. A few weeks later it was Fourier's turn to go to Dieuze to buy, at the time of curfew, a second house 'attached to that which Madame de la Ruelle gave to the sisters'.[192] Alix, thinking she should compensate Fourier for his travelling expenses, slipped two gold pieces into her letter, and had in reply a letter in which irony does not quite conceal a touch of irritation:

> You call me 'poor' – if you called me 'stupid' I should bear it better, for our good father St Augustine in his sermon 8 *de Verbis Domini* commands me strictly and narrowly so to call myself both before God and before men. If it were 'fool' I would still bear it, the great king David certainly takes this name in Psalm 72. But 'poor'! with two great pieces of gold to tempt me, that I cannot endure. This is why I send them back to you and complain loud and strongly and demand reparation of this wrong by some *Ave Maria* which you will say for our parishioners who certainly need it. At Mattaincourt, 5 August 1621.

He adds this postscript, apparently regretting his sharp tone:

'I praise Our Lord for the excellent letter from Monsieur le Primat. And I thank you very humbly for those two handsome gold pieces. Although I cannot use them at present, thank God, and send them back to you. But I am grateful to you, and have greater things to ask of you'.

What were these 'greater things' he asks of Alix? We do not know, but it is important to notice how the founder and foundress work together 'with a good will and for the love of God' (*C.* 1, 359). Here is one more example: there was a house for sale in the Old Town and the Nancy sisters 'have taken it into their heads to buy it', wrote Fourier on 29 July 1621. The business was tempting, for since the sale of Our Lady's Cloister the children of the heavily populated area of Saint-Evre had no school. Fourier put forward sensible objections and, without forbidding the purchase, only asked for prayers. Relying on 'heaven's great help', Alix made the bargain and bought it, established an 'open house' and in charge of it put two secular sisters. In this way she hoped to deal with the inconvenience of enclosure and to create a day school for working class children. Subsequent events demonstrate the good sense of her plan, whose only fault was to be ahead of its time with regard to people's attitudes and to canon law. In 1622 the two sisters in charge asked permission to enter a convent, threatening to leave the house empty and unpaid for. Fourier now championed Alix's idea. He tried to stop the sisters leaving their school, not hesitating to postpone their solemn vows. When it came to selling the building for lack of money to pay the dues, he wrote to the sisters at Saint-Mihiel, '[...] it seems that we do not trust Providence, very rich, very wise and very powerful [...] and then this would ruin one of the finest, most fruitful and most flourishing schools in your Congregation in the first town in the land' (*C.* 2, 31). He even picked up Alix's bold suggestion that they should put into temporary 'residence' some professed nuns from Nancy to keep school. Before seeking support from church authorities, Fourier had made sure in August 1626 that he had the approval of Duke Charles IV.

Saint-Nicolas, Epinal, Dieuze, Nancy – every one of these is a clear example of the way the founder and foundress worked together. We must be careful not to set them in opposition to each other. To those who claim that they did not get on well, we can say that the facts prove them wrong. During the years, even the months, before Alix died they shared roles, shared anxieties, competed with each other in praying that God would enlighten their decisions. Their disagreements, visible but always temporary, arose from the difference in their temperaments, as Alix, with her accurate intuition and more venturesome trust in God, would always be a step ahead of Fourier's prudent calculations. Both found that they rejoiced together in the fact that 'all things work together for good for those that love God'.

CHAPTER FIFTEEN

Mother Teresa of Jesus

'Pray God that I may please him'

Alix might have borrowed from Teresa of Avila and called her *Relation*, the *Book of the Mercies of God*, but more concisely she avoided digressions, and said as much to Father Guéret: 'I should have much to say if I wanted to talk at length all that divine Providence sends upon us, but this not being necessary for what I intend, I only pray to your Reverence, as I often do to Our Lord, to pray to him that I may please him, and that, knowing his ways and deep judgments, he may spare neither the green nor the dry[193] in sending evils and afflictions upon me' (*Rel.* 51). In rather complex terms Alix explained what she intended: she would not emphasise the favours God had granted the Congregation, she would only speak of the 'infinite mercy and kind goodness of God towards her' (*Rel.* 51). Only one thing mattered to her: to please her Lord, and to this end to allow him to use whatever means he thought best and so to accept as coming from him the 'evils and afflictions' he would heap upon her. Realising the boldness of her prayer, she added humbly, 'I tremble in saying this, for my untamed nature dreads them marvellously, but I hope, if it shall please him to give me opportunities, that he will give me the grace to bear them with patience, provided I can obtain from him one last mercy, to praise him for ever; this is my one ambition' (*Rel.* 51). Her thirst for suffering was based on her trust in divine grace which would grant her the supreme favour of praising God for ever in the heavenly Jerusalem.

This passage, occurring in the final pages of the *Relation*, marks a pause in the record and inverts the timing. Abandoning memories of the past, Alix turns to a future which she intends to live generously, inspired only by her wish to please God, however hard may be the tests he will send her. If we accept that these lines were written in 1618, the final years towards which she looked would indeed contain a rich measure of 'evils and afflictions'. Some of the saddest were, as we have seen, the disputes over union of the convents. She was unhappy about the 'disagreements' between the sisters which uncompromisingly drove her into the Lenoncourt camp, where she was far from comfortable. She and Fourier had the same problem: one cannot openly oppose the primate. Obedience, which ought to lead her along a path of peace, placed her between diverging authorities, that of the founder, her beloved and loving spiritual father, that of the convent's protector, Lenoncourt, powerful and ambitious, and that of Father Guéret, her confessor, her last court of appeal.

Her health was seriously damaged. She was so ill during the convent's building that doctors gave up hope, but she told Angélique Milly, who was already weeping for her death, 'Don't worry. I shall live another four years in the new convent'. For her companions too the noviciate had not begun well. Settled too soon into newly built premises, they fell ill. All of them, however, strove heroically to prepare for their perpetual profession which was to take place on 2 December 1618, the first Sunday of Advent and the feast of St Francis Xavier.[194] Both the primate and the bishop of Toul being absent, it was Fourier who received their vows. Among the eight women making their profession were Alix and Claude Chauvenel. Gante André and Isabeau de Louvroir attended as guests, so that the four first founding sisters were present together, and their founder gave them the *Constitutions de 1617* which confirmed for centuries to come the union of all the convents, in spite of the apparent rupture. On 8 December 1618 Alix was unanimously elected to be the Superior of the house in Nancy, and from then on was known as Mother Teresa of Jesus.

Alix herself allows us to follow events of her inner life after her move to the new house on 11 November 1617, as she for once mentions periods of time. She wrote: 'A week after our entry into this convent, temptations began again and troubled me for ten whole months with very little respite', adding for Father Guéret, 'as I have told you and I dread even thinking of this again' (*Rel.* 58). As this memory was so painful for her, it is tempting to think it cruel of Father Guéret to require it. But the consequence shows his good sense, for it was in the depths of her dereliction that Blessed Alix received her greatest mystical grace. She acknowledged her wretchedness and the Lord heaped his mercy upon her. As for the prince of darkness, he worked in the shadows. One night when Alix had struggled till two in the morning with his dreadful temptations, she at last fell asleep, after begging Our Lady 'for a bit of a truce' (*Rel.* 9). When the bell rang at four o'clock to wake them all, she opened her eyes. 'One could see clearly', she wrote. 'I saw the Virgin present in the middle of the room. I called out to her, "Our beloved Mother and Mistress!" I was very sorry afterwards, as she immediately vanished. And I felt in my soul a new confidence in her, and am sure she got me the tranquillity I have had since her Nativity'. As she had done on 8 September 1609 at Mattaincourt, Mary on that same feast day in 1618 delivered Alix from the temptations which had tormented her during the first ten months of her noviciate in Nancy. But the knowledge that she was soon to make her solemn vows plunged her into fresh anxieties, which she described, at once adding, 'Being in my room the same day very sad and in difficulty about making profession, it seemed to me that having doubled the vow of chastity I had already made, this being solemn, the sin would be greater, and seeing myself so wretched on every side I did not dare hope for sufficient grace of God as not to offend him'. In a slightly tangled style she here sets out her case of conscience – will she have strong enough grace to resist a more serious fault? Her Jesuit confessor must have taught her to distinguish between sufficient and efficacious grace, but she did not push the subtle casuistry much further as her thinking was suddenly broken into by the presence of God:

> As I was in these troubles my spirit was suddenly withdrawn and I was rebuked for the little trust I had, with the certainty of Our Lord's grace. I found I was shedding sweet tears, a thing unusual with me for any reason at all, unless it is in a similar encounter which I suppose to be from God to support my weakness, thus making me feel the marks of his very great mercy. (*Rel.* 60)

Alix considered that doubting God's grace deserved a rebuke, one given so kindly that tears sprang from her eyes. Like those children who expect to be scolded but find in their parents' arms that the worse the offence, the more they are loved, so Alix was moved by God's goodness towards her. Though she acknowledged that such tears were unusual, she let it be known that a 'similar encounter' did 'sometimes' occur. Without realising that she had already said a good deal about this, she emphasised the frequency of these divine visitations. 'For', she continued, 'these withdrawals that happen, most often numbing all my external senses, always leave my memory filled and my will enkindled with the love of God, with a great longing that he should always accomplish his holy purposes in me'. She describes here in a few lines the mystic experience which Teresa of Avila expounds more fully in the Fifth Mansions of the *Interior Castle*. Employing unusual means, God granted her a mystical gift of grace, taking, as the Spanish Carmelite expressed it, 'a shortened path'. God's possession of her soul was accompanied by a numbing of her outward perceptions which Teresa of Avila noted as follows: 'All our outward powers are put to sleep, deeply asleep even, with regard to all things of the world'.[195] Although Alix in her humility did not assert that this encounter was 'from God' and was content merely to 'suppose' it, she was made sure of his visitation by the change it effected in herself.[196] Wholly invaded by God, she surrendered herself to his good will. She had taken the first steps along the mystical path and had now reached the union of the will. The Lord had spoken to her and his words were set fast in her memory. Like the disciples on the road to Emmaus, her heart burnt within her as she listened. Now, eager to prove her love, she gave herself to his 'holy purposes' for her.

Thinking back over the characteristics these withdrawals had in common, Alix mentioned the times when they occurred. 'They do not stop coming to me during my great temptations, not in the renewed feelings of rebellion of the flesh but after my soul has been much humiliated and most often also in considering the infinite merits of the holy life and passion of my Lord, which I would wish to be continually in my memory' (*Rel.* 60).

The correspondence in time which Alix establishes between the temptations and the mystical grace enables us to see how completely free from any unhealthy 'admixture' was her experience. 'A singular gift of spiritual health springs literally from a text like hers where all the evidence shows that there is no attempt at rhetoric, but rather a reflection of the light of a pure look which focuses wholly on God in his ways, sometimes so disconcerting'.[197]

God took the initiative in invading Alix's soul; she in reciprocal love welcomed his visitations. The holy Scriptures provided her with a simple path to such meetings. Trained to meditate on the life and passion of her Saviour, she knew that the purpose of every word and act of the Christ was to save those to whom they were addressed. She also knew that even though his human deeds took place once and once only, they were still eternally acts of God and possessed a healing strength which made them 'salutary', that is to say, 'causes of grace'. Therefore she wanted to hold them constantly in her mind so as to benefit from them. Influenced by the spirituality of Bérulle, she saw them, 'not as things past and lifeless but as things alive and actual, even eternal, from which we can gather present and eternal fruit'.[198]

Alix might have ended her *Relation* with these mystical encounters with Christ which left her 'burning for divine love', but she did not wish to omit any part of her inner life, so added one more episode, the most recent, she said, before she gave the manuscript to Father Guéret. Here it is:

> The last time I was most agitated by these temptations was when one evening, going into my room, with my mind quite at peace, no trouble or anxiety, I seemed to see a dark phantom in a corner where I normally took the discipline. I doubted whether I should take it or not; nonetheless I decided to take it in order to subdue my imagination. Suddenly I felt such strong temptations that I did not know where I was with this; and they continued at me all night. (*Rel.* 61)

Did Alix include this paragraph to offset the mystical gifts of grace she had just described? In any case the passage is in no way a repetition and includes interesting elements. It is written with her normal command of narrative according to the rules – introduction, peripeteia, resolution – and with her accurate choice of words, worthy of the classical writers of that century. To each of her faculties she attributes the emotion that stirred her – 'I doubted' relates to her intelligence, 'I decided' to her will, and 'I felt' to her sensibility. Such lucid inner vision during an experience so extraordinary as the sight of a dark phantom calls us to affirm that her mind was perfectly normal, but that external causes were at work, disturbing her imagination to such an extent that it forced on her, although awake, the images we normally see in nightmares. And naturally the demon seized his advantage and made a sudden attack. In trying to convince Alix that her thirst for penance was useless, he sought to pervert her behaviour and make of it an occasion of sin. Thoroughly discomforted, Alix was flung into a no man's land without signposts. 'I did not know where I was with this', she wrote, but we can be sure she was valiant enough to hold the devil at bay all night long.

Her inner radiance

It is a remarkable coincidence that we have evidence from Alix's companions to confirm what she herself told us of her inner life. As pictures gain depth when placed one on top of another, so these external comments confirm the traits which the author of the *Relation* took care not to stress, and give us a lively portrait.

She was one of those beings whose presence attracts eyes and hearts. The habit she wore clearly indicated her dedication to God, an identity she embraced wholeheartedly. Tall and fragile, she was an upright figure, with lively movements and expressive features which revealed her vivacious temperament. Nothing was lost of her natural charm, a harmony of opposites, distinction and simplicity, firmness and kindness, gravity and gaiety. Her friendly approach and great evenness of temper made her accessible to all, and although she loved recollection best, she excelled in social contacts because she knew how to talk and how to listen. Here lay the original character of her personality: she was a true mystic through the exceptional gifts of grace God lavished on her, and she fulfilled her vocation as a teacher by passing on to others what she had received.

Alix's comrades wrote a great deal about her union with God, stressing and perhaps exaggerating what seemed to them to be the clearest sign of her holiness. 'The Mother was a daughter of great silence, always in recollection and retreat', they said. 'She was so much engaged with God that one could say her prayer was almost unceasing'. And elsewhere: 'She was so engaged and absorbed with God that she often had to force herself to turn away from him and deal with external duties'. Such concentration has its inconvenient side, as the chronicle does not fail to tell us. One such occurred during the retreat before taking the habit, when one day Alix at two o'clock rang the bell to start the meditation each would do in her own cell, and then sank into prayer and forgot to ring for the end of the exercise, which lasted until compline.[199]

More significant than this anecdote is the witness of those close to her, who perceived the divine presence within her. Her comrades understood this clearly. 'When you saw her or met her', they said, 'you felt something of God, indefinable, and it led you to withdraw into yourself, to think about, adore, and revere the divine Wisdom which was her life and worked so efficaciously in that great soul'. They noticed that this radiance shone more brightly in certain circumstances. 'On the days when she made her communion', they wrote, 'you would see her so attached to and so absorbed in God that she seemed to be animated by a spirit not her own, there was even something indefinable in her face, majestic, divine, which called those who looked at her to recollection'. It needed no more than this for the spiritual prestige of their Superior to take shape in her daughters' eyes in the form of an extraordinary light encircling their mother's brow . . . 'Two of the nuns, reliable women', it was said, 'saw her one day at prayer in the choir surrounded by light as brilliant as the sun'.[200] We are free to correct this portrait of Alix which turns her into a stained glass window saint, imagining for preference her serene look, her gracious smile and her direct gaze. But fortunately the facts are there to bear witness that contemplation and action had their right place in her life.

Her active charity

All day long Mother Teresa of Jesus was busy in her large convent where she freely gave the comfort of her presence. In the morning she attended the opening of the doors, a strategic place where the rules of enclosure had to be strictly observed. She visited the kitchen, making sure that the sisters 'should always have good food, sound, properly and cleanly kept, and above all that the bread should be good and well made'. She was anxious about the diet of the sick, for whom she ordered 'delicate food and some other sweet things according to the illness'. She went to the larder, where one day, drawn towards the turn[201] by the sound of loud voices, she found the convent's bursar (*la soeur procureuse*) arguing vigorously with a village woman who had brought goods to sell. The woman swore she had not been paid; the nun declared that she had given her the money. The Superior tried in vain to calm the village woman and in the end said to the nun, 'Give her what she is asking'. Then she knelt down and begged God to enlighten the thief.

Hardly had the woman turned the street corner when remorse seized her and she came back to return the money, which Alix refused. 'Your repentance is enough for the dear Lord', she said to her. 'Go, and do not start again'.[202]

Mother Teresa of Jesus went every day to the novices' house, where she liked to talk with the mistress of the novices, for example about how they should teach the girls to pray. We must try to make them love it, she advised, by leading them to it, 'gently and sweetly, not forcing their minds'. She recommended simplicity of spirit to the novices, wanting them to be sincere in word and act and that their intention 'should always go straight to God'. She was concerned for the training of future teachers and drew up a programme for this. To the curriculum of subjects taught, Christian doctrine, reading, writing, arithmetic, manual work, she added practical tests, going herself into the classrooms to encourage new teachers, 'showing them in practice the methods needed'. More important than techniques for success, she considered respect for the teaching vocation, requiring the novice mistress 'to instruct [the young sisters] well as to the importance and excellence of this calling, making them understand that they could not do any service more pleasing to God (after the care of their own improvement) than to teach children to know him, to fear, love and serve him, above all striving to keep them innocent through the strong fear of sin they must give them, and the means too by which they can be restored when unhappily they fall into it'.[203]

Alix herself took charge of the sisters' training in liturgy, 'settling them [in the choir] in their places and showing them what they must do'. Her companions tell us that she 'had a very beautiful voice' and that being a musician she could give the novices good singing lessons, teaching them 'to sing with order

and measure, setting the pitch and keeping them steadily to the
task. She often told the choir mistress that she must make sure
that they always sang and chanted the psalms in an even tone,
neither too high nor too low, so that they sang them lightly'.

To these vivid images of Mother Teresa of Jesus teaching the
young sisters we can add a last sketch taken from life. The
scene is played out in the kitchen garden where the day's work
consisted in covering or uncovering asparagus beds. The Mother
Superior, a commanding woman who thoroughly understood
the nature of gardening, handled the manure, took hold of it
and spread it, under the somewhat disgusted gaze of the novices,
to whom she wanted 'to give an example of self control' in this
trivial matter. Stripping caterpillars off cabbages required similar
self-command. Therefore, says the chronicle, 'when she saw
them afraid to touch one, she would pick it up in her fingers to
encourage them to do the same'.

In her relations with the sisters of the community Alix
applied to the letter the principle she had expressed in one of
her writings: 'The Superior will try in her ruling to be more
loved than feared, so that they may all have the confidence to
turn to her as to their kind mother in all their needs and
troubles, spiritual and corporal'. It was no trouble to her to
create these mutually affectionate relationships, and people
were glad to send her the most awkward cases as her sweet
nature and kindness used to transform them. She had the
ability to 'heal religious illnesses', but did not plume herself on
that, for it was, she said, 'a gift from God'. What means did
she use? She revealed at least two, one being discretion, that is
to say discernment, being able to see who it was that needed
help, and as well as that, being herself 'so kind and friendly
that she is not ashamed to open her heart to you'.[204]

In the notebook where Alix described her way of ruling, she

stresses the feelings Superiors must have for the nuns of their community.[205] 'They must excel in charity', she wrote, 'must have for them a more than motherly affection'. Her great tact and long experience as a Superior lead her to list all the forms this affection, this tender affection, she says, must take forms whose names have all but vanished, though perhaps the practice of them has not: sweetness, gentleness, leniency, affability, compassion. When they copied the notes written in Alix's own hand, the sisters at Nancy testified that they had seen their Mother putting into practice the principles she wanted to see in her community. And the chapter they wrote of her virtues, entitled 'Of her charity towards her neighbour',[206] shows that Mother Teresa of Jesus practised what she preached, for it tells us that she helped those around her 'in things temporal and things spiritual, in all the ways her charity led her to invent'. It was indeed an inventive charity, one based on careful attention to other people's needs.

Alix was also very attentive to any who were ill, visiting them frequently, undertaking her share of the most physical necessities and serving them 'dinner, to encourage them to eat'. Nothing repelled her, not even the sister sick with the plague whom the rest were afraid to go near. She wanted, she said, to comfort her in her trouble. If she saw one of the teachers suddenly exhausted, she would take over her class and give her some hours of rest. She knew that 'the trouble inferiors feel in subjection is always heavy, according to nature', even though grace and virtue lighten the burden for them, and she tried to make the practice of obedience 'sweet' to them. She trusted her office-holders and allowed them to fulfil the 'extent of their charges' without interference, except in case of need. She detested particular friendships and never believed reports made by one individual against another but paid attention to the opinions and complaints of each. She did not blame those who failed, said no evil of anyone and lived 'in good understanding and trust' with the older sisters. She had the same friendship for each one and for the community as a whole. Her welcome was famous in the Congregation – when for instance nuns arrived from other houses she welcomed them with warmth and joy. She prepared hot baths with flowers and sweet smelling herbs for travellers and one day when a poor serving woman came back soaking wet and muddy to Nancy from Pont-à-Mousson she washed her feet, giving them a refreshing bath. She was accessible to all, thanks to her even temper and calmness. 'No one ever saw her upset or agitated because of hurry or anxiety, whatever happened to her', says the chronicle. Unchangingly gentle, her constant prayer enabled her to see God in her neighbour. She loved others with the same love she gave God.

CHAPTER SIXTEEN

Writing the 'Relation' [207]

Written to order

After Father Baccarat had observed Alix in a trance in the Cloister of Our Lady, the Jesuit fathers began to wonder about her strange ecstasies. Some suspected her of imposture, others even thought she was possessed. It is not surprising that her director, Father Jean Guéret, better informed than they, asked her to write down everything 'rather unusual' that had happened in her soul. Obediently she began her *Relation*, probably during her noviciate in Nancy (21 November 1617–2 December 1618), a suitable time to review her life in the light of grace received.

Father Guéret at the period was already well known. He had joined the Jesuits when he was twenty, and was teaching in Paris at the Clermont College when in 1594 one of his former students, Jean Châtel, tried to assassinate the king, Henri IV. Unjustly tortured and exiled with other colleagues from the kingdom of France, Guéret arrived in Lorraine in all the glory of a martyr. In 1602 he was appointed rector of the Jesuit noviciate in Nancy and from then on played an important part in the life of the Congregation of Our Lady, acting as an intermediary between the primate Lenoncourt and Pierre Fourier. His position became more and more awkward, as the prelate used the Jesuit in his attempts to oust the founder. In 1621, for example, Guéret was to produce 'declarations' with regard to the Constitution, a piece of work rejected by the sisters.

What was he for Alix in 1618? A guide sent her by Providence. She lived at a time when the ideas of the Council of Trent had become habitual, when 'a personal encounter with God cannot take place except through hierarchical mediation'.[208] Submission to the judgment of confessors and theologians was evidence of submission to the will of God, expressed by the very mouth of his ministers. Alix, aware of the shattering nature of the experiences she was living through, warned Father Guéret that she was writing, 'to be corrected and advised, if she has misunderstood anything, or to be somewhat relieved in certain doubts' (*Rel.* 1). Seen thus, the *Relation* was an act of humility and of faith in the role of the director. It was a call for help, and she expressed it so that he could advise her on a certain point: should she record the 'two or three examples' in which it was clear that her trust in God had obtained miracles? She admitted that she was 'a little mortified to have difficulty in telling them' because while affirming that there was 'nothing but evil' in the affair for herself, she was afraid of letting it appear that she had had any merit in it. It was for Father Guéret to help her out of her 'perplexity', 'so that Your Reverence', she told him, 'may judge it all and advise me about the things I should put in order, the better to please God' (*Rel.* 63). Then follows the description of the three episodes in question (*Rel.* 63, 64, 65), so that we may presume that the director gave her an affirmative answer which she does not mention. This work, the *Relation*, is a dialogue with only one voice. The presence of the silent partner is often felt, as when Alix speaks to him about the Jesuits, saying 'your Reverend Fathers', 'your Company', 'one of your houses', and so on. But the director does not interrupt. We do not know what 'advice' he gave his penitent when she asked for it. Nor do we know what he or any of the other churchmen thought of Alix's text. Father Guéret merely countersigned the manuscript, guaranteeing that he had received it 'written in Alix's own hand'.

Only one thing mattered to her, 'to please God better', and help in achieving this was what she wanted from her director. She 'trembled' to ask Our Lord for 'ills and afflictions' which would let her prove her love for him, but she told Father Guéret very precisely what she wanted of him: 'I pray to Your Reverence, as I often do to Our Lord, to pray that I may please him' (*Rel.* 51). But as she was obedient to the Holy Spirit she did not need to toil up the ladder of human consultation. Thus when she and her comrades held doggedly to their new vocation, in spite of the objections raised by churchmen, she presented her director with a *fait accompli* and spared him the trouble of making a decision: 'What I have said so far', she pointed out to him, 'is in order to make it clear to Your Reverence that this vocation comes from God'. (*Rel.* 17) She is shown in the *Relation* as so intent on discerning the will of God and so swift to perceive it, that we can forget Father Guéret and hear only the voice of Alix talking with her God.

An exercise of the memory

To respond to her director's request, Alix had to look back over the past: 'I shall begin with shame to say what I think I have received from this good Lord to withdraw me from sin and my vanity, everything that I shall recall that was rather unusual for the good of my soul and my vocation' (*Rel.* 1). Yet the *Relation* does not read like an exercise for the memory, one in which she would list, carefully framed in a sort of organised journal, the significant events of her life. Her memory was selective, she would only recall the episodes in which God had shown himself to be, as she put it., 'greatly zealous for my soul' (*Rel.* 1). The chronological order is not followed, but there is no disorder or confusion. She composed her text with easy competence, not because she scorned the rules of rhetoric but because her interest lay elsewhere. In her opening lines she announced the rule she chose: 'To make this declaration as briefly and truthfully as I can, knowing that God who searches our hearts cannot be deceived' (*Rel.* 1). The theological truth, that God knows all, was for her a stylistic principle which she easily reconciled with another, natural to her character and to the literature of her time when classicism was coming to birth: to write as briefly as possible. It was a contradiction she resolved with skill, so that her pen and her memory are never at odds with each other. Here is one of the many examples which prove this: being the chief inspiration for a new religious order, Alix could well have been tempted to describe its development. She avoided this and held firmly to her purpose, that of recording the mercies God had shown her. 'I could say a great deal', she said, 'if I wanted to go into detail about the marks of divine Providence upon us, but this is not necessary for what I intend' (*Rel.* 51). The history of the congregation is perceived through that of Alix herself. In so far as she was part of the original founding project, the two themes are linked. The account of her own first commitment is followed by that of her companions, and where Alix at first spoke of 'my vocation' she now said 'our vocation, our plans, our inclinations'. She mentioned the 'little upsets and dis-agreements' among the sisters because of the effect they had upon her (*Rel.* 57). But her brevity is constant. Thus she notes that 'While sleeping, things that are to happen to me are shown to me, both concerning myself and those that touch our Con-gregation' (*Rel.* 44). But she does not develop the theme, merely noting that premonitions are useful because they enable her to bring these things to Our Lord. She adds, 'They usually happen as I have seen them'.

Having no literary pretensions and being well able to notice any awkwardnesses, she picks up what she has omitted. After narrating events during her stay in Verdun (1613–1615) (*Rel.* 56), she goes back to the years 1606–1607 (*Rel.* 57), and we can see why. The chronological order gives way to the inner truth; she recalls distant memories to prove that in spite of 'disagreements' then as now God protects the Congregation and gives it hope. Another return to the past described her encounter with St Clare and St Elisabeth who revealed her teaching vocation to her (*Rel.* 45). This time-shift is also partly due to the grouping together of episodes which were spread out in time but all relate to an 'inner light', (*Rel.* 42–50).

She was not writing as an historian and did not bother with dates or accurate periods of time – 'Sixteen or seventeen years, nineteen or twenty years, five or six years, six weeks or two months, two or three months earlier . . .', and so on. But she did mark precisely the dates of significant events. The liturgical year and the religious office provided her with shining reference points: feasts of the Blessed Virgin (2 February, 8 September), Easter day, high mass on a Sunday, office of the Hours recited in the choir.

She did not laboriously think back into the past and would link different episodes quite vaguely: 'After that, another time, one day . . . ' But within an episode she excelled at noting the movement of time in a wide range of phrases which expressed suddenness (all of a sudden, at once, immediately, the same instant, at that moment . . .) or frequency (often, very often, most often, sometimes, occasionally, several times . . .), or duration (day and night, a long time, a very long time, some time . . .). This economical usage in the treatment of chronology favoured a psychological time-scale and could even set the episodes outside a time frame.

With places she was more exact. She could locate her spiritual journey on a physical path which established its reality. In a few short words she would characterise a town according to her experience there. Remiremont lay under 'the darkness of ignorance', Mattaincourt was alive with 'rumours and calumny' against her, later home to the good father. There were Poussay, at first so welcoming, Ormes, a village she did not name because she could say nothing good of it, Nancy, dangerous for its crowds and the ducal court, Verdun where the threat of the Poor Clares loomed, almost as terrible as passing troops, and Châlons, 'the great French town set in a plain, far from Verdun', a far journey. Alix did not linger over picturesque descriptions. These brief phrases worked for her as catalysts to stir the emotions she had felt there and in which alone she was interested.

Alix's memory was at the service of her spiritual powers, for her encounters with God involved her whole self, body and soul together. Her visual memories, when she is describing her visions, are always spiritually significant, and often depend on a contrast of light and dark. On at least nine occasions her inner battle takes place at night, or includes 'the darkness of ignorance, obscurities of the soul' or of the understanding. But God's light always shines through this darkness, as clear to her as the light of the candle in the inn at Châlons. She describes the inspiration of the Holy Spirit as a light which enlightens the eyes of her soul. She said, for instance:

Another time my soul was flooded with a great interior light. I was at that moment meditating on some subject, I forget which, and this light overwhelmed me and I saw all my nothingness, surrounded as I judged myself to be, by so many faults and imperfections. (*Rel.* 43)

This is a notable use of sensory vocabulary to convey an inner perception. With Augustine she could say to God, 'Thou didst call me and thy voice broke through my deafness, thou didst shine and thy brilliance banished my blindness . . . ' (*Confessions*, X, 27, 38), for she knew that her 'ears were stopped up by vanity, and her heart, 'wrapped in darkness, could not yet receive the light' (*Rel.* 7). Meditation on the Scriptures following the Ignatian principles of the composition of place, had accustomed her to seeing 'the Word made flesh' by means of images which must have owed much to contemporary representations. We know that Teresa of Avila received the grace of definitive conversion at the sight of a statue of the suffering Christ, an *Ecce Homo* covered in wounds, and we may suppose that Alix's devotion to Christ had filled her mind with similar images. But over and above the emotion these aroused, she meant to keep hold of the spiritual fruit they brought her. Twice (*Rel.* 60 and 70) she prayed that the infinite merits of the holy life and passion of the Saviour should be fixed forever in her memory. From the conversations she had with Christ, with the Virgin or the saints of heaven – Anne, Elisabeth, Clare or Ignatius – she retained precise memories which allowed her to evoke the whole of the forceful phrases she had heard. She introduced them quietly – 'I was told inwardly . . . ', 'and one said to me . . . ', 'it seemed to me that my Lord rebuked me, saying to me . . . '. She spoke of these familiar conversations so simply that the heart to heart with God no longer seemed a privilege reserved for mystics but a grace available to any who made themselves able to hear the Word, by listening.

In noting down her feelings, Alix was always succinct, but never hid their intensity. A single strong word did the work: she had an *aversion* to subjection to a husband, a *horror* of joining the Poor Clares, she knew *bitterness, despair, repugnance.* As an adolescent she felt the emptiness of perishable goods, 'My soul was very sad among the vanities', she said, but unlike the Romantics who much later would spend long pages analysing 'le mal du siècle',[209] she took no pleasure in describing her 'actions de légèreté', deeds of vanity, but preferred to show how God had given her the fullness of joy.

The word 'joy' itself does not occur in the *Relation,* but its meaning runs all through it like a watermark. In her honesty and humility Alix described her quest for God as so beset with hardships that we are in danger of not noticing that it resulted in the happiness she found in God. She gave an absolutely clear account of her moral distress. Without attempting to quantify it, she used a single adjective and spoke of her 'great temptations, great anxieties, great troubles'. Without lingering morbidly or taking pleasure in the task, no tautology or amplification, she recalled the 'temptations, annoyances, afflictions and difficulties' which upset, thwarted or oppressed her. But after every descent into the abyss she made note of the return to peace. 'I felt my spirit strengthened by fresh hope', she said, after her temptations to mistrust and impatience (*Rel.* 57). The dominating note of her soul does not sound here but in another register, one of trust, hope and consolation. At that period the word *consolation* had more than the purely emotional sense it has now. It meant 'an inner movement which suddenly takes hold of the entire person, peace in the depth of the soul, rest for the heart in which a presence dwells'.[210] This is what Alix felt as she held the Child Jesus in her arms (*Rel.* 22) or received the Eucharist (*Rel.* 25). She kept in mind these joyful moments, which supported her desire for heaven – an immense desire, for Alix could not be half-hearted in any such emotion. She told us that she 'gave great sighs in her desire for death' (*Rel.* 68), but soon added a correction: 'These desires were sometimes excessive'. Her natural sense of measure controlled her memory. She wrote down what she recalled, neither enhanced nor diminished. Anything else would have been dishonest.

A mystical text

Alix's frank clarity demonstrates that she habitually looked at her life in the light of God. Naturally honest, she had a passion for truth in any situation, beginning with knowledge of herself. Regular examination of conscience, general confession, 'spiritual psychoanalysis',[211] the Jesuits' *Exercises of St Ignatius,* all these gave her excellent training in inner awareness. Love of silence and the *lectio divina* developed her capacity for self-knowledge. The *Imitation of Christ,* strongly recommended by Fourier, had taught her that 'humble knowledge of oneself is a surer way to God than profound scientific research'.[212] Writings of the saints told her just the same. We can be sure she had read the *Confessions* and *Soliloquies* of St Augustine, which Fourier said should stand next to the Bible on a bookshelf. Like the bishop of Hippo, she followed the road which led to the mystery of God by way of the mystery of the self, and reached the same end: 'Withdraw into your own heart, the image of God is there'.

It was Teresa of Avila who showed her the way. Reading her books, which were published in Paris in French in 1601, Alix embarked on a friendship with the Carmelite nun which went well beyond bookish sympathy. The period she spent in Paris in 1615 confirmed her in this affection, for there she was in the centre of the 'mystical constellations' which circled around Madame Acarie who brought the Carmelite movement to France.[213] By that time Madame Acarie had entered the Carmel, under the name of Mary of the Incarnation, but Alix met other followers of the Madre, in particular Monsieur de Bérulle. She

visited the Paris Carmel, meeting both Spanish and French
Carmelites, and learned about the life of Teresa, finding in her
a sister soul. There was so much she had in common with
Blessed Teresa! [214] Young and physically attractive, this girl had
become a highly talented nun and when the time came had
proved herself a woman of action, well able to establish new
houses for the salvation of souls. It was above all in reading the
Autobiography, also known as the *Book of God's Mercies*, that
Alix felt closest to her. It taught her an essential lesson, and we
may wonder whether without Teresa Alix would have been so
quick to reach excellence in the recall of her mystical experiences.
The Madre taught her, not by using scholarly theories but by
describing her own case. In a context often like her own, Alix
learnt to speak the language of mystics, to identify correctly
'raptures, withdrawals, trances' and to distinguish them
from their opposites, 'imaginations and illusions'. Like her
predecessor, she could 'thumb her nose at the devil'. As for
ecstasies, she took her stand with Teresa, maintaining that the
essential was the grace of light and love that God poured into
the soul, while the suspension of faculties was merely the result
of their inability to transmit such grace.

Reading Teresa's books was a help to Alix, but she did not
try to imitate her. They were similar in that they recorded the
same experience of God with the same love of truth, but each
did this in her own way. What was unique to Alix was the
transparency with which she showed God's action in her.
Making no claims for herself whatever, she described the graces
of the union granted her. She did not try to convince her
confessor of the depth of the mystical communication she was
granted but simply stated the facts. Father de Goedt, analysing
the 'charm' of the *Relation*, wrote, 'The spiritual fruit is always
visible, recognisable, clearly described. The strength of the

spiritual intention within Blessed Alix, which is the work in her of the Holy Spirit, the candour and absolute renunciation of herself in what she entrusts to her confessor, this mixture or rather this union is what creates the clear yet indefinable charm of these pages'.[215]

A love story

In her *Relation* Alix moved step by step through her mystical journey, so that it reads as a narrative, a narrative of the great love between God and herself. Without attempting to search the depths of her relationship with God, which must always remain mysterious, we can pick out points of light and wonder at them. They agree perfectly with her *Spiritual Writings* and with the testimony given by her sisters. Using these sources we can have a clearer idea of the 'entire love' which burned in her and which she wanted to see burn in her daughters.[216]

Called as she was to intimacy and familiar talk with God, she was still fully aware of his transcendence. He was the supreme and only good, able, she affirmed, to fulfil all our aspirations because 'the soul will never have rest until it is united with him'.[217] She tells us that she was carried 'to things very high in the knowledge of God' and that she had contemplated 'a little scrap of his greatness and perfection' in the Holy Trinity. She never lost this vision, for she added, 'this greatness stayed with me always, as if imprinted on my mind' (*Rel.* 23). With a sure touch she analysed the effects of these mystical graces which sometimes came to her: 'It spread lights in my soul which made me long and sigh for the divine perfections . . . ' (*Rel.* 33).

She perceived the Absolute in God, offering him respect and reverence. In the opening words of her *Relation* she gave him the title borne by monarchs in those days: 'God, in the presence of whose majesty I am as a little flea'. The realistic comparison demonstrates her 'lowliness', which she felt the more strongly as God's greatness was revealed to her more clearly. Thus when the evil spirits attacked her with horrible temptations, she wrote, 'During this time my mind was so confused, humbled and full of mistrust that I did not dare lift the eyes of my thinking towards God' (*Rel.* 27). But faith in his mercy gave her fresh confidence and she came to be glad of the circumstances which brought home her 'lowliness' to her. During periods of spiritual dryness, for instance, she had 'great devotion to the psalm *De profundis,* because', she said, 'from the depth of my nothingness, my void, I called out to the God of majesty and greatness beyond understanding' (*Rel.* 34). God appeared to her as supremely desirable and at the same time transcendent and therefore inaccessible. She apprehended him as the Other in the very action by which she raised herself towards him.

She delighted in 'always looking at the infinite beauty and goodness of God',[218] and would joyfully contemplate one or another of his attributes: eternal truth and wisdom, power, immense charity, patience to put up with us, endless providence, mercy. She advised her daughters to choose the perfections of God as a subject of prayer, and so taught them her own spiritual paths: to know and therefore love better, to love and therefore to know.

Her mystical experience of God, Three in One, led her to 'the holy humanity of Jesus Christ', to which she vowed passionate devotion, although we cannot, as we can in the life of Teresa of Avila, know the circumstances of what was 'a mystic marriage'. It was Mary who told Alix that the Lord had looked at her, when she said to her that 'You did what pleased my Son in making your confession' (*Rel.* 4). Thus the Virgin was present at the start of the loving relationship between her Son and Alix, and she continued her role as mediatrix. Young

Alix confessing the wretchedness of her soul learnt to know the Saviour's mercy, and her humility opened the gates to a flood of grace. All her life she continued to beg Jesus that he might be pleased 'to restore her soul to its first purity' and always he would respond to her prayer and enfold it in his holiness.

It is these graces of liberation and light that best reveal to us the radiant clarity of Alix's soul. Admittedly she spent more time in the *Relation* making avowal of all that humbled her – doubts of the faith, despair when she was harassed by 'the hellish flames of the flesh', discouragement when her plans were uncertain. But all these dark passages break through into light, the presence of the Lord filled her with strength and guaranteed her victory over the evil spirits. In this way Mary's promise to her was fulfilled, Jesus was indeed her hope.

She needed this presence, welcomed his sudden visitations and thanked him for coming to the help of her 'lukewarmness'. But she did not overestimate these unusual favours, as we can see from a remark she made to one of the sisters, 'I have more respect for a scrap of humility than for a hundred ecstasies'.[219] Evidence gathered from her contemporaries draws the same picture, in her daily life she was the same woman whom we meet in the *Relation*. She practised and taught simple methods of living in the presence of God. Meditation on the Scripture, prayer using the Psalms, and above all the Eucharist were occasions of meeting him. She saw him in the service of our neighbour and served him with equal delight as Martha and as Mary. The liturgy of the Hours, spiritual conversation, direction given to those who turned to her, all these added an ecclesial, a communal, indeed an apostolic dimension to her personal devotion. Representations of Christ and the Virgin provided her prayers not only with images to contemplate but with models to imitate. During Holy Week in the Nancy convent she staged the passion of Christ so that the sisters should relive the Saviour's sufferings in their own hearts and bodies. She herself acknowledged that her greatest mystical graces came to her from the contemplation of such scenes, 'in considering the infinite merits of the holy Life and Passion of my Saviour, which I would wish to have continually in my memory' (*Rel.* 60).

Just as love feeds on the presence of the beloved, so there is nothing more painful than its absence. Alix knew this pain when she felt 'dry, without devotion, the understanding darkened, full of confused thoughts'. But on reflection she saw that this dryness was not important as long as it did not stop her 'persevering in serving God well' (*Rel.* 34). From her insatiable longing for the divine Presence came her desire for heaven, a desire whose development she noted. Her wish for death, she said, came to her first because of her distress at living in this world 'where so much is done that displeases the divine Majesty' (*Rel.* 18). Later her feelings became purer, and twice (*Rel.* 25 and 68) she thought she heard the Lord tell her inwardly, 'When I am with you, that must be enough for you, but there is still much self-seeking even in this'. Then Alix revealed the secret of her inner peace:

> And since then these great desires have moderated, for when they appear they are instantly followed by a sweet and calm resignation to God's will, with a stripping away of the self-love which this Truth teaches me inwardly: that one must love God for love of him. And I am very happy not only to stay here as long as it shall please him but even, when it shall be his good pleasure to call me from this world, I am very happy, if such were his will, not to enjoy the glory of the blessed as long as I can hear them praising and blessing him. (*Rel.* 25)

What Alix called 'a sweet and calm resignation to God's will' shows another dominant characteristic of her soul. These words do not express some every day passiveness in the face of what cannot be changed but betray a dynamic conception of holiness and the main thrust of her life. From the moment of her conversion, her decision was taken: 'I planned that from now on I would do [...] everything that was most pleasing to God, even if it should mean death' (*Rel.* 6). This constant desire marks its rhythm on every stage of her life – 'To know and do God's will' (*Rel.* 16), 'to accomplish his holy will' (*Rel.* 22), 'to know God's will' (*Rel.* 55), 'to know what I could do that be most pleasing to Our Lord' (*Rel.* 67) – these frequent expressions show that she tried first of all to see clearly and then to go on. A wholehearted love of God meant for Alix to achieve such concord with him that her own will should be transformed into his, so that one would no longer know 'what we do or do not wish'.[220] Her perfect submission to the will of God gave her sweetness and calm in her soul, even in the midst of battles. Her inner joy was assured by the divine indwelling Presence. Attentive to the voice of the Spirit which taught her inwardly, she gathered from Truth itself the definition of wholehearted love by which she meant to live, that 'one must love God for love of him'.

This disinterested love, free of any touch of egoism, gave Alix her passion for God's glory. Her burning desire was to praise him and to make him known and loved. She adopted the words of St Ignatius and strove to act always 'for the greater glory of God'. As did Fourier, she saw the teaching mission of the Congregation of Our Lady as a means to this end. The Virgin Mary herself, when she entrusted her Child to her so that she should nourish him and help him grow, had shown her the deep meaning of her apostolic calling, and Alix understood the significance of the message, 'this meaning that I should win him glory' (*Rel.* 23).

CHAPTER SEVENTEEN

The last offering

Nancy, spiritual pole

We must not suppose that Alix, ever more strongly possessed by God's presence and struck by the disease which would soon take her away, lived her last years withdrawn into herself. Her flourishing convent in the duchy's capital was producing the fruit of her holiness and making the town a centre of spirituality. The form of religious life she established there astonished and attracted people. It was, she said, a 'mixed life' because the sisters divided their time between prayer and teaching, and as soon as Rome authorised this novelty, new vocations came flocking into Nancy. On 26 January 1621 Fourier wrote, 'It is a marvel to see these excellent young women coming forward. God be blessed!' He repeated this to the sisters at Châlons on 11 September and in fact between 1618, date of the first profession, and Alix's death in 1622 six such ceremonies followed one after another, in which altogether seventeen novices made their perpetual vows.[221] When they were asked why they were doing this, all replied that they wanted to win salvation by avoiding the dangers of the world and to do all possible good by consecrating themselves to the teaching of young people.[222] And as God sent workers for the harvest, so did the number of students increase, for as soon as it opened the school profited from the interest aroused by Fourier's teaching methods, now tried and tested over more than twenty years. One of his innovations, much appreciated, was the 'simultaneous method', in which a mistress would teach a small group of girls who were all at the same level, using a blackboard and identical copies of one book. In the street where the Congregation was housed, people admired the girls who came out from their classes 'in order, without making a noise or pushing each other'. The kind behaviour of the teachers, never threatening or angry, was so much prized that parents did not hesitate to enrol little girls as boarders, although by the strict terms of the bull of institution, they would not return to their families during the whole period of their schooling. According to the chronicle there were between forty and fifty of them, and Alix put Angélique, tireless and enthusiastic, in charge.[223] The number is confirmed by a letter of 4 June 1620 quoted by Mother Louis de Gonzague in which Alix asked the sisters at Mirecourt, 'Have you plenty of boarders? We have forty at Nancy'. [224]

This spread was in part due to the presence of Alix but also to action of Antoine de Lenoncourt, primate of Lorraine, who was proud of his role as protector of an establishment so well in line with the Council of Trent, and regularly brought important churchmen to visit it. No doubt when they went there they also met the Superior. In 1620 the famous Jesuit Pierre Coton (1564–1626), former confessor to the king Henri IV and afterwards rector of the college of Bordeaux, preached in the chapel of the ducal palace during the octave of the Assumption. Alix sent to tell Fourier of this but the message did not reach him in time (*C.* 1, 438). Perhaps this preacher's visit would inspire them to read or reread his best known book, *L'Intérieure Occupation d'une âme devote (The Interiour Occupation of the Soule)*, in which he describes for those who live in the world a mystical life directed towards action.

In the 1620s we can be sure that the example of Mary Ward (1585–1645) stimulated lively discussion among the Jesuits in

Nancy and in the Convent of Our Lady. This brave English-
woman, very like Alix in her calling as a teacher and in the role
she advocated for women in the Church, was engaged in the
creation of a teaching Order based on the Jesuits' Rule. This
was opposed in ecclesiastical circles on the grounds that
she wanted to establish a centralised system and to abandon
enclosure and the wearing of a religious habit, so that in
December 1621 Mary Ward travelled to Rome to defend her
cause, passing through Nancy on the way.[225] Alix must have
been too ill to meet her English counterpart, but she followed
with great interest the debates aroused by the rulings of the
Church which forbade nuns to teach. Did Bérulle, whose discussions with Fourier took place in 1620, call in to see Alix? It
seems very likely.[226]

It was in this period that Elisabeth de Ranfaing (1592–1649)
was in the news, and came to know Alix. She was younger than
her countrywoman, having been born in Remiremont in 1592.
Wife of an evil man who died in 1616, she hoped to place her
two little daughters aged seven and three with the sisters at
Nancy, but the younger child was not old enough and this
did not occur. In Nancy once again in 1619 she and Alix
became confidential friends. The unhappy woman then suffered
appalling troubles which can only be accounted for by the
epidemic of accusations of witchcraft which was then raging
in Lorraine. Victim of malevolent accusations made against
her by the man whose advances she had rejected, she was said
to be bewitched, possessed, hysterical, mad, or a witch. In
order to release her from demoniac possession the bishop of
Toul ordered exorcisms to take place, and these were performed
several times a week in the chapel of the Jesuit noviciate in
Nancy. The sessions were open to the public, and crowds
flocked in – the curious, the devotees greedy for emotion,

grandees from the Court, and religious from every Order.
Father Guéret was present, and so for one day in order to obey
his bishop, was Pierre Fourier.[227] In front of this mixed bag
of an audience Elisabeth de Ranfaing performed all sorts of
extravagances. She flung and twisted her arms and legs about,
she raved in fury, shouted insults, denounced hidden vices and
unknown secrets. Those who watched this display came to a
variety of conclusions. Some were shocked, others puzzled, said
she was mad or that this was the act of Satan. Yes, they said, this
woman is possessed, the devil has taken over her body but not
her soul. They wondered at her patience, her submission to
God's will, and counted her among the martyrs. That was
Fourier's opinion, full of pity for the woman they called 'the
Nancy demoniac'. And where did Alix stand? She welcomed
Elisabeth after the exhausting exorcisms, and gave her all the
peace and reassurance she could. She understood her friend's
anguish and how tempted she was to despair and could comfort
her, when she talked of the demon's foul attacks upon her body
and how she resisted him, by reminding her of Father Coton's
words to her, 'It is in his infinite love that God permits these
works of the Evil One in you. It is better to have this in the
body than a single mortal sin in the soul'. This is what the
famous Jesuit said to Elisabeth in July 1621 after he had taken
part in the exorcisms, and Alix repeated them to her guest
together with others, such as, 'The holy angels are encamped
around you to save your soul and your body too'. Another was,
'The true Master of the house is the one you often receive in
the most august sacrament of the holy Eucharist, who by his
presence purifies and sanctifies his tabernacle'.[228] Their horror
of sin led both women to the same compassion for sinners and
to a similar desire to atone for their offences by sharing in the
redemptive work of Christ. Alix told Elisabeth that from the

very start of her vocation she had declared herself ready 'to give her life many times to save the souls of those who rise up against the will of God' (*Rel.* 23), and Elisabeth told her that she when very young had accepted 'the quality of victim' in reparation for the sins of men. Recognising the mystical grace they had received, both gave thanks to God. Then Elisabeth left the parlour, followed by an affectionate look from Alix, who took up again her close colloquy with the Lord. Some years later, by the kindly intervention of the Virgin, the 'demoniac of Nancy' was released from the indwelling demon. She devoted herself then to the founding of a religious congregation, Our Lady of Refuge, to take care of prostitutes. She may well have discussed the urgent need there was for this mission with the woman who had founded the sisters of Our Lady.

The court of Lorraine could not be indifferent to the convent that gave such glory to Nancy, and the community could not fail to take an interest in matters touching the ducal family, for which it was bound to pray. At the heart of this relationship stood Pierre Fourier, counsellor to the dukes in things both spiritual and temporal, and anxious that his nuns should be aware of their country's situation. When Count François de Vaudémont, general of the Catholic League, and his son Charles were fighting Protestants in Germany, Mattaincourt's parish priest became worried and in a letter to Alix on 26 September 1621 asked her 'if anyone has heard news of the health of my lord the Prince. You said in your last letter that people were anxious because two of his staff had come without mentioning it'.

But the great affair now was the succession to the ducal throne, a question which gave Alix another occasion to demonstrate her love of her country. Twenty years earlier she had prayed fervently that the duke Henri II should not marry the Calvinist Catherine de Bourbon, and now she prayed with equal vigour that Princess Nicole should not marry a stranger to whom she would give Lorraine as her dowry. Eventually in 1621 Nicole married her cousin Charles, son of François de Vaudémont, but this marriage raised other problems. Not only was the prince of an adventurous nature, but his right to the succession was not certain, and the same was true of Nicole, who was ousted on the grounds of the Salic law. The duchess Margherita di Gonzaga (1590–1632), niece of Marie de Medici, queen of France, did not merely choose Fourier as her director of conscience but was glad to visit Alix in her convent and ask her advice on the problems connected with the marriages of her daughters Nicole and Claude. But the most frequent of her noble visitors was François de Vaudémont who often went to ask for her prayers. One day, hoping to obtain from her a special grace, he said to her, 'Mother, I have great confidence in you and I think you a saint'. Taken aback, Alix then retorted, 'My lord, when we come before God, many will be undeceived'. As she left the parlour she burst into tears, because, says the chronicle, 'she had not liked this praise'.[229]

At this period a Carmelite arrived at the court in Nancy, Father Dominic of Jesus and Mary, already famous for his holiness and miracles. All those who had fought in the battle of Prague on 8 November 1620, such as Charles de Vaudémont and his men, were talking of this man's most recent exploit. He had marched at the head of the Catholic troops carrying a picture of the Virgin and encouraging them in the final attack. Everyone attributed to his prayers the overwhelming victory of the White Mountain, where the duke of Bavaria, the emperor's ally, defeated the elector palatine.[230] Nancy welcomed the Carmelite with awe and it is not surprising that Alix wanted to see him. But when she spoke of this, one of her nuns dissuaded

her, saying that 'the Father is surrounded by a n
impossible to speak to him'. Nevertheless he wa
would like to meet him and he promised to go
had to be cancelled as she was too ill. Yet som
told her nurse that she had seen Fr Dominic in the spirit, and
that he had answered all she asked. For whom did she intercede?
Perhaps for Elisabeth de Ranfaing, in whose exorcisms the
Carmelite took part?

Body and soul, a hard diagnosis

Time passed, and the sisters knew that their mother was dying.
They remembered what she had said, 'I shall live more than
four years in the new convent', and to them this seemed to
mean, 'not much longer than four years'.

We have no way of knowing about Alix's last years except
from the recollections provided by her contemporaries and
written down in the first biography, which appeared in 1666.
These pages are strongly marked by the ideas of that epoch,
especially in the importance they attach to the devil's assaults
on Blessed Alix. This can largely be explained by the historical
context – between 1580 and 1635 Lorraine was in the grip of a
most improbable 'crisis of Satanism'. At that period when there
was no frontier between the natural and the supernatural, God
and Satan were forever intervening in the course of events
and in people's actions. The law claimed it could control this
phenomenon by repressing it, while the Church had recourse
to supernatural methods such as prayer and exorcism. The
exorcisms to which renowned churchmen subjected Elisabeth
de Ranfaing took place in Nancy in 1620, and these must have
affected the recollections of Alix given by the sisters there. Just
as the woman who would one day found Our Lady of Refuge
emerged strengthened from the machinations of hell, so would

Alix's holiness blaze out more brilliantly from her repeated victories over the devil and his minions. So thought Angélique Milly, the chief if not the only author of the pages we read, and this is why she takes the trouble to give detailed accounts of the torments the demons inflicted upon Alix. They redoubled their efforts, she wrote, they did not give her a moment's rest, they appeared to her day and night in horrible and terrifying shapes – satyrs, wild animals, snakes – which gave her great anxiety and inner distress; they raced about inside the building, sometimes like big dogs, they invaded the infirmary, opening doors and banging them shut, they alarmed the nuns and terrified the boarding pupils.[231] Therefore, explained Angélique, 'in order to divert her from these distressing visions', her confessors allowed her to confide in one of the nuns (herself, although she does not say so) so that she could tell her about the 'unusual disturbances which happened to her, both in body and mind'.[232] A wise decision, we think, good therapy. In her conversations with Alix Angélique discovered the kind of temptations that were attacking her friend, temptations of which no one, she wrote, had the least idea, 'she was so reserved in her speech and so wise in her behaviour'. After this praise of Alix's discretion, Angélique went on to say that 'these had always been taken for bodily infirmities, and that if her confessors had not ordered her, in the last years of her life, to talk about them to the said nun, she would never have done so'.[233] Her confidant, the only one who knew about the hidden link between the sick woman's illnesses and the demon who caused them, was now going to reveal in this first biography the secret with which she had been entrusted. And in order to denounce the trouble-maker more clearly, she described his devilish machinations at length. In this way she transformed what may have been nothing more than a dreadful nightmare caused by fever and delirium into a hell rew of sorcery. The sorcerer was the demon himself who stood in the shape of a man in the centre of her room and drew a great circle with a staff, muttering as he did so words which the sick woman did not understand. Immediately, says the narrator, she felt temptations so furious and extreme that they altered her face till she became unrecognisable, with these strange pains all over her body, followed by strong convulsions which continued long after the temptation had passed'.[234]

The duke's medical adviser was called to Alix's bedside, and he gave the same diagnosis, though more calmly expressed and did not mention the setting which Angélique provided for her friend's nightmare visions. Considering the great pain [the patient] was suffering and the convulsions and contractions of the nerves she was experiencing, the doctor declared that they were 'caused by the fears and extreme apprehensions she felt in her temptations, and the violence she was doing to herself in body and mind in resisting them'.[235]

It is remarkable that both Angélique and the doctor noted the physical manifestations of the sick woman's inner tensions at a time when the domain of the psyche and its repercussions on the body were so little known. Alix's disease looks very like a psychosomatic illness caused by the violence of her inner struggles. Like Teresa of Avila and many holy women, Alix fought her psychological battles in her body. 'Wanting to do too much, she broke herself like a bow bent too far'.[236]

Angélique highlights the vigorous resistance Alix made to her temptations, and here her evidence agrees with what we know from the *Relation*. This is the Alix we know, and her words, directly quoted, have the ring of truth. She was not afraid of the demon but dreaded his perverse incitements to sin. 'Gladly', she said 'I would choose to die a thousand cruel deaths rather than suffer even the slightest of those attacks'. And again, 'My mind is firm: I would rather God should eternally exercise his justice upon me than offend him even once'.[237] To repel the demoniac hordes she used holy water in Jesus' sacred name and with the sign of the cross, which brought her, she said, 'great relief'. But there were moments when her strength abandoned her. Her weakened body would no longer obey the commands of her will and darkness clouded her mind. 'In the abyss of such exhaustion', reported Angélique, 'she often cried out, "My God, my God, why hast thou forsaken me?" ' She used the Saviour's own last words from the cross, uniting her dereliction to his. Amongst the readings from holy Scripture the passages she most often asked Angélique to read were from the Book of Job and the narrative of the Passion. The suffering Christ was her model. She told him that she loved and trusted him, and although she repeated, 'Yes, I know, I deserve hell', she would add, 'but I have always hoped in your mercy'. She liked to repeat the penitential psalms in Latin or in French, especially the *Miserere* and the *De profundis*, making the penitent psalmist's humility her own.

Angélique described one episode as evidence of Alix's humility. One day, she wrote, finding her sad and depressed, the doctor indicated a picture of St Catherine of Siena on the infirmary wall and by way of comfort said, 'Take courage, God made that great saint undergo trials like yours'. Disturbed by this comparison, Alix wanted to point out the difference, and summoning her strength, exclaimed, 'Catherine of Siena was exercised by love to glorify God, but for me, wretched sinner, it is by justice as punishment for my sins'.[238] A long commentary follows this in the 1666 *Life*, but it was not included in the Evreux manuscript and therefore was not written by Angélique.[239] Its authors assert that in view of the great glory that would accrue to God through Alix's indomitable endurance of her temptations, he had 'given hell a free hand', that is to say full permission to torture her. After this they acknowledge that they have not said all they know about the 'bitter struggles' of the Blessed lady against the 'importunate attacks of her raging enemies'. They have only spoken 'very much in general terms so as not to alarm the weak'.[240]

But the demons themselves took care of the publicity. During the public exorcisms of Elisabeth de Ranfaing they reported 'from end to end' all that had happened as Alix came home from Châlons in 1614. God had delivered her to them, they said, and with their whole power they had tormented her. Asmodeus[241] and his legions had invaded the hotel bedroom but the Great Mistress, as they called Our Lady, kept Alix so well protected that their enterprise turned to confusion. They had not been able to drag from her the smallest consent to sin and they judged her courage to be invincible.[242] The diocesan exorcist, Monsieur Viardin, impressed by this revelation, wanted to check it and visited the convent during the Superior's last illness. The nun whom he questioned was Angélique herself, who had been there on the Châlons journey and had received Alix's confidences, so was able to confirm that the demons were telling the truth. But the matter was not generally known at the time, and it was not until the sisters at Nancy began to collect their memories together for a publication that the heroic strength Alix had shown in combating the forces of evil could be unveiled. We can believe that, as they said, they did not repeat every detail, but we may think that they revealed enough. And we share their conclusion: 'Alix's courage was so strong', they wrote, 'that it seems to go beyond example and beyond belief. It is enough to say that she suffered as did the saints'.[243] We do indeed believe this, and it is enough.

'When it shall be his good pleasure to call me . . . ' (*Rel.* 25)

The disease continued its advance. At the beginning of 1621
Alix was so weak that she could barely walk, but still took part
in the activities of community life. She even increased her
austerities, in spite of all attempts to persuade her to reduce or
abandon them. 'I cannot neglect what God requires of me', she
said. By September she did not leave her room, exhausted by
the phthisis which was killing her. When the nurse out of
kindness suggested she should not take the opiates[244] which
did nothing but disgust her, she answered gently, 'If they don't
help the body, they will help the soul. We must obey to the
end'.[245] To the sisters who went to see her she gave unstintingly
both her advice and her smile. Mother Mary Ignatius, novice
mistress, given up by the doctors, later testified that she owed
her recovery to Alix's prayers, seemingly more effective in
heaven as she withdrew from the earth.[246] 8 December 1621
was the third anniversary of her appointment as Superior. After
months of asking to be relieved of this post, her wish was
granted and on 19 December Angélique Milly was chosen to
replace her. Fourier was satisfied, because as he knew, 'everyone
there approves of her' (*C.* 1, 302).

All those in Nancy who revered her were moved by the news
of her extreme illness. The duchess of Lorraine, Margherita di
Gonzaga, and the princesses Nicole and Claude exercised their
right of entry to the Cloister and were taken to her room. Every
day they took her light dishes but received from her more in
exchange, for Alix gave them her fervent love of God. Like a
candle which blazes up and lights other flames before it goes
out, she never relinquished her apostolic vocation.

She could do nothing on her sick-bed but suffer and pray,
and there she once again saved her Congregation in a critical

situation. Father Guéret, asked to do so by Lenoncourt, but without consulting the founder, drew up a set of Constitutions, and the sisters were invited to put forward their comments. Six months passed, and they stayed silent. The primate was annoyed and rebuked Fourier for failing to come to Nancy to meet the Jesuits and discuss the affairs of his Congregation, including especially the setting up of a Mother General and a 'universal noviciate' (*C.* 1, 275). In fact Fourier had been more than ever at the service of all his convents. At the end of September 1621 he travelled to Verdun and Bar. From there he went to Châlons and on to Soissons with a view to a foundation, then returned through Verdun and Saint-Mihiel, after being present at the enclosure of the house at Bar on 11 November. During this time Alix's condition deteriorated. Bishop Maillane went to see her several times and gave her general absolution, at the same time asking this woman whom he saw as a saint to pray for him. After these visits his attitude changed, he rejected Lenoncourt's prejudices and trusted Fourier again. What is more, feeling that the Jesuits were trying to remove the Nancy house from Fourier's control, he briskly dismissed them and ordered an Oratorian priest to help Alix. She, two weeks before her death, expressed her urgent wish to talk to Fourier, who at once hurried to Nancy, not giving a thought to the fatigue of such a journey in addition to his already burdensome ministry. He did not, however, visit Alix until he had had a written order to do so from his bishop.[247] Angélique Milly said of their meeting, 'She saw him two or three times, made her confession to him and talked with him at leisure about the state of her conscience and other things concerning the Congregation'.[248] What did they say to each other? Perhaps they talked about the burning question of the way the Congregation should be governed. Pierre Fourier, just back from an extended tour among the convents in France and in the duchy of Bar, could have told her about the problems of a centralised system dependent on a Mother General resident in Nancy. Neither the bishops nor the French *parlement* nor the Roman Curia would accept it. Alix, now freed from the influences that had bullied her, would hear and accept his wise words. Like him, she would understand that time would do her work for her. That being so, it was better not to rush into a dangerous centralisation, better to avoid a definitive rupture between the convents. Although Alix had once envisaged a system different from his, although she had even maintained her ideas too forcefully, now they reached a perfect understanding and her imminent departure gave their conversation a prophetic note. She was, said Fourier, 'about to pass from death to life' [249] and they could both rejoice at this prospect. Like Augustine and Monica, 'talking sweetly together in Ostia', they might wonder 'what is this eternal life of the saints which the eye has not seen nor the ear heard nor the heart of man known within him'.[250] Together they opened their hearts 'to the running waters of the source of life which is near God'. In this foretaste of heaven, they could part joyfully. Then Fourier went back to Mattaincourt where he was needed as Christmas drew near.

Eight or nine days before she died Alix was enfolded in God. 'What are you thinking about?' Angélique asked her. 'I am talking with God, from whom now nothing distracts me'. 'Are you afraid of dying?' asked her friend. 'No', said the sick woman. 'For a long time I have been trying to prepare for it. I used to be afraid of God's judgment but now I trust his goodness and I am sure of his mercy'.

Being asked by the Superior to say a few words to the sisters gathered in her bedroom, she began by asking their forgiveness, then promised to pray for them. To this she added a last message: 'Always keep together in complete unity, and use love towards each other, for love and unity are the only way to maintain the Congregation'. [251]

Angélique asked her to bless the sisters around her, and she did so, asking God to extend this blessing beyond the limits of space and time. Peace shone from her face and her lips murmured verses of the psalm *Ad te domine clamavi in toto corde meo*. Although the doctors could do nothing for her, they constantly visited her sickroom, wanting, says the chronicle, 'to wonder at the marvels of God in her'. On Epiphany 6 January 1622 she was given the last unction, and every day received the eucharist as a viaticum. Would she have the strength to reach the forty-sixth anniversary of her birth and baptism? No, she would celebrate 2 February in heaven, but when on Sunday 9 January Angélique suggested that they should postpone the conventual mass so that the sisters could stay with her, she refused, and promised to wait till they came back. Thus she united her death to Christ's sacrifice, celebrated on a Sunday, the day of his resurrection. After a short and gentle agony, she died, giving 'three short sighs' and uttering the names of Jesus and Mary. She had heard her Lord's call and chosen to obey it. Her delight in living united to God was transformed into eternal blessedness.

We have more evidence of her last days in a letter Angélique sent on 29 January to Mother Charlotte of the Cross, Superior at Verdun. Part of it reads: 'Her body was opened but no cause of death discovered, she was quite healthy throughout . . . and was only slightly affected in the lungs. A fortnight before her death she felt such heat in her left side that cloths soaked in cold water had to be applied to both temples.' She added a hagiographic detail in the 1666 *Life*: 'When dressing her to put her in the coffin, they found clear marks of her extreme and rigorous penances in the scars seen on her body'.[252] There is also an important passage which did not appear in the chronicle, a proof of the uneasy relationship between the Nancy house and the founder. The following significant paragraph is found in the Evreux manuscript:

> The day before her death the Mother Superior had sent express to Mattaincourt to warn the Reverend Father the founder that the Mother was nearing her end and could not live past Sunday. He set off at once and made such good time that he reached Nancy on the Monday at eleven in the morning, and went straight to the sacristy to prepare to say mass for the dead woman, and he put on a white chasuble even though the church was all hung with mourning; this was noticed by many there, because the Father was always held to be a saint, illumined by light from God.[253]

What a significant gesture this is, telling us what Fourier thought about Alix! He placed her among the elect who have received their reward and for the mass of thanksgiving he celebrated in her honour, he wore festal robes, not clothes of mourning. The whole of Nancy felt just the same and hastened to venerate 'the saint', so that for three days a solid crowd was crammed in around her remains which lay on view in the convent chapel behind the choir grill. Those she had loved and helped filed past, the duke's family, princes and princesses, nobles and grandees, but also poor people, the sick, the prisoners, school pupils and their relatives. On the day of the funeral still more came, twice as many, to say a last farewell before she was placed in the coffin, an event which took place outside the Cloister to satisfy the townspeople's piety.

The fallen grain

Although Alix wanted to be buried in the convent's small cemetery, Monseigneur de Maillane asked that her leaden coffin should be placed in a vault inside the chapel, underneath the altar of the nuns' choir. It was a comfort to the sisters to have their Mother near them, as we can see from a letter Angélique wrote to the Superior at Verdun, telling her that 'I promise you that I have often pleaded for you beside her tomb, asking her to obtain from Our Lord all that you need'.

There is a chance reference to this tomb in the 1666 chronicle. When Alix was leaving Saint-Nicolas in 1620, we are told that she said to Claude Chauvenel to comfort her, 'Don't cry. You will come back to Nancy to accompany my body, carrying a lighted candle and singing *Laudate dominum*'.[254] As it happened, Claude Chauvenel was not in Nancy when Alix was buried in 1622. But in 1626 this prophecy came true in every detail. Construction work meant that the height of the nuns' choir had to be raised, and the coffin was removed 'to put it somewhere else', and the sisters accompanied it 'in procession, singing'.

Its later history was more eventful. In the eighteenth century a learned man, mentioning the fact that the tomb of Alix Le Clerc was venerated, recorded the epitaph, but not the tomb's whereabouts.[255] When the nuns left their convent in 1792, driven out by the Revolution, two inventories were made, and in the year IV a plan was drawn, but with no reference to the tomb. The convent buildings, now the property of the nation, were divided up and sold, ceilings were installed in the chapel vaultings and a second storey made. Yet in spite of all these changes and successive sales, local opinion insisted that Alix's tomb had remained inviolate after the nuns were scattered. All through the nineteenth century the tradition persisted, because from one generation to the next information was handed down from those who had bought parts of the convent and described themselves as keepers of the tomb. Excavations took place in 1849, 1904, and 1934, but without success. When Pius XII beatified Alix in 1947 no one had any hope of finding her remains. But then on 2 May 1950 a chance discovery brought attention back to 'the only place to which a careful examination of the texts should have led: a wide vault underneath the nuns' choir'.[256] Young people intending to lay a dance floor in a cellar at 9 Rue Maurice-Barrès brought out a lead coffin containing a human skeleton and a heart encased in lead. Ten years of scientific research by historians and doctors led in 1960 to the conclusion that the skeleton was certainly the remains of Alix Le Clerc: its age, size, and diet were in accord with all records of Alix at the time of her death and the pieces of cloth and of a rosary also found in the coffin were of her period , everything was correct. Abbot Jacques Choux, then conservator of the Museum of Lorraine in Nancy, reconstructed events as follows: after being moved from its place because of works in 1626, the coffin was then left in a kind of crypt, not buried but accessible to all who came to pray there. During the Revolution, perhaps immediately after the nuns had gone and certainly as privately as possible while there was danger of profanation, pious hands moved the coffin into a corner of the crypt, put into it the heart of the primate Lenoncourt, which he had chosen to give to the sisters at Nancy,[257] and covered the hole with some fifty centimetres of earth. The chance laying of a floor in 1950 revealed the secret and allowed Christians once again to venerate the woman whose humility was thus thwarted. The leaden coffin in which the remains of Alix Le Clerc had rested for more than three hundred years now lies in the crypt of the abbey church at Remiremont where she was born. Her relics were kept in a shrine standing in the chapel of the school of Our Lady St Sigisbert in Nancy. They have now been moved to a side-chapel in the basilica of Nancy. The crystal flame which rises above the coffer of silvered bronze containing her bones reminds all who see it of the burning desire Alix felt when she offered God her 'body to be crushed into a thousand pieces' rather than lose the glorious purity of her baptism.

The cult of Alix Le Clerc

The duke's family was the first to make plain its reverence for Alix. Duke Henri II and his brother François de Vaudémont sent Claude Deruet, court painter, to paint a portrait of her.[258] He represented her as he had seen her on her death bed, eyes half closed, a crucifix in her hands, her expression soft and peaceful. But Count François' veneration needed more than a portrait and he wanted a book recording her virtues. In it should be collected the evidence of those who knew the saint, and he began by consulting Fourier. What did he and the Jesuits who supported this request want of Fourier? Not that he should produce a personal testimony which might be indiscreet or partial, but that he should pass the request on to the sisters. They were asked to send him 'all the virtues and the holy actions they have observed in Mother Alix, so that the legend can be written'.[259] This was because, he wrote to the sisters at Soissons on 10 March 1622, 'they consider her a saint and want to cast light on her life'. Many have seen this reply as evidence of enmity towards Alix. They pile up complaints against him and accuse him on the one hand of lacking zeal and on the other of not making enough of Alix's holiness. But they forget that Fourier's humility did not let him behave in this way and that a cheerfully brusque manner can often hide deep emotions.

Here is an anecdote in evidence – one day some Jesuits visiting Mattaincourt begged him, saint that he was, to give them his blessing. 'My good Fathers', he exclaimed, laughing, 'if I did not know you were intelligent people, I should think you were off your heads!' In fact Fourier, understanding what was likely to happen, thought this glorification of Alix was premature. Angélique Milly, Superior of the Nancy house, had given the Count de Vaudémont a manuscript entitled *Note on the Virtuous Acts of the Mother and of some unusual graces, taken from the recollection of nuns who lived with her and who heard her talk about the said virtues in every day and in private conversations.* The prince was full of admiration and wanted to claim for Alix the honours of the altars. But the movement towards Alix's beatification was very soon interrupted. Monseigneur de Maillane died on 4 September 1624, and the whole ducal court was in any case thrown into confusion by the death of Duke Henri II three months earlier and the question of the succession. No one now gave a thought to the beatification of Alix Le Clerc, not even Mother Angélique, who had gathered together the documents submitted to the prince and now only wanted to find an author who could write the Life of her holy friend. None came forward, except for one who promised but then did not perform, said Bedel, and Angélique decided to publish the collected pieces of evidence just as they were. Her death in 1660 delayed the publication, which emerged from the Charlot Press in Nancy in 1666 with the title, *Vie de la Vénérable Mère Alix Le Clerc, Fondatrice, première Mère et Religieuse de la Congrégation de Notre-Dame.*[260] The memory of Alix was still greatly venerated as long as her tomb was there for the public to visit, but the Revolution put an end to these devout pilgrimages and it was another hundred years before a passionate admirer of Alix, Count Gandelet, succeeded in having her declared Venerable by Pope Leo XIII on 21 February 1899. The first world war delayed the issue of the usual decretals and not until 15 March 1932 did Pius XI proclaim the heroic nature of Alix's virtues, a first step which led to her beatification by Pius XII on 4 May 1947. Would she come closer to us if she were canonised? It is rather for us to move closer to her, by praying to her and by living the message she gave us.

CHAPTER EIGHTEEN

The spiritual writings[261]

The seeds in the 'Small Notebook'

As well as the *Relation*, which of itself is enough to bear witness to the depth of her mystical experience, Alix left some spiritual writings, short but rich in meaning. Angélique Milly gathered them into a *Small Notebook* written in her hand and faithfully copied these and other documents into another manuscript, found at Evreux in 1937.[262] The sisters at Nancy had published them in the first biography of the foundress in 1666, arranging them under certain titles but without altering the text, so that there is no reason to doubt their authenticity. They wanted to make it clear that Alix was the author of these pages, and introduced the first text as follows: 'Here is reported her method of governing as it is found in a notebook written in her hand, composed according to the light God gave her and which the nuns saw her practise'. An additional note reads: 'Also taken from her daily writing', and then advice, 'To understand and heal spiritual infirmities'. These are instructions addressed to the superiors of communities, in which Alix shows shrewd psychological insights as a director of souls. One general title covers another five texts: 'Her thoughts about some particular virtues, taken from a small notebook written in her hand', together with a few pages called 'The Mother's thoughts about the Institute'.[263] These six texts were published by the Congregation of Our Lady with an Introduction by Sister Marie-Madeleine Cord'homme in 1968.[264] By now it was all complete;

together with this biography the Editions du Cerf published her *Relation autobiographique* and the *Notes de ses cahiers* in the collection 'Sagesses chrétiennes' (2004).

As our predecessor wrote, 'Reading these pages provides our truest contact with the soul and thought of Blessed Alix Le Clerc, and with her spirituality'. These are work notes which Alix collected for the talks she gave the sisters to initiate them in the spiritual life. Some passages may have been taken from such and such an author. Her choice of these is significant, and if she does not name her sources, this is because she has assimilated them to the point where she can use them as her own. She expresses herself like a teacher, used to giving talks to her girls, the nuns of her 'little Congregation'. Her direct style – rhetorical questions, exclamations, supposed objections and so on, reveal the oral basis of the writing. There is no heavy rhetoric, only a clear purpose, sharply indicated: the *Little Notebook* contains, she wrote, seed for the most essential virtues, seed which she hopes 'with the grace of God to cast upon our barren lands, so that all the other [virtues] may sprout and grow with these'. This is her true voice, admitting that all of us, she and we ourselves, resemble the barren lands where only the Lord can make the seed sprout and grow.

Of inner peace

As in an exercise of St Ignatius, Alix starts by addressing God in a prayer appropriate to the subject of her meditation. Here it is in a modernised style, as appointed for the Office of Readings on the feast of 9 January:

My God and Lord, send me the light of your holy and blessed Spirit, that I may find the path of Peace which you declared to us on the day of your holy Nativity by the voice of your Angels. If You, eternal Truth, had not told us to seek it, we should not be able to find it; we are in this world surrounded by so many enemies, very strong and very daring, ready to attack us on all sides, while we are very weak and lazy in resisting them.

... It is therefore in You, O my God and my strength, that I mean to find all I seek; your eternal Wisdom has taught us how to possess our souls in peace in the midst of war. I implore you, my God and Saviour, to grant us all such grace that we may walk by the road it has pleased you to tread for us, by your example and by the merits of your blessed Mother, whom we long to imitate, assisted by her power. In this hope we wish to die beneath the shelter of her name and protection.[265]

Of the deceit of those who seek a false peace

Having established the preliminaries, Alix goes back to the problem: many deceive themselves and think they are in peace because everything is going well for them. She gives these only a few lines and then comes to the sisters who are seriously guilty ('Woe betide them!' she dares to write) because, 'enlightened by the true light and withdrawn from the blindfold of the world to seek the real truth', they intend 'to possess peace before they have won it in battle'. Now she describes the meaningless contentment of a nun who is pleased to have an easy life without trouble or temptation. After vigorously rejecting this false peace, she answers the question:

What is true peace? In this life our peace consists in a great deal of patience; to attain this, great grace from God is needed, and will not be refused to those who have the will to profit from it.

. . . If there be any good in this world, it is the man of
peace who has it, for the Kingdom of God is peace and joy
in the Holy Spirit. The soul which does not have inner
peace is like a boat tossed by winds and storms, always in
danger of perishing, of shipwreck; it can do no good for
itself or for others because it takes such care to think about
itself that this is where its trouble arises. To put this right, we
must remember that Our Lord said, "He who would be my
disciple must renounce himself, take up his cross and follow
me".[266]

Ending her meditation with practical resolutions, Alix reminds
the sisters of the three postulates proper to their Congregation:
to seek the honour and glory of God, to work at their personal
salvation and become saints, and to help their neighbour. By
suggesting collective resolutions, Alix turns her piece into a
community exercise.

The framework of this meditation on a traditional theme[267]
tells us more than we might expect about Alix's soul. She had
herself experienced the paradox she puts forward: true peace is
enjoyed in spiritual conflict. She denounces with conviction the
pursuit of false peace and reminds her daughters of the demands
made by their calling. But does she not speak to every Christian
when like St Paul she uses 'the language of the Cross'?

Let us seek the centre of our soul which is God

Mystics are not afraid to look at the outside world and find that
it echoes the inner life. In this way Alix, believing that 'every
created thing has a centre' to which it returns as being the place
of its happiness, sees here for every human an invitation to look
for 'his aim and purpose and place of rest'. She uses the natural
elements and asserts that fire, earth, water, birds and fish obey

this principle, even though their real purpose is to be created for the service of mankind. This anthropocentric view of creation leads her to establish a hierarchy among all created things in which the superior beings command the inferior. From this, she says, 'it follows that man, whose spirit is immortal, must be superior to mortal beings'. Pushing her logic all the way, she comes to the conclusion that man cannot find true peace in that which is less than himself but certainly 'in God, infinite in every perfection'. Then like the psalmist she takes flight, saying, 'Oh for the wings of a dove to fly away and find rest' (Ps. 55:7). And as soon as she sees the promised rest, she gives the heartfelt cry, 'Oh end most worthy to be longed and sought for! Blessed may you be, my good Lord, in that without our deserving it, without having worked for it, you have given us so happy an end and supreme repose for ever, which is yourself. Oh that my heart were able to express what it conceives of this future good!'

Alix's thought here takes a strongly Augustinian tone. Like Augustine, she takes her point of departure from experienced fact. What he called 'happiness' in his treatise *De beata vita*, she calls 'true peace' and like him she declares that any good thing which will perish leaves us anxious and unsatisfied. 'All abundance which is not my God to me is indigence',[268] he said, and like him she concludes that the end of man is God himself. Swift to go in search of 'Him who made us', she sought to take her companions with her. Using the metaphor of the road, so frequent among mystics, she invited them to set off: it remains for us now to take the road of peace for our souls, although it is long and hard for those who love themselves; the further we get away from self-love the shorter we make the road leading to the love of God, which is the most effective way of establishing holy peace within us. Let us love him, no one but him. This love of God means that we always look at infinite beauty and goodness, and teaches us that nothing is worth being loved, esteemed or desired except himself; let us desire him, only him, for the sake of his love. Let us say to him, in love and from the heart: Grant me, Lord, that you may be in me and I in you, and that being so joined, we may always stay together. For you are truly my beloved, chosen amongst thousands, in whom my soul has delighted to stay and rest all the days of its life. Truly you are my peace and my love[269] in whom is true rest; without you there is only labour and pain. (*Rel./Cahier* 2004, pp. 108– 9)

Here Alix reveals the depths of her soul, and the revelation is the more precious because the *Little Notebook*, unlike the *Relation*, contains not confidences but instructions of value to all the sisters, among whom she includes herself, as is shown by her constant use of the pronoun 'we'. In this passage the word 'I' breaks surface, expressing a personal witness she could not restrain. Very significant too is the change from 'vous' to 'tu' when addressing God, as is the mystic 'beloved' (*bien-aimé*) she uses of the Lord. After this outburst, she returns to instruction, although without losing the tone of personal witness.

> Let us run after him then, like the thirsty hart which desires the springs of fresh water, but let us go gently for fear of stumbling, and do not let us deceive ourselves when we feel our affection united with God, for in order to reach perfect unity we must by repeated practice mortify all our emotions and subject them to the superior part of our souls, and our will must be always united to that of our God with such perfection that we no longer know what it is we want or do not want. Those of us who seek him by this road will be truly peaceful in their souls, because the Master of peace will have taken his place in their hearts.

A mistress of the spiritual life, Alix Le Clerc could present in a few sentences the great stages of the Christian's journey towards God – purification, requiring the stripping away of self-love; illumination, leading to love of God. She used the direct and simple terms of a good teacher – 'Go gently for fear of stumbling'. But prudence and gentleness do not exclude uncompromising demands, for it is 'perfect union' that must be sought. To reach it, she denounced the illusions offered by emotion and recommended the renunciation of ourselves in daily life. She expressed in her vivid manner and with striking imagery the constant effort required to 'seek the things that are above'. Picking up the spatial metaphor of our progress 'towards the centre of our soul, which is God', she spoke here of 'subjecting our passions to the superior part of our soul', a phrase like that in the *Relation*, 'To render the flesh subject to the spirit and the spirit to God, seeking him and loving him in everything' (*Rel.* 11). This setting in order, an exercise in Christian discipline, attains the same summit as mystical grace: the Master of peace dwells in our heart.

Alix rejoiced in this certainty and echoed the heartfelt words of St Paul: 'I myself live no longer', she says, 'but Jesus Christ lives in me'. And she sang of the joy of a soul that has reached true peace:

All the powers of hell will not be able to shake her, for she holds Jesus crucified within her and believes that he has power over all the demons and evil spirits. But will not the wind of vainglory, the reputation for sanctity, the visions and divine consolations, the gift of prophecy and of performing miracles, tear her away from the holy crucified one, her beloved? No, for she desires to follow him along the way of the cross and of scorn of oneself; and her greatest longing is that she be found worthy to suffer something for his love. (*Rel./Cahiers* 2004, p. 110)

Here we can recall a confidence Alix made. She was discreet and did not talk about herself but did base her teaching on experiences of her own. Developed and generalised, these could be useful to others. Now she made clear the secret of her dauntless resistance to the demon and the strength she drew from the Cross of Christ. Having been ordered to describe the wishes of her soul in the *Relation*, she provided a key to the contents of the *Little Notebook* when she explained the exact circumstances in which she received her greatest gifts of mystical grace: 'It was', she said, 'most often in considering the infinite merits of the holy Life and Passion of my Saviour, which I would wish to have continually in my memory' (*Rel.* 60). Committed to following him on the road of the Cross, she exulted, as had the apostles, that she was judged worthy 'to suffer for love of him' (Acts 5, 41).

Then, not losing sight of the every day world, she gave practical advice to her nuns: walk sincerely and simply in his presence, care nothing for any creature except for love of him, see in them only the image of the Lord, his power, goodness and wisdom'. Then from these principles to applications: the soul which recognises the greatness of God, she said, desires his honour and glory. Speaking as she was to nuns who recited or chanted the Holy Office, she showed them that this prayer was a way of celebrating God's glory, as long as it was done 'with reverence and modesty', here meaning dignity. We need to remember that for the young Congregation of Our Lady, lacking any monastic tradition, recitation of the office in the choir was a new thing which had to be learnt. Pierre Fourier in his *Le Primitif et Légitime Esprit* devoted long pages to suggesting how the sisters could occupy their minds during the hours of the breviary.[270] Alix, more briefly, referred to 'the spirit of distraction' which derived, she said, from 'our sex's ignorance'. Did she mean that knowledge of Latin, uncommon among women in the seventeenth century, would enable nuns to understand the text and prevent minds wandering, as female minds can do? She recommended a method used by someone she knew, who used to recite each psalm while giving thanks in turn to each Person of the Trinity.

She had taught her daughters how to speak to God; now Alix asked them to speak about him. She knew from her own experience: 'One who is aware of God present in her soul cannot help often talking about him'. The mission of the word was for her of the greatest urgency, one which the sisters could not avoid. She wanted their zeal for souls to have a universal dimension, so that everyone 'should know, honour and serve this great God'. But she felt that this mission should begin with the near neighbour, within the community, in 'ordinary conversations': conversations, not learned discourses, in circumstances where the subjects discussed usually arise spontaneously. Alix defined their nature – each sister would try, she said, 'to throw out sparks of holy fire, gathered in holy meditation and in contemplating the works and perfections of God'. Nothing could better describe Alix's own work in her *Little Notebook*.

Preparing a place for God in our soul

Once we have sought for and found Our Lord, who is our true peace and rest, we must take the trouble to rejoice in his blest presence and to prepare for him a dwelling fit for his greatness. We must not be daunted by our poverty, as he himself will provide us with all we need to perfect our work. All he asks of us is faithfulness and a little effort to make good use of the talent he will put into our hands. And let us not be like the man who hid his talent in the ground so that he was scorned by his master whereas the others were praised for having brought forth fruit.

In this section of the *Little Notebook* Alix clearly had in mind the text from St John, 'If anyone loves me, he will keep my word, and my Father will love him, and we shall come to him and make our home with him' (John 14:23). She followed the evangelist and St Teresa of Avila in using the image of the inner dwelling place, the part of ourselves to which God comes as guest. Unlike St Teresa, whose entire *Book of Mansions* describes the journey of the soul up to the seventh Dwelling of the *Interior Castle*, where it finds its centre, which is God, Alix succinctly describes this progression by using the parable of the talents. Employing Christ's images, she explains how we can prepare a dwelling place for God in our soul. He is the master builder and we the workers, to whom he allocates the means of completing the task. Since we shall have to give an account of the gifts received, she makes us look them over once again, 'so that through this knowledge,' she says, 'we shall be moved to love and be grateful to him'. As a teacher she understood the connection between 'to love' and 'to know'. She therefore used a method common in her time and drew up an almost complete list of all the truths of the faith. First came our free will, strong to do good and avoid evil. Second came the being God had given us, adorned 'with its own life and its living image', preserved by divine Providence. Thirdly Alix celebrated the Christ who came to save us; and fourthly she marvelled at the graces bestowed on us through the sacraments, especially that of forgiveness. At the end of this summary, almost a catechism, she moved into prayer:

Oh how good and generous you are to us, my God, in all the good you constantly do us, in your patience in enduring our ingratitude and lack of faith. You do not scorn to inspire us continually with your holy and blest Spirit, which shows us your holy will. And to preserve these graces he has in his pure goodness added the religious calling, the true mark of our predestination, if we live according to the aims for which this state was established.

And she settles the balance-sheet in a form of prayer:

You will be well satisfied with us, my God, if we manage it all so that the major profit comes to you. For yourself you ask only our heart, but it must be whole, and free from any affection for your creatures, clinging only to you in love, so that you may dwell there and take your delight.

Then let us turn to and build him a temple in our hearts, so that he may rest there in peace and we too may rest in him in this world and in his eternal kingdom for ever.

This meditation, which shows the balance Alix thought should be kept between action and contemplation, is typical of her spirituality. She indicates the effort demanded of us by verbs of action – we must 'seek, prepare, take trouble, make an effort, build, erect a building' – but she also uses peaceful verbs – 'receive, love, know, cling to, rest, dwell, take delight', because God rewards our good will by a closer union. She expresses the mutuality of this love by the phrases, such as 'Myself in God and God in me'.[271]

The virtue of humility

Alix knew for certain that no one could be called humble except the Christ. He, possessed of all glory and honour, for love of God his Father chose to renounce these in order to satisfy divine justice. To drive this message home she recalled the words of St Paul as he presented the Easter mystery to the Philippians (Phil. 2:5–11), or demonstrated in his letter to the Romans (Rom. 8:3) how Christ, being without sin, had taken on our sinful condition to set us free. She spoke of Mary, purer than the stars, who yet acknowledged her unimportance (Luke 1:48). She talked of the small children we are called on to imitate. Except in this last instance, she did not give references. Holy Scripture nourished her soul so that her writings are as it were impregnated with it. From the revealed Christ she looked at the sisters as they lived their daily lives, then returned her gaze to the Saviour's humility and tried to see how it could be copied. Her meditation moves forward in this double form.

Next she asks what we are to do, confronted by the humbleness of Christ? Nothing more or less than to acknowledge our condition as created beings and the consequences this entails. Five or six times she repeats the exhortation that we should have 'true knowledge of ourselves'. She does not take pleasure in painting a dark portrait but stresses our 'lowliness, wretchedness, smallness', glad, it seems, to unveil a truth which ought to be blindingly obvious. To admit that we are sinners was also for her to know that we have received everything from God and that he loves us, in spite of our limitations. This inspires in return our love and gratitude towards the author of 'all we have that is good'. It gives him, she says, the opportunity to grant us freely, 'without our asking', all we need.

Alix wanted these ideas of the faith, firmly based on a strong scriptural foundation, to be part of the living breathing life of every day. She could always offer excellent practical steps but made sure they were never cut adrift from the acts of spiritual devotion which must inspire them. The image of the humble Christ must always dwell in the hearts of the sisters, and in contemplating it they would realise how much they fell short. A

perceptive psychologist, used to the direction of souls, Alix
sketched out some pictures of nuns who lacked humility, and
for each one she supplied an appropriate remedy. To end, she
gave them a contrasting portrait:

> A humble man is loved and held dear by all: he is glad to be of
> service, gives way to all, great or small, does not make himself
> important, makes no account of his nobility or the other
> good qualities he may have, covers and hides the good he
> does, even from himself, does not care about greatnesses of
> this world but values them for what they are, true folly,
> considers his own faults and imperfections, thinks more
> often about his own shortcomings rather than noticing his
> neighbour's faults . . .

In these pages humbleness can be reconciled with the thinking
of those who consider it 'a synonym of self-annihilation of the
creature, confronted with God who is all, and of the diminution
of the self in relation to others'.[272] There is much to be learnt
from the way Alix approached the subject. Avoiding narrow
moralising, she defined this virtue as a manner of being inherent
in our nature, and recommended that we make the effort to
think clearly in order to understand our created condition and
its limits. Humility, she considered, was the good ground, the
soil in which all the other virtues could grow.

Alix's text and vocabulary contribute to the outdated impression her works convey. Spiritual writings age fast and
demand of us an effort in understanding them which makes
them doubly useful. Certainly we no longer talk about 'vainglory' (*la vaine gloire*), a traditional theme which Alix develops
when discussing those who plume themselves on their work
and boast of their achievements, but we can agree in denouncing
'vanity', 'the temptation to define oneself on the basis of what

one does, of one's employment, one's works'.[273] Alix already
insists that we do not confuse being and doing, making it clear
that success, efficacy, is not the best criterion on which to base
a judgment. Her thought seems modern indeed in her idea
of humility, seeing it not as one particular virtue or as a step
in self-improvement, but as an element essential to a life in
common. When she denounces the great blindness which
prevents us from seeing our true selves, she is also fighting
against the pride which stops us seeing the true nature of others
and of God.

'The Mother's thoughts about the Institute'

The sisters at Nancy did well to collect and write down their
memories of what Alix said to them about the Institute. She
casts light on the novelty of the Congregation which she and
Fourier founded, creating a body in which professed religious
also taught children. She deals at once with this very point,
defining the sisters' way of life. It was, she said, 'a mixed life', a
phrase which in the seventeenth century marked a revolution.
This 'mixture' linked together two elements which until then
had always been supposed to be irreconcilable for women
living in convents, those of contemplation and action. Pierre
Fourier and Alix Le Clerc, neither of them a friend to half
measures, took up the challenge and created a form of religious
life in which the fervour of contemplation supported the zeal
of mission. In Alix's time the sisters made solemn vows, lived
in community in an enclosed cloister where they devoted
themselves to prayer, completely cut off as advised by the
Council of Trent. But they were able to take this consecrated
life, dedicated to God, and with the same generous spirit to
consecrate it afresh to their neighbour, choosing for their chief
mission the education of young girls.[274] In the text quoted

below Alix does not touch on the debates with Rome as to the legality of this innovation, she was only concerned with the spiritual problem, how best to lead this 'mixed life'. Here is her opening passage:

> If the nuns of the Congregation who are living a mixed life do not begin by establishing a firm basis (*un grand fond*) of spirituality, they will risk being easily distracted and diverted by their teaching activity. But if they can manage the great talent of their vocation well, they will one day know the grace God has done them in calling them to such a worthwhile task. Their first care must be to work to honour the plans of Our Lord and keep the souls of little girls in a state of innocence by impressing on them in good time the fear of God and a horror of sin.[275]

Alix, who had learnt as a mistress of novices the importance of early training, advises young nuns to lay down this 'firm basis of spirituality', a solid foundation which will guarantee the strength of the building they are to erect. The eye of faith with which the novices will learn to look at everything during their time of probation, will turn them towards God (this is what the word 'conversion' means) and will prevent their being turned away, diverted, by the variety of their teaching work. Like Pascal, Alix used the word 'diversion' (*divertissement*) for all that is merely additional, that distracts from the essential, in this case from the purpose of education. When she defines 'such a worthwhile task', she links it to the Saviour's redemptive mission, as the sisters are working to foster the grace of baptism in children's souls. In fact she could not say more clearly that 'the apostolic activity of the Sisters of Our Lady is part of the very nature of their religious life', to quote the words of the conciliar decretal of Vatican II, *Perfectae caritatis*.[276] The 'mixed life' established by Alix is exactly that of apostolic nuns, as laid down by the Council.

Nor did she have any trouble proving its excellence, for as she said, Our Lord and his Mother led this 'mixed life', 'in order to show us the way to the highest perfection'. She gave supporting examples and suggested to her daughters that they should 'represent to themselves' those people in Scripture who would confirm them in the choice of life they had made. In this she was using a sure and simple method that many saints – Bernard, Francis of Assisi, Ignatius de Loyola – had employed successfully to instruct the faithful. Like them, Alix advised her daughters to use their imagination and step into the gospel scenes. She took them into the desert to listen to John the Baptist revealing the greatness of the Messiah, hidden from men but known to God. She led them to Nazareth to contemplate God made man, despised and reviled, and urgently begged the sisters to do as he did and love persecution. This imaginative work is effective – spectators become actors in the imagined scene, it becomes new, actual, and offers a model of conduct for daily life.

The process is clearer still in the final example: an apocryphal story which places Mary in the Temple in Jerusalem, living the same life as the other little girls there except that she would withdraw at a set time to pray. This devotional exercise of the imagination enabled Alix to point out the parallel between the Virgin's use of time in the Temple and that of the nuns in their convent. They would pray, meditate, and sing God's praise 'in order to receive', she said, 'the heavenly dew and manna which they must then share out among their little scholars, as the Virgin did in the Temple'. Clearly, the sisters were not only to share Mary's life in their imaginations but must continue to share it in their every day life.

At the end of this section Alix teaches her daughters how to live in union with God in their outward actions. We should bear her striking phrases in mind: to have the intention and spirit raised in God, to seek him in simplicity of heart, to work to save souls, one of which is worth more than a whole world.

Sometimes we regret that Alix died too early to take part in the drawing up of the definitive Constitutions of 1640, but a text like this one tempers our disappointment. It shows how thoroughly the founder and foundress shared ideas, as here where we see how firmly the sisters' apostolic vocation was rooted in the reality of the Incarnation. Like Alix, Fourier defined the sisters' chosen life as 'mixed'. He wrote:

> Of the three forms of religious life, the active, the con-
> templative, and that which partakes of both, they chose
> the third as the most excellent . . . the most useful in these
> days . . . and to try to reconcile the different functions of
> Mary and Martha in such a way that action does not hinder
> contemplation, nor contemplation action.[277]

As for being able to live a 'mixed life' in holiness, Fourier and Alix agree in stating that the surest road to this is by contemplation of Christ in the Scriptures. Like good teachers, they both suggest how this is to be done, each according to his and her temperament. Alix with her feminine sensitivity turns to the imagination and recommends that we stage the gospel stories in our minds; Fourier looks more generally on the whole life of Christ and in his abundant flow of words reveals the joy he finds there:

> They thirst to follow Our Lord wherever he may go . . .
> knowing that all his deeds, all his words while he was alive
> and visible here on this earth are given them for a rule and for

instruction . . . they look closely at all they can learn of what
he did and said there, and at what he taught, honoured,
advised, counselled, embraced, practised, such as poverty, toil,
hunger, thirst, zeal for souls, an insatiable longing to do in all
things the will of God.[278]

They had the same purpose, Alix and Fourier: through
contemplation of our model, to succeed in making our life
like his.

Epilogue 2004

Alix had written, 'It came into my mind that the vocation I should follow would suffer much persecution without being destroyed and that Our Lord would make it firm and stable' (*Rel.* 45). This promise has been kept for four hundred years, for 'the faithfulness of the Lord endures from age to age'.

In 1650 the Congregation had fifty-nine establishments in France, Luxemburg, Brussels, Val d'Aosta and Germany. In 1747 it entered Hungary. In 1789, out of ninety houses the Revolution closed the seventy-five in France. Once the storm had passed, some of these reappeared. At the beginning of the nineteenth century Napoleon I closed the German convents, but in 1833 one of the sisters' former pupils, Karolina Gerhardinger, was inspired by Fourier's educational work to found the 'School Sisters' who are now active in thirty-two countries. At the end of the nineteenth century there were closures and re-openings in Germany, while in France at the start of the twentieth century the Combes laws expelled all teaching Congregations. This led the sisters to make new homes in England, Belgium, the Netherlands and Hungary, before returning when they could do so to France. In Hungary and Slovakia it was not until 1989 that the nuns were able to reopen their schools, closed in 1950. Although the different houses always kept in touch with each other, there was no legal union until the twentieth century. The Union of Jupille in 1910 reunited the daughter houses of the Jupille convent in Belgium, founded from Trèves in 1878, while the Roman Union, recognised by Rome in 1931, gradually collected the houses of several different countries. A German-speaking federation was formed in 1961, and in 1963 the Unions of Jupille and Rome joined forces. The creation of unions and of a more centralised governing body encouraged the Congregation to grow world-wide – to Brazil in 1906, Vietnam in 1935, the Belgian Congo in 1940, Uganda in 1960, and after 1963 in Algeria, Hong Kong, California, Mexico and Chad. In 1969 the Chapter of *aggiornamento*, required by the Council of Vatican II, declared unanimously that 'apostolic action is part of the very nature of the religious life of the Congregation'. The sisters in 1987 drew up a new constitution which was approved by Rome in 1987 and allows them to discover new expressions of communal life, prayer and teaching.

Well aware that the founders' God-given power to arouse devotion and enthusiasm is a gift of the Spirit to the Church, the sisters of Our Lady do all they can to deepen these and to share them. The teaching spirit of Pierre Fourier and Alix Le Clerc flourishes in their schools and in France the Congregation supervises sixteen educational establishments and their more than twenty thousand students. As nuns and teachers, the sisters strive in all their different tasks, in schools and elsewhere, to foster the growth and development of the person. Pierre Fourier's purpose, to help individuals become their true selves, is a very present need, so much so that across all the immense needs of our world everyone, believer or not, can hear the call.

Epilogue 2014

The author Marie-Claire Tihon adds for the English edition:

La publication de la biographie de la Bienheureuse Le Clerc en langue anglaise dix ans après son édition français se situe dans le grande mouvement de retour aux sources de leur spiritualité que le concile Vatican II a réclamé de tous les ordres religieux. La Congrégation Notre-Dame est entrée avec joie dans cet élan, heureuse de découvrir toujours plus la richesse inépuisable de la vie et des écrits de sa fondatrice.

Conscientes de posséder en la sainteté d'Alix un trésor culpable de communiquer à d'autres dans l'Église universelle un peu de son amour entier pour Dieu, les religieuses de Notre-Dame n'ont voulu garder dans la chapelle de leur école de Nancy les reliques de la bienheureuse. Elle les ont offertes à la cathédrale de la ville où, le dimanche 14 octobre 2007, Mgr Papin, évêque de Toul et Nancy, les a accueillies. Cette présence d'Alix sur sa terre de Lorraine nous tourne vers le passé mais nous pousse en avant car selon les mots du pape François, 'La joie évangélisatrice brille toujours sur le fond de la mémoire reconnaissante. C'est une grâce que nous avons besoin du demander.'

Janet Shirley translates:

The publication of the life of Blessed Alix Le Clerc in English ten years after its appearance in French is part of the great movement of return to the sources of their spiritual life which The Second Vatican Council required of all the religious orders. The Congregation of Our Lady has been delighted to share in this initiative, joyfully discovering ever more of the inexhaustible riches of the life and writings of their founder.

Knowing that in her holiness they possessed a treasure well able to pass on to others in the universal Church something of her total love of God, the sisters of Our Lady decided not to keep the relics of Blessed Alix in the chapel of their school in Nancy. Instead they gave them to the cathedral where, on Sunday 14 October 2007, Mgr Papin, Bishop of Toul and Nancy, received them. This presence of Alix in her own land of Lorraine turns our thoughts to the past but also makes us look ahead because, in the words of Pope Francis, 'The joy of declaring the Gospel always shines out on a background of grateful recollection. This is a grace we should ask for.'

The Congregation of Our Lady Canonesses of St Augustine is international and its Sisters are to be found in twelve countries across the world.

Address of the governing body:

50/52 rue Louis Auroux
94120 Fontenay-sous-Bois, France

Website: www.cnd-csa.org

Associates' website: www.alix-pierre-associated.org

Endnotes

Chapter One: *'A good and devout girl in everyone's opinion'*
   pp. 17–30

1 Guy Cabourdin, *Encyclopédie illustrée de la Lorraine*, Paris, les temps modernes, vol.1 'L'affaire de Remiremont', p. 95.

2 *Vie*, 1666, p. 70.

3 Pierre de Gonneville, *Vers la béatification* . . . (articles in *La Croix de Lorraine*, Epinal, published separately 1947; and 'La famille Le Clerc d'Hymont', *Annales de l'Est*, 1965, n. 3, pp. 217–33. An abstract of these articles by the abbot of Gonneville appears in the journal *Généalogie Lorraine*, December 2000, n. 118, pp. 4–7)

4 Guy Cabourdin, 'L'expédition des reîtres', p. 117; Jean-Marie Constant, *Les Guise*, Paris, Hachette, 1984, pp. 90 and 160.

5 Guy Cabourdin, 'Le passage des gens de guerre', p. 103.

6 Pierre de Gonneville quotes the in-folio 25 leaf register kept in the archives at Epinal (CC 51), 'Compte de Jean Clerc, en l'année 1587'.

7 A. Guinot, *Etude historique de l'abbaye de Remiremont*, 1859.

8 See P. de Gonneville, quoting Bergerot, *Les Institutions municipals de Remiremont*, 1901.

9 *Remiremont, l'abbaye et la ville*, Actes des journées d'études vosgiennes, 17–20 April 1980, Michel Parisse, University of Nancy, II, 1980.

10 A prebend is the revenue allocated to a canonry, for a canon or canoness, paid out of the chapter's income from rents, here appropriated to the use of Noble Ladies.

11 The four noble chapters of Lorraine were known as the Ladies of Remiremont, the Damsels of Epinal, the Chambermaids of Bouxières and the Servant Girls of Poussay.

12 Michel Pernot, 'Catherine de Lorraine, abbesse de Remiremont, Réflexions sur l'échec d'une réforme', in *Remiremont, l'abbaye et la ville*, p. 100.

13 Georges Poull, 'L'église et la paroisse Notre-Dame de 1570 a 1630', in Actes des journées d'étude vosgiennes, pp. 250–62. The church of Our Lady was demolished in the Revolution, when the former abbey church became the parish church and after the chapter ceased to exist in 1790 was given the name Notre-Dame-en-sa-Nativité.

14 Jean Delumeau has a chapter on sacrilegious confession in *Le Péché et la Peur*, Paris, Fayard, 1983, pp. 517–35.

15 This word was often used in the plural – the vanities, vain things – and refers to appearance, to what is derisory, attractive but disappointing, ephemeral, illusory. Mystics used it of the nothingness of being. Pascal would later use it frequently in his pages on human unhappiness.' Paule Sagot, Présentation de la *Relation d'Alix Le Clerc*.

16 *Vie,* 1666, p. 70.

17 Jean Le Clerc died at Hymont in 1602. His widow went to live at Mattaincourt, where she died in 1609; see P. de Gonneville.

Chapter Two: *Conversion,* pp. 31–41

18 Of some thirty visions, eighteen are introduced by such expressions as *It seemed to me* (*Rel.*4), *I thought I saw* (*Rel.* 19), and so on.

19 Fr Poulain in *Des grâces d'oraison, Traité de théologie mystique,* (Paris, Beauchesne, 1931, p. 312) explains: 'In French we usually say 'imaginary', not 'imaginative' (*imaginaires, imaginatives*). I have made this change in our tongue as the word 'imaginary' almost always indicates some lapse of the imagination, it is used of things which do not exist, whereas 'imaginative' implies a healthy act of the imagination.' According to Alain Guillermou (*Ignace de Loyola,* Paris, Tequi, 1991, p. 102), the word 'imaginary' means not 'fictitious' but 'which moves in the imagination's world of images'.

20 François de Sales, *Introduction à la vie dévote, Œuvres,* Paris, Gallimard, coll. 'Bibliothèque de la Pléiade', pp. 222–5.

21 This late fifteenth century masterpiece is in the church of Bar-sur-Loup, a village in the Alpes-Maritimes. A thirty-three line poem in Provençal describes the scene.

22 We should note the religious connotations of the vocabulary used in such works as the *Relation.*

In the catechesis of that time, simple persons (as distinct from 'les savants', those with knowledge) were 'les rudes', the ignorant, the unschooled, as receptive as children. Both words could describe Alix, taking these first steps on her spiritual journey. The white veil is a symbol of baptism.

23 'J'avais un grand regret de n'avoir pas gardé la pureté de l'âme dès mon enfance (*Rel.* 69).

24 *Vie*, 1666, 'Remarques des actions des vertus que la Mère a pratiquées', p. 327.

25 *Ibid.*, 'Sentiments de la Mère sur l'Institut', p. 226.

26 He later founded the Congregation of Our Saviour.

27 This way of describing her conversion allows us to date the composition of the *Relation* to about 1617 or 1618.

28 This was not a mystical levitation but an imaginative vision, affecting not only ears and eyes but the whole body. Alix began her account with the words, '[It] seemed to me that . . . ' and did not claim to give a scientific explanation. She wanted to make clear the harmony between her impressions and what they symbolised.

Chapter Three: *'This vocation is from God'*, pp. 42–55

29 Comte A. Gandelet, *La Vénérable Alix Le Clerc*, Paris, 1906, p. 48.

30 At the time of the Counter-Reformation the French word, *Religion*, meant an institution in which solemn vows were made.

31 Here this simply means 'nuns'.

32 Historians do not agree about their names. As the three 'shock troops' are generally thought to be: Alix Le Clerc herself, Gante André and Isabelle de Louvroir (that is, Alix, with Gante and Isabelle from Mattaincourt) the third girl she mentions here as coming to her is less certain; but see the beginning of Chapter Fifteen.

33 Some biographers say that Claude Chauvenel joined the group.

34 Jean Bedel, *La Vie du Très Révérend Père Fourier*, Pont à Mousson, 1656, p. 126.

35 These sisters were not enclosed.

36 In Lorraine, then independent.

37 See the *Dictionnaire de spiritualité*, Crèche.

38 See *Mirecourt et Poussay*, Journées d'études vosgiennes, 22–23 May 1982, Nancy University Press, 1984: M. Parisse, 'Poussay au Moyen Age'; F. Boquillon, 'Le chapitre a l'époque moderne'; and J. M. d'Harreville, 'La vie des Dames du Poussay'.

39 See Abbot C. Chapelier, *Le R.P. Jean Fourier de la Compagnie de Jésus, 1559–1636*, Remiremont, printed Kopf-Roussel, 1900.

40 E. Renard, (*La Mère Alix Le Clerc*, Paris, J. de Gigord, 1935, p. 89. This may have been Père Nicadese, 'as there was only one Père Nicaud in the company, unlikely to have known Fourier, not living at Pont and too young to be consulted'. See too L. Carrez, *Histoire du premier monastère de la Congrégation Notre-Dame*, Châlons-sur-Marne, Martin frères, 1906, vol. 1, p. 6.

41 Alix addresses her *Relation* to the Jesuit Father Guéret, so refers to his fellow Jesuits as 'your Fathers, your Company'.

42 Quoted by Rogie, *Histoire du B. Pierre Fourier*, Verdun, 1887, vol. 1, p. 557.

43 Fourier's letter of 17 September 1627 (*C*. II, 351–53) includes this text entitled 'Extrait du règlement provisionnel que gardaient les filles de la Congrégation de Notre-Dame avant qu'elles fussent religieuses'.

44 Among these the canon of Remiremont, who in 1766 wrote *La Vie de la Vénérable Mère Alix Le Clerc*, includes 'two great men, among the first in learning, in experience and in holiness of life', Sinçon and Comelet.

Chapter Four: *'Apparently small beginnings'*, pp. 56–65

45 Mgr Fourier-Bonnard, *Les Relations de la famille ducale de Lorraine et Saint-Siége, dans les trois derniers siècles de l'indépendance*, Nancy, 1933.

46 *Vie*, 1666, 'Sommaire du dessein des Filles de la Congrégation de la Bienheureuse Vierge Marie', p. 119.

47 *Constitutions de 1640*, part 5, chapter VI, 'Du devoir des religieuses envers les grands qui gouvernent les peuples, et pour le spirituel et pour le temporel'.

48 *Recueil de plusieurs monuments historiques*, quoted in: J. Rogie, *Histoire du B. Père Fourier*, Verdun, 1887, vol.1, p. 555.

49 J. Bedel, *La Vie du Très Révérend Père Fourier*, Pont-à-Mousson, 1656, 'De la Mère Gante André', pp. 149–58.

50 Mère Louis de Gonzague, *Alix Le Clerc, dite en religion Mère Thérèse de Jésus*, 2 vols. bound as one, Liège, 1889, pp. 82–3.

51 Chanoine de Remiremont, *Vie de la Vénérable Mère Alix Le Clerc*, Remiremont, 1766.

52 *Quelques remarques de la vie et des miracles de notre B. Père Instituteur*, manuscript collection made by sisters of the monastery of Saint-Mihiel, 17th Century copy in the Archives of the Congrégation Notre-Dame, p. 3.

53 *Mirecourt et Poussay*, Journées d'études vosgiennes, 22–23 May 1982, Nancy University Press, 1984, p. 146.

54 Quoted by J. Rogie, vol. 1, p. 192, referring to A. d'Hangest, *Histoire générale du B. Pierre Fourier* bk. IV, article II.

55 E. Renard, *La Mère Alix Le Clerc*, Paris, Gigord, 1935, p. 112, referring to d'Hangest, bk. IV, article II.

56 Some soon did so: Anne de Choiseul joined the Carmelites at Nancy; the younger sister of Madame de Fresnel chose the Annonciades of Saint-Mihiel; Henriette and her sister Elisabeth de Beauvau-Craon opted for the Dames de Sainte-Marie in Paris.

Chapter Five: *For or against a 'new house'?*, pp. 66–78

57 After the dedication, D.O.M. (*Deo Optimo Maximo*) and the date, *1719*, six lines read [in translation]: 'Here is the cradle of the holy Institute / founded upon zeal for salvation./ it is 120 years since, in this small place,/ the Congregation of the Mother of God,/ in this enclosed garden where their house stood,/ began with fervour their holy teaching'.

58 When he heard of the death of Jeanne Brégeot (soeur Ignace de Saint-Jean), Fourier wrote on 6 February 1639 to the sisters of Mirecourt, 'She was a good pillar of your Congregation'. To the sisters at Bar, whose Superior she had been, he sent his funeral eulogy, a magnificent example of his letter-writing art (*C.* 4, 495).

59 'Never in this Congregation shall the superior of a monastery . . . take the name of abbess or prioress, nor of My Lady nor Lady . . . They shall restrict themselves simple and permanently to the

beautiful name of Mother'. *Constitutions de 1640*, part 4, chapter VI, p. 3.

60 *Vie*, 1666, p. 208.

61 *Constitutions de 1640*, part 4, chapter VI, p. 22, 'De la Mère Supérieure'.

62 Jean Bedel, *La Vie du Très Révérend Père Fourier*, Pont-à-Mousson, 1656, p. 146.

63 *Op. cit.*, Bedel, p. 362.

64 Quoted by R. Taveneaux (*C.* 1, XVIII, n. 42) referring to Rogie, vol.1, p. 216.

65 The Franciscans, much involved in Catholic reform, between 1580 and 1630 created several reformed branches: Recollects, Cordeliers, Capuchins, Tertiaries and Minims.

66 Ignatius de Loyola, *Spiritual Exercises*, First exercise, first preface, 47.

67 'Much comforted' translates the expression 'se consolant beaucoup', and the author adds a footnote explaining that the word *consolation* at that period had a wider sense, implying 'peace in the depths of the soul, a heart at rest and indwelt by a Presence'. See Paule Sagot, Présentation de la *Relation*, 1996.

68 *Vie*, 1666, pp. 336–8.

69 See, for example, letter of 12 April 1622.

70 *Vie*, 1666, p. 90.

Chapter Six: *The first flight*, pp. 79–91

71 'Congregation' here refers to a monastery which was one of a closely united network, ruled by a temporary superior, not by an abbot elected for his lifetime.

72 *Vie*, 1666, p. 217.

73 *Quelques remarques de la vie et des miracles de Notre Bienheureux P. Instituteur, le Rme Pierre Fourier*, IV and V.

74 René Taveneaux, *Jansénisme et Réforme catholique*, Nancy University Press, 1992, 'La vie intellectuelle à l'abbaye bénédictine de Saint-Mihiel aux XVIIe et XVIIIe siècles', p. 105.

75 *Vie*, 1666, 'De sa foi', pp. 372–4.

76 *Ibid.*, p. 375.

77 The sisters' first house to which they came in 1603 stood between the streets now called Rue Saint-Julien and the Rue des Dominicains. Behind the present Town Hall and the Post Office were the Saint-Julien hospital and the House of the Grey Sisters.

78 *Ibid.* 'De ses prédictions', p. 382.

79 *Conduite de la Providence dans l'établissement de la Congrégation de Notre-Dame,* 2 vols. bound as one, Toul, 1732, pp. 9–22.

80 Under threat from contending armies, the sisters at Pont-à-Mousson had complained affectionately to Fourier that he had left them to themselves during this storm. Impossible, he replied, for they are the source of solace…

81 *Translator's note*: At this period the duchy or Bar had its own currency, also used in Lorraine.

82 Odile Kammerer-Schweyer, *La Lorraine des marchands à Saint-Nicholas-de-Port, du XIVe au XVIe siècle,* Connaissance et renaissance de la Basilique, Saint-Nicholas-de-Port, 1985.

83 'Copies' are the prepared sheets the sisters handed out to each pupil for writing practice, with carefully drawn lines for the children to write on.

84 'The little girls' translates Fourier's 'les petites nunons', a Lorraine word for small children.

Chapter Seven: *God can bring good out of evil,* pp. 92–102

85 Jolain or Gauzelain, a tenth century bishop of Toul, founded a Benedictine monastery at Bouxières in Meurthe-et-Moselle.

86 *Vie,* 1666, pp. 357–8.

87 *Ibid.,* p. 384.

88 *Ibid.,* pp. 297–9.

89 The seven psalms specially calling on God's mercy, numbers 6, 32, 38, 51, 102, 130 and 143 in the Hebrew numbering.

90 Mother Louis de Gonzague in her *Life* of Alix (Liège, 1889, p. 245) identifies this relative as Jacques Sagry, cousin on his mother's side of Madame Le Clerc, secretary to his Highness, formerly *enseigne* of Epinal and ennobled by Duke Charles III in 1607.

91 *Vie,* 1666, p. 280.

92 *Ibid.,* p. 288.

93 Jean Bedel, *La Vie du Trés R. P. Fourier*, 2nd ed., Pont-à-Mousson, 1656.

94 Published anonymously, *Alix Le Clerc, dite en religion Mère Thérèse de Jésus*, 2 vols. bound as one, Liège, 1889.

95 *Panegyrique de la Bienheureuse Alix Le Clerc*, delivered at *Saint-Louis-des-Francais* by His Excellence Mgr. Blanchet, Rector of the Catholic Institute of Paris, in Rome, 6 May 1947.

Chapter Eight: *The mystical path*, pp. 103–113

96 Teresa of Avila, *Lettre au Père Rodrigue Alvarez, Oeuvres complètes* Paris, Ed. du Seuil, 1949, p. 518.

97 St John of the Cross distinguishes between: communications which reach the soul through outward physical senses; those created supernaturally in the imagination such as in imaginary visions; and finally the clear and distinct knowledge which by a supernatural path, reaches the understanding in intellectual visions. Fr. Surin (1600–1665) defined ecstasy as 'a failure of the heart attacked by love'. According to St John the ravishment, on the contrary, is to do with the understanding. *Guide spirituel*, VII, 4–5.

98 Quoted by Christian Alexandre, *Etre mystique*, Collection 'Foi Vivante'. Paris, Ed. du Cerf, p. 178.

99 Ecstasy of 1 February (*Rel.* 23). See above Chapter Five, p. 76.

100 *Vie*, 1666, p. 363.

101 *Ibid.*, pp. 360–1.

102 François de Sales, *Traité de l'Amour de Dieu*, bk. VII, chapter VI, Paris, Gallimard, coll. 'La Pléiade', p. 682.

103 *Vie*, 1666, pp. 359–60.

104 *Ibid.*, p. 362.

105 *Ibid.*, p. 329.

106 *Ibid.*, p. 329.

107 *Ibid.*, p. 330.

Chapter Nine: *Alix in distress*, pp. 114–125

108 'Lavatories' translates Alix's 'lieux communs', which a footnote in the French text gives as 'lieux d'aisance, cabinets'.

109 The word 'illusion' generally refers to diabolic deceptions. Alix never uses it in connection with heavenly visitations, except in section 22 of *Relation* when she quotes Fourier telling her that a vision may be nothing more than an illusion.

110 *Dictionnaire de sapience*, Troyes, 1604, quoted by Jean Delumeau, *Le Péché et la Peur*, Paris, Fayard, 1983, p. 238.

111 *Vie*, 1666, p. 29.

112 *Summarium additionale exhibens levia discrimina inter editionem anni 1666 et novam editionem anni 1882 quod attinet* Relationem *a V.D.F. traditam Confessario*, Sancti Deodati seu Nanceyen. Count Gantelet, quoting the bishops who authorised the reprinting in 1882, points out that they all disapproved of the suppressions.

113 A religious house normally has an 'extraordinary' confessor as well as the regular 'ordinary' one. Alix's experience shows how useful this can be.

114 *Vie*, 1666, p. 32.

115 Hélène Derréal, *La Bienheureuse Alix Le Clerc et ses écrits*, Nancy, Société des impressions typographiques, 1947.

116 St Bernard, in *Sermon sur l'Annonciation* in *Ecrits sur la Vierge Marie*, Paris-Montréal, Médiaspaul, p. 72.

117 John Paul II. *Vita consecrata*, 1996.

Chapter Ten: *Mattaincourt and Pont-à-Mousson*, pp. 126–137

118 *Vie*, 1666, p. 227.

119 *Ibid.*, p. 322.

120 Edmond Renard, *La Mère Alix Le Clerc*, Paris, Gigord, 1935.

121 *Vie*, 1666, p. 297.

122 *Ibid.*, pp. 299–300.

123 *Ibid.*, 'Les sentiments de la Mère sur l'Institut', p. 226.

124 See Hélène Derréal, *Un missionaire de la Contre-Réforme*, p. 247, where she dates to 1607–1611 a constitutional plan contained in the Balaincourt manuscript.

125 Pius V was more rigorous than the Council of Trent. He insisted that all monastic houses be strictly enclosed and in his encyclical *Circa Pastoralis* of 1566 he abolished tertiary orders who took

simple vows, by requiring them to take solemn vows and accept enclosure.

126 *Vie*, 1666, pp. 312–3.

127 *Vie*, 1666, p. 102.

128 Archives Meurthe-et-Moselle, H 2576. 'Barrois' was the currency of the duchy of Bar.

129 Hélène Derréal supports this, referring to the choice of Pont-à-Mousson, a university town where the Jesuits and the Premonstratensians had put their seminary. See *Un missionnaire de la Contre-Réforme*, p. 240.

130 Dieulouart, district of Nancy, 7 km from Pont-à-Mousson.

131 *Vie*, 1666, p. 299.

132 In Alix's time lepers still lived a segregated life in lazar houses, all contact with the outside world forbidden.

133 *Vie*, 1666, p. 302.

Chapter Eleven: *Verdun (1612–1615)*, pp. 138–152

134 *Vie*, 1666, p. 376.

135 Louis Châtellier, 'La sainteté au quotidien, saint Pierre Fourier d'après sa Correspondance', *Annales de l'Est*, 2, 1989, p.108. To be exact we should say, 'the first women in Lorraine', as Jeanne de Lestonnac, foundress of the Compagnie de Marie-Notre-Dame, in 1606 was using the Exercises recommended by a Jesuit in Bordeaux with her small group of sisters. See Françoise Soury-Lavergne, *Chemin d'éducation, sur les traces de Jeanne de Lestonnac, 1566–1640*, C.L.D., Chambray, 1985.

136 'Bushels' loosely represents the word 'rhez', an old measure of Lorraine, equivalent to some 120 litres.

137 St James in French is Saint Jacques, so that Dominicans who lived in Verdun or in Paris, both situated near churches of St James, came to be known as Jacobins.

138 *Constitutions de 1640*, part 4, chapter VI, no. 7, 'De la Mère supérieure'.

139 *Vie*, 1666: 'La vertu d'humilité décrite par la Mère dans un cahier écrit de sa main'. p. 257.

140 A doll dressed in the habit of the Order was usually kept in a convent, to avoid changes.

141 Dorothy of Lorraine (1545–1621), youngest sister of Duke Charles III, and aunt of Duke Henry II.

142 *Vie*, 1666, pp. 379–81.

143 *Ibid.* 'Les sentiments de la Mère sur l'Institut'. p. 225.

144 See Paule Sagot, 'L'inspiration augustinienne chez Pierre Fourier', in *Notes sur la spiritualité des fondateurs*, C.N.D., no. 33, April 1986, p. 1.

145 *Vie*, 1666, 'Les sentiments de la Mère sur l'Institut', p.231.

Chapter Twelve: *Foundations in France*, pp. 153–168

146 *C.* 1, 33.

147 Ghislaine Boucher, *Dieu et Satan dans la vie de Catherine de Saint Augustin, 1632–1668*, Montréal-Tounai, Bellarmin-Desclée, 1979, p. 77.

148 Juliers, in German Jülich, a town in Germany NE of Aachen. On this conflict see Henri Bogdan, *La Guerre de Trente ans, 1618–1648*, Librairie académique Perrin, 1999, pp. 34–46.

149 Antoine Vergote, *Figures du démoniaque, hier et aujourd'hui*, Brussels, Facultés universitaires Saint-Louis, 1992, 'Anthropologie du diable, l'homme séduit et en proie aux puissances des ténèbres, p. 93.

150 Georges Viard, 'L'installation de la Congrégation de Notre-Dame en Champagne et saint Pierre Fourier, 1613–1640', *Saint Pierre Fourier en son temps, Actes du colloque de Mirecourt*, April 1992, Etudes réunies par R. Taveneaux, Nancy University Press, 1992, pp. 111–26.

151 'Les Ursulines s'installent dans le diocèse de Langres, à Langres en 1613, à Chaumont et à Châtillon-sur-Seine en 1619, à Tonnerre en 1627, à Bar-sur-Aube en 1628', Georges Viard, *ibid.*, p. 115.

152 Georges Viard, *ibid.*, p. 119.

153 *Constitutions de 1640*, part 4, chapter VI, art. 29, 'De la Mère supérieure'.

154 *Vie*, 1666, pp. 347–8.

155 R. P. Dorigny, *Histoire de la constitution de la Congrégation de Notre-Dame*, Nancy, 1719.

156 The famous abbey of St Vanne was founded at Verdun in 952. One of its two towers is the only part of the former monastery that survived Vauban's rebuilding of the citadel.

157 Alix said that she saw Verdun in a vision three years before going there, that is in 1609. She seems to have seen both towns at once from the St Vanne height.

158 *Vie*, 1666, 'remarques omises par mégarde', pp. 402–3; the citizen rescued at the roadside.

159 If a sorcerer uses 'charms', he does so by means of occult powers granted him by the devil, whose 'baleful miracle-worker' he is. See Etienne Delcambre, *Le Concepte de sorcellerie dans le duché du Lorraine au XVIe et XVIIe siècle*, Nancy, 1949.

160 *Vie*, pp. 105–10.

161 An *Agnus Dei* is a small packet of holy wax taken from an Easter candle.

162 On p. 56 of the 1666 *Vie* this passage is emended, and the last section omitted. It reads: '[…] until the fire of rebellion in the flesh was so strongly alight that I would not have been afraid to throw myself into a blazing furnace in order to put out these inner flames and as I feared that these violent feelings could become intentional, it was principally from this that the scruples arose that were gnawing at my mind'.

Chapter Thirteen: *Fresh openings, Paris, 1615*, pp. 169–184

163 J. Rogie, *Histoire du B. Pierre Fourier*, Verdun, 1887, vol. I, p. 284; L. Carrez, *Histoire du premier monastère de la Congrégation de Notre-Dame*, Châlons-sur-Marne, 1906, vol. I, p. 17; E. Renard, *La Mère Alix Le Clerc*, Paris, 1935, pp. 295–7.

164 H. Derréal, *Un Missionaire de la Contre-Réforme*, Paris, 1965, 'Remarque sur l'auteur de la postulation du bref de 1613', pp. 404–8.

165 J. Dorigny, *Histoire de l'institition de la Congrégation de Notre-Dame*, Nancy, 1719, pp. 144–53.

166 H. Derréal suggests 9 September 1614, not 1613, for this undated letter, which would not allow time for the different stages of Isabeau's temptation.

167 Schools in pre-Revolutionary France were almost all fee-paying, in town or country. Payment was made not through taxes but by donors' charity.

168 *Conduite de la Providence dans l'établissement de la congrégation de Nostre-Dame*, Toul, 1732 (two vols. bound as one), pp. 23–38.

169 *Vie*, 1666, p. 139.

170 See Marie-Andrée Jégou, *Les Ursulines de faubourg Saint-Jacques à Paris, 1607–1662*, Paris, Presses universitaires de France, 1981.

171 The *approbation* of 1603 authorised the sisters of Our Lady to receive income, and the bulls of 1615, 1616 and 1628 repeated these clauses.

Chapter Fourteen: *The teaching nuns cloistered*, pp. 185–203

172 This text is in the *Constitutions de Nancy*, 1647.

173 Lorraine's troubles delayed the building of a primatial church in Nancy until 1742 in the reign of Stanislas. It became a cathedral in 1777 when Nancy was made an Episcopal see.

174 *Vie*, 1666, 'De sa confiance en Dieu', p. 359.

175 *Vie*, 1666, 'De sa patience'.

176 *Vie*, 1666, p. 148.

177 *Cérémonial des religieuses de la Congrégation de Nostre-Dame*, Châlons, 1663, 'De la vêture des novices', pp. 42–3.

178 They would have to wait until 1660 before getting a house suitable for a monastery.

179 Edmond Renard, *La Mère Alix Le Clerc*, Paris, Gigord, 1935, p. 375.

180 This refers to the colours of the habits.

181 Jean Bedel, *La Vie du Très Révérend Père Pierre Fourier*, Mirecourt, 1869, p. 128.

182 *Constitutions de Verdun (dites du Père Lebrun)*, 1, 1643.

183 Edmond Renard, p. 376.

184 *Constitutions de 1640*, part 6, 'De l'union de tous les monastères'.

185 'De la Congrégation des Filles externes', 25 articles attached to *Usages des Religieuses de la Congrégation de Notre-Dame*, Châlons, 1690, pp. 289–300.

186 See Patricia Simpson, *Marguerite Bourgeoys et Montréal, 1640–1655*, McGill-Queen's University Press Montreal, 1999.

187 H. Derréal, *Un Missionaire de la Contre-Réforme*, Paris, Plon, 1965, p. 282.

188 *Vie*, 1666, p. 157.

189 The German-speaking federation was constituted in 1961, and in 1963 joined to form a single body with the Union of Jupille-sur-Meuse and the Roman Union.

190 Letter quoted by Mère Louis de Gonzague in *Alix Le Clerc*, Liège, Dessain, 1889, vol. II, p. 219.

191 *Vie*, 1666, 'De sa devotion envers la Sainte Vierge', pp. 355–6.

192 Archives of Meurthe-et-Moselle, series H, box 2536.

Chapter Fifteen: *Mother Teresa of Jesus*, pp. 204–216

193 *N'épargner ni le vert ni le sec*, to use every possible means.

194 *Vie*, 1666, p. 154: an anachronism, repeated by Alix's biographers; Francis Xavier was not beatified until 1619. See Eric Suire, *La Sainteté française de la Réforme catholique, XVIe-XVIIIe siècle*, Bordeaux University Press, 2001, p. 150.

195 Teresa of Avila, *The Interior Castle*, Fifth Dwelling Places, chapter I.

196 Teresa of Avila put it well: 'God establishes himself in the intimacy of this soul in such a way that when it returns to itself it can have no doubt whatever but that it was in God and God was in it,' *ibid.*

197 Commentary by Fr. Michel de Goedt, o.c.d., 'En marge de la *Relation* d'Alix Le Clerc'.

198 Quoted by Yves Krumenacker, *L'Ecole française de spiritualité*, Paris, Ed du Cerf, 1999, p. 190; reference to Bérulle, *Oeuvres de piété*, 111, 1666.

199 *Vie*, 1666, *passim*, pp. 359, 331, 332.

200 *Ibid.*, pp. 409, 341, 333.

201 The 'turn' was a pivoted cupboard, accessible from either side.

202 *Vie, passim,* pp. 220, 209, 308–9.

203 *Vie,* pp. 367, 289, 310.

204 *Vie,* pp. 347, 348, 275, 219, 293, 225.

205 *Vie,* 1666, 'Here is described her system of government, found in a notebook written in her hand, composed according to the lights God gave her and that the nuns saw her practice', pp. 204–213.

206 *Vie,* 1666, pp. 296–311.

Chapter Sixteen: *Writing the 'Relation',* pp. 217–231

207 The complete text is published in the collection 'Sagesses chrétiennes'.

208 Yves Krumenacker, Paris, Ed. du Cerf, 1999, p. 333.

209 The reference is to nineteenth century writers who adopted Chateaubriand's disillusion: 'We live with full hearts in an empty world'.

210 Paule Sagot, Commentaire de la *Relation d'Alix Le Clerc.*

211 Jean-Jacques Antier, *Thérèse d'Avila, de la crainte à l'amour,* Paris, Perrin, 2003, pp. 158.

212 *Imitation of Christ,* bk. 1, ch. 3.

213 See *Dieu au XVIIe siècle,* 'L'invasion mystique' en France au XVIIe siècle' by Dominique Salin, ed. Facultés jésuites Paris, 2002, p. 249.

214 Teresa of Avila was beatified by Paul V in 1614 and canonised by Gregory XV in 1622, the year Alix Le Clerc died.

215 Commentary by Fr. Michel de Goedt, o.c.d., *op. cit.*

216 4 June 1610 at St Nicolas, Alix used to end her letters to the Mirecourt sisters with the words, 'I beg you to pray God for us. I beg Him that He may be your whole love.' See the facsimile of her letter and analysis of her handwriting in A. de Remiremont, *Mère Alix Le Clerc, 1576–1622,* CND, 1946, pp. 239–44.

217 *Ecrits spirituels,* 'Cherchons le centre de notre âme qui est Dieu, et l'honneur et gloire d'iceluy'.

218 *Ibid.*

219 *Vie,* 1666, 'De son oraison', p. 363.

220 *Ecrits spirituels,* 'Cherchons le centre de notre âme qui est Dieu, et l'honneur et gloire d'iceluy'.

Chapter Seventeen: *The Last Offering,* pp. 232–252

221 See Marie Elisabeth Aubry, *Le Monastère nancéien de la Congrégation de Notre-Dame aux XVIIe et XVIIIe siècles,* degree thesis Nancy 1970; this discusses the *Livres des interrogatories,* H 2571 in the Archives of Meurthe-et-Moselle.

222 'It is certain that the teaching vocation of the Congregation de Notre-Dame so new at that period, acted as a real magnet', *ibid.* p. 77.

223 *Vie,* 1666, 'Recueil des plus signalées et éminentes vertus de la Mère Angélique Milly', p. 10.

224 Mère Louis de Gonzague (who did not put her name to her book), *Alix Le Clerc, dite en religion Mère Thérèse de Jésus, fondatrice de la Congrégation de Notre-Dame,* Liège, 1889, bk. 2, p. 219.

225 See Emmanuel Orchard, *Till God Will, Mary Ward Through Her Writings,* London, DLT, 1985.

226 H. Derréal, *Un missionaire de la Contre-Réforme,* Paris, Plon, 1965, p. 287 & 310, n. 111, on the beatification process begun in Toul in 1682.

227 Bedel gives a well known account of this in his *Vie du très Révérend Père Pierre Fourier,* Pont-à-Mousson, 1656, p. 429.

228 C. Dussaux, *Vie mystique au pays vosgien,* III, 'Elisabeth de Ranfaing', pp 17–68. The letter from Fr. Coton is given in full.

229 *Vie,* 1666, "De son humilité" p. 280.

230 A battle in the Thirty Years War (1618–1648) between Catholics, Imperialists and Lorrainers on one side and German Protestant princes on the other. See Henry Bogdan, *La Guerre de Trente Ans,* Le Grand Livre du mois, 1999, pp 78 & 86.

231 *Vie,* 1666, pp. 165–8.

232 *Vie,* p. 164.

233 *Vie,* p. 174.

234 *Vie,* p. 167.

235 *Vie,* p. 169.

236 Jean-Jacques Antier, *Thérèse d'Avila, de la crainte à l'amour,* Paris, Perrin, 2003.

237 *Vie,* 1666, p. 166.

238 *Vie,* p. 179.

239 See H. Derréal, *La Bienheureuse Alix Le Clerc et ses écrits,* Nancy, 1947, p. 18.

240 *Vie,* 1666, p. 180.

241 Asmodeus, whose name may mean 'bringer of destruction'. See the apocryphal Book of Tobit, where he appears as a demon of impure pleasures.

242 *Vie,* 1666, pp. 111–13.

243 *Vie,* p. 181.

244 In an electuary, a honey or syrup-based mixture containing opium.

245 *Vie,* 1666, p. 175.

246 *Ibid.,* pp. 398–9.

247 This has been explained as being due to his wish to avoid breaking the rules of enclosure without special permission, but may also have been meant as a reminder that such a visit formed part of the task entrusted to him by the bishop, to visit his convents and help his nuns.

248 *Vie,* 1666, p. 182.

249 *Constitutions de 1640, part 2.* Ch. XXIII, 'Du devoir envers les Filles de la Vierge lorsqu'elles sont passées de la mort à la vie'.

250 *Confessions,* IX, X, 23.

251 *Vie,* 1666, p. 184.

252 *Ibid.,* p. 188.

253 Ms d'Evreux, folio, 60 – 61. See Hélène Derréal, *La Bienheureuse Alix Le Clerc et ses écrits,* Nancy, 1947, p. 18.

254 *Vie,* 1666, p. 388.

255 J.- J. Lionnois, *Histoire des Villes vieille et neuve de Nancy,* written 1788, published 1811.

256 Jacques Choux, *La Découverte et l'Identification du corps d'Alix Le Clerc,* Nancy, 1960.

257 Mgr. de Lenoncourt had wanted his heart placed in the convent chapel at Nancy as a token of his attachment to the Congregation

of Our Lady, while his body was buried in 1636 in the church of the Jesuits' novitiate, which he had founded.

258 The portrait passed through many hands, was given to the Congregation and in 1978 went back to Nancy, in an almost miraculous sequence of events. It then hung in the chapel at 26, rue de Médreville, Nancy and is at present at Fontenay-sous-Bois.

259 Legend, from the Latin *legenda*, 'that which must be read', in this context, the lives of the saints read daily in the convent refectories.

260 This is the document often referred to here as 'the chronicle', abbreviated to *Vie*, 1666.

Chapter Eighteen: *The Spiritual Writings*, pp. 253–270

261 These are published in the collection 'Sagesses chrétiennes'.

262 The sisters at Nancy probably gave this manuscript to their foundation in Vernon. After the Revolution the books were scattered and it ended up in the city library in Evreux.

263 These six texts are on pages 225–66 of the 1666 *Vie*.

264 *Ecrits spirituels d'Alix Le Clerc*, Congrégation Notre-Dame, 1968.

265 *Textes propres pour la Messe et la Liturgie des Heures*, Congrégation Notre-Dame, 1991, p. 16.

266 *Ibid.*, p. 17.

267 See *The Imitation of Christ*, 'In what consists true peace and real progress of the soul', III, 25.

268 St Augustine, *De beata vita*, XIII, 8, 9.

269 'My peace and my love' translates *mon pacifique amateur*, to which M-C. Tihon adds a note explaining this as meaning 'one who loves with a loving preference which brings peace', and refers to the *Imitation of Christ*, IV, 13, 'The Faithful must wish with all his heart to be united with Jesus Christ in the Communion', also noting that Alix added an ontological dimension to this text.

270 *Le Primitif et Légitime Esprit de l'Institut des Filles de la Congrégation de Nostre-Dame* by the Very Rev. Fr. Pierre Fourier